THE PACIFIC
ISLANDERS

PEOPLES OF THE WORLD SERIES

Editor: *Sonia Cole*

The People of America
by T. D. Stewart

The Pacific Islanders
by William Howells

THE PACIFIC ISLANDERS

William Howells

Professor of Anthropology,
Harvard University

CHARLES SCRIBNER'S SONS

NEW YORK

GN
662
.H68

To my wife
who has helped me so much

Contents

Plates

Between pages 110 and 111

Skull of Solo Man, Java, reconstructed by F. Weidenreich (*American Museum of Natural History*)
Skull from Keilor, Australia (*N. W. G. Macintosh*)
Skull from Niah Cava, Sarawak, reconstructed by D. Brothwell (*British Museum, Natural History*)
Skull from Kow Swamp, Australia (*Dr Alan Thorne*)

Australia and Tasmania

Aboriginal baby, Alice Springs, Central Australia (*Muriel Howells*)
Group of the last surviving Tasmanians (*Tasmanian Museum, Hobart*)
Tiwi, Melville Island, Northern Australia (*William Howells*)
Groote Eiland, Northern Australia (*William Howells*)
Arnhem Land, Northern Australia (*William Howells*)

Melanesia

Girls from Mount Hagen, New Guinea (*William Howells*)
Ufeto villager, near Goroka, Eastern Highlands District of New Guinea (*Muriel Howells*)
Tolai, near Rabaul, New Britain (*Muriel Howells*)
Baegu girl, Malaita, Solomon Islands (*William Howells*)
Man from Tanna Island, New Hebrides (*Public Relations Office, Suva*)
Girl from Trobriand Islands, Papua (*B. J. Adams*, courtesy of *Pacific Islands Monthly*)
Men of Espiritu Santo, New Hebrides, with masks and figures produced for export (*Pacific Islands Monthly*)
Woman and child from New Caledonia (*Qantas*, courtesy of *Pacific Islands Monthly*)

ix

Maps

Figures

Preface

Some ten years ago I wrote a short handbook for the sub-department of anthropology of the British Museum (Natural History). This was in the days when the word 'race' was innocent of many of its present connotations and the booklet was entitled *Races of Man*. After it had been published, and as a result of my frustrations when trying to compile it, I realized that outside the major groups of Caucasoid, Mongoloid and Negroid there are no such things as 'races of man'. There are populations, there are ethnic groups, but they grade into one another to such an extent that races or sub-species, as normally defined in zoology, are really meaningless when applied to anthropology.

So, out with races, on with peoples. But call them what you like, there are obvious differences between them. You don't have to be a physical anthropologist to recognize that a Japanese, an Englishman and a Kikuyu don't *look* alike (probably they won't think alike either, but that is a question of culture and not genetics). Yet, as a statement drafted for UNESCO by fourteen physical anthropologists put it: 'Some biological differences between human beings within a single race may be as great as, or greater than, the same biological differences between races.'

There is no problem in finding a book on the birds of Europe or the mammals of Africa, but when it comes to human beings it is quite a different matter. Man is seldom included with other mammals, partly because of our conceit but mainly because the book would burst its binding. It was this lamentable lack which made me realize the need for world-wide coverage on people. To do justice to the subject, it would have to be in several volumes. As divisions based on 'race' presented such difficulties, the boundaries would have to be geographical.

The books would have to be written by specialists. Clearly they would have to be trained in physical anthropology, but they would need to be far more than just skull-measurers.

They would have to describe characteristics and relationships of the present populations of each continent, based on the latest findings of human biologists and geneticists. They would have to try and discover how people got where they are and how they coped with and were moulded by their environment. This would involve the whole pageant of migrations and invasions, conquest and trade, throughout history. It would also mean examining the hardware of preliterate societies, their tools, weapons, art and other artifacts. The origins of the diverse populations of today would have to be traced back to a handful of bones in the grey mists of prehistory.

The setting would also be important, taking in geology, climatology, ecology and many other -ologies. The animals man hunted, the vegetable foods he gathered and later cultivated, would all have to be brought in.

It would be hard enough to find authors competent to discuss all these varied aspects; but the geographical boundaries of the proposed volumes presented yet more difficulties. An anthropologist who had specialized, say, in the sophisticated cultures of Chinese or Indian civilizations might have little knowledge of, or interest in, the seal hunters and reindeer herders of northern Siberia; yet all these peoples, and many more, would have to be included in the one volume on Asia.

There was still another very important qualification that these paragons of authors would have to possess, perhaps more daunting for some than anything else. This was the ability to turn a mass of scientific data and statistics into a readable and stimulating book, of real value for serious students and at the same time appealing to non-specialists.

Naturally, each author would ride his favourite hobby-horse to a certain extent; indeed one would want them to, for enthusiasm is infectious. Each author in this series has in fact treated his subject with a different emphasis, one underlining the historical background, another the genetic aspects and so on. These various approaches will emphasize the wideness of the topics under discussion and perhaps enhance the interest.

SONIA COLE

Foreword

Having agreed to do this book, at the welcome invitation of Sonia Cole, I began trying to write it in the summer of 1967. I now see this as the equivalent of starting to write a history of trench warfare in 1913. I had not even completed certain studies of my own in physical anthropology. Some important work of the linguists had just reached the library shelves, but other major contributions were still to come; and the outpouring of new information from the archaeologists had not begun. Symposia on Pacific matters mushroomed in the next few years, putting new ideas together and suggesting still newer ones. Friends and strangers came to my help with copies of their latest published and unpublished papers, without which I would never have finished.

Not that I have 'finished'. The same thing still goes on: one linguist, in sending me a still unpublished study, wrote apologetically that it was already about four years out of date. I can hardly wish it all to stop while I publish a book, and anyhow the atmosphere of 'What next?' is particularly exhilarating just now. So I have tried to pull the facts together, and put some of my own interpretations on top of those of others, at what does seem like an opportune moment. I cannot say too positively that almost every good idea has already been suggested, some of them long ago, and that I am sure to have thought thoughts which seemed to me more original than they are. I apologize to the many authors I have not quoted or credited, as well as to those I have not read at all, if I seem to be assuming too much. And I thank not only those who have helped me directly but also the many who have been gathering the simple facts, to be used by all of us, for over a century.

These are my main creditors, the people who have read parts of the book, given me advice and ideas, shown me or told me about new evidence, or sent me their latest writings, often not yet in print:

At Harvard, Douglas Oliver, Einar Haugen, Jonathan Friedlaender and, over the years, Carleton Coon. At Yale, Kwang-chih Chang. At the Irwin Memorial Blood Bank, San Francisco, Melvin S. Schanfield. At the University of Hawaii, Wilhelm G. Solheim II, Byron W. Bender, Michael Pietrusewsky. At the University of Iowa, Richard E. Shutler. At Australian National University, Jack Golson, Rhys Jones, Alan Thorne, L.M. Groube, James Allen, R.L. Vanderwal. At the University of Sydney, N.W.G. Macintosh. In Melbourne, at the Archaeological Society of Victoria, Alexander Gallus; at the National Museum, Edmund Gill. At the University of Auckland, Andrew Pawley. At the University of Otago, Chester Gorman. Sonia Cole, the book's godmother, gave it the benefit of her editorial talents; Gurdon Metz and Judith Neal did the same.

It would be ungracious not to mention the granting agencies of my government, the National Science Foundation and the National Institutes of Health. They are, of course, not in the business of directly supporting books like this one, but rather of funding original professional research. It remains true that I owe much of my recent education in Pacific studies to what they have aided, be it my personal research projects, or the Harvard Solomon Islands Project or, above all, the encouragement of work by many new and young professional anthropologists. Such help has been a major factor in the scientific progress and burgeoning of information which has made this book possible now.

THE PACIFIC
ISLANDERS

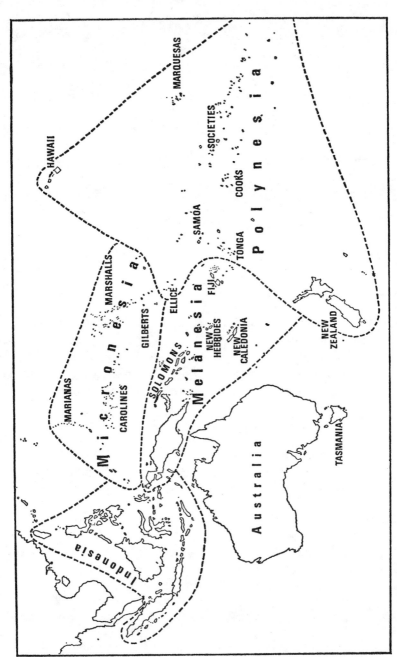

1 Islands of the Pacific.

I

Taming
the wild surmise

Then felt I like some watcher of the skies
    When a new planet swims into his ken;
Or like stout Cortez, when with eagle eyes
    He stared at the Pacific – and all his men
Look'd at each other with a wild surmise –
    Silent, upon a peak in Darien.
(*from Keats, 'On first looking into Chapman's "Homer"' '.*)

We may excuse Keats's own surmise that it was Cortez, not Balboa. The grand surmise – in my schoolbooks and in encyclopedias – that a European 'discovered' the Pacific is the less excusable, for Europeans were particularly late in finding their way to this great ocean, already replete with human settlers. Perhaps the earliest discoverer, a million years before, was our small-brained, thick-skulled forerunner, Java Man. But it was men of our own kind who first moved out into the islands and to Australia during the last great cold phase of the Pleistocene or Ice Age something like forty thousand years ago. Further to the east, problems of water distances and available food long delayed occupation of the rest of the ocean, and it may have been within the last thousand years that Hawaii was reached. Nevertheless the Asiatic shore and the nearer islands as far as New Guinea and beyond had been alive with activity for several millennia before. We Europeans, last and most foreign of all comers, should be more humble.

But Europeans are both inquisitive and acquisitive. Other 'discoverers' continued to marvel. Fired to explore by the sight of South American gold, Mendaña in 1568 was the first to reach the middle of the Pacific and left Spanish names we still use for the

islands of Guadalcanal, Santa Ysabel and San Cristobal. Gold
does exist, but all they found was a little fool's gold (pyrites) in
native ornaments. None the less the belief grew that the land of
Ophir was in this new part of the world, and Mendaña's archipelago came to be called the Isles of Solomon. Two centuries later
the British and the French found other major groups throughout
the ocean, bringing back, from the freshness of contact, reports,
objects, and natives themselves, which set off a whole new literature in philosophy, natural history and primitive anthropology.
Only after two more centuries was the wonder wiped away, when
well-inoculated tourists, in well-indoctrinated groups, could jet to
Easter Island or, still in their Honolulu clothes, could travel in the
interior highlands of New Guinea, first visited a mere thirty years
before. If a tourist were lucky, he might yet see a New Guinean
coming into town in pig grease and plumes, aiming to change to
the more forward-looking costume of a cotton undershirt and
khaki shorts.

While the old surface glamor is faded and mildewed, an inner
one remains and grows in the people themselves. They are still
there, speaking their languages and acting out patterns they
have not forgotten. What grows is the surprise and interest
scholars find in unraveling the Pacific past. That is what this book
is about.

The curiosity has always been there. Early scholars satisfied the
pangs with such conjecturing as their scholarship allowed: listening
to myths, classifying people into races and so on. Much of this
came out of their own minds, casting about to make connections
with other parts of the world. Some of it sounds rather lunatic
now, the kind of 'scholarship' or non-science which projects a
hypothesis of what might have happened, and looks everywhere
for facts, however questionable, which might support it. Science,
by contrast, projects a hypothesis from the facts at hand, and then
looks for evidence which would disprove it. If the evidence is
forthcoming the hypothesis is modified or discarded, a very painful
thing to do as everybody knows.

In all ways anthropology today has far better means of being
'scientific', of finding the needed facts. Archaeologists have learned
how and where to dig in the most careful and effective way; how to
evaluate their results from earlier work in objective fashion; and
how to get absolute dates in the past from the now well-known

method of radiocarbon (if they can produce charcoal, bone or shell). From this comes the kind of testimony which is very hard to shake, and which knocks down old wrong guesses and ideas like tenpins. Linguists have worked out the difficult business of recording and analyzing newly encountered languages (or old ones, from bibles translated into great numbers of Pacific languages); and they use computers for some ways of comparing such languages. By this means they can construct family trees of a sort, and can estimate dates when two groups who spoke one language separated and allowed their respective tongues to drift apart.

Physical anthropology, as I shall soon show, can also apply computers to make trees of a similar kind on data both from living people and from skulls of known populations, and can even make mathematical judgements as to prehistoric skulls. Such trees will not give dates, only relationships. But in this and other ways physical anthropology co-operates with its sister branches of anthropology. For example, although a language may be borrowed outright in the course of a few years by some community with a history entirely different from that of the lender, nevertheless, the leopard cannot change his spots, and, if all they borrow is language, the borrowers keep their essential physical form. On the other hand they may become hybridized with the lenders, a fact which might not show up in the languages – linguists do not hold with 'mixed' languages in the basic sense. So one kind of evidence balances another and possible hypotheses are narrowed down.

In fact, an important 'new' thing, apart from new methods and training, is the sharing of information all around the profession. The surprise and wonder that students are experiencing lies both in the parts, such as the very recent pushing back of Australian prehistory to at least 30,000 BC, with its great implications, and in the whole, in the fact that so much information can be pulled out of sources once thought to be rather barren – information which allows the putting together of major patterns of the past, such as the peopling of Polynesia.

The Matter of Race
New knowledge, not special to the Pacific, has made it possible to get rid of some bothersome old fallacies. One such is the Long Migration: finding the Lost Tribes of Israel in the American

Indians is an example. Because of a cast of countenance, a religious rite, a misread myth, some tribal group is cut surgically out of its natural habitat and transported across the ages and the continents back to Xanadu. The actual event, of course, is surmised to be the reverse. The ancestral group begins its journey, for reasons seldom gone into, traversing one environment after another and, most important, going through country which must already have had its load of inhabitants, although the consequences of this, in hindrance or mixture, seem not to matter. The chosen group finally arrives in its new home, in good enough repair to reflect the culture, or the physique, or both, with which it started. Now of course people have migrated: the Indians to America, the Bantu-speaking tribes all over East, Central and South Africa, and very ancient Australians to Australia. But we take these to have started from naturally available homelands, and to have moved under circumstances appropriate to people in their conditions of culture. I am referring instead to writers who explained the Polynesians as at least partly a movement from dynastic Egypt, or else as the remnants of Alexander the Great's fleet. Good grief! Still, these writers were honorable and pleasant gentlemen, and their names will not be handed over to obloquy.

A boon companion of the Long Migration is the 'Pure Race', a fallacy deeply embedded in anthropology from its beginning. This is the compelling notion that a race has a basic type and that some of its members, from simple anthropological description or from everyday observation, are more typical Polynesians, let us say, or Navahos, or 'Nordics', than are most. The intellectual consequences of this have been several: above all the attempt to define the 'pure' type anthropologically, and then to classify the races of man. At once there follows the surmise that any actual population you are studying is a mixture (since its members are not all of one proper type) of Pure Races, which separately made Migrations, often Long ones, to the place where your mixed population now is.

This is an overdrawn picture but it does contain the kernel of much older thought about race. Anthropologists of the past failed to notice two points. All peoples are now 'mixed', and none are 'pure', even in the places where long migrations, or short ones, might have started. And thus it is impossible to count, or classify, original pure races. I am not going to dwell on the general matter of race, but I must make the above points. For the question

4

only too often put to an anthropologist is, 'What race are the Polynesians?' I cannot answer; I do not know.

This fallacy was undermined by the reshaping of zoology and anthropology through understanding of Mendelian genetics. The biological nature of a human (or animal) community rests on its shared pool of varying genes. Genes, as any schoolboy knows, are paired, which was Mendel's central discovery; and the particular pair, one coming from either parent, rules the development of some trait of an individual, wholly or in part. Skin color is evidently ruled by several different pairs of genes. In African and Melanesian populations the whole set of genes is prevailingly composed of those for heavier pigmentation. In Europeans the pool is of genes nearer the low end of the pigment scale. In any pool, however, there is a degree of variety in the genes. This is the main point: for a given population there is no 'typical' assortment or arrangement of such genes, and so no typical color for a 'race', only some colors (as with some face forms, or other facets of appearance) which result from commoner gene combinations, just as the number seven comes up most frequently in rolls of two dice. A child less 'typical' in features of his community is not more 'mixed' because of a rarer gene combination he happens to have, any more than there is something 'mixed' about a roll of two or twelve with the dice. None of this makes it a sin to describe a community in terms of its average or most common features, and its variation in these. But it is a mistake to chop it up into 'types', and to try to run these down in different corners of the earth.

So interest has shifted from racial types to population structure. In a simple culture stage like that of the pre-Magellanic Pacific, people are not distributed as smoothly as butter on toast but sort themselves out into small groups such as villages or hordes. Seldom are there supergroups of any importance – loose tribes at best – and so the little groups are kept in relative isolation, fostered all the more by language differences or traditional hostilities. That is exactly what exists in New Guinea, heavily populated though it is.

And this makes a laboratory for small-scale evolution. Some differences may come about by natural selection, perhaps through adaptation to high altitudes. Two other things also lead to physical differences: inbreeding and accident. The inbreeding is not especially close, but it does prevent the wide mixing of genes. It keeps them at home, as Hulse [127] puts it, which is more effective if any genes are unusual; and it also leads to a more frequent pairing of unusual genes, which is like increasing the unusual rolls of dice. As to accident, its name is genetic drift, meaning that by chance some of these unusual genes become more numerous here, less numerous there, another result of the isolation. In the Italian part of Switzerland where Hulse worked, he noted the folk recognition that villages have their special physical marks. 'Everyone knows, for instance, that the people of Moghegno have big noses – and, as a matter of fact, they do!'

An occasional extra squeeze or puff is put into this. A ferocious typhoon struck the atoll of Mokil in Micronesia in 1770, leaving alive only three family groups, less than thirty persons [161]. Mokil is the very type of an isolated and inbred community of two or three hundred people; idiosyncrasies in its stock and proportions of genes would likely be enhanced in a residue of three families – things do run in families, because they are only small samples of populations – and so, when they once more increase to replenish this little bit of earth, their gene stock might drift sharply in a new direction. And, once in a blue moon, just such a small group may rapidly expand in open territory into a large population, large enough to be called a race in the proper sense, having the special characters of its patriarchal band. Remember that, when we put together the history of Polynesia.

This picture of checkerboard isolation is a little too rigid, since it is always modified by marriage across group lines: a creep of genes which does not blot out local differences but does put a common complexion over a considerable area as well. Such are the elements in the whole population structure, the nature of things which gave rise to the people we shall be seeing. They are not, we can now believe, the result of mixtures of Caucasoids, Veddoids, Papuans, Melanesians, Negritos, Proto-Malays, Deutero-Malays – all the 'types' or big and little races abounding in the older literature. The reality of such ingredients has always been inferred, never proved. I must confess that I have in the past done some inferring of this kind, but the rise of genetic theory and present methods of analysis of material show that it must be abandoned.

I am not saying there are no races in the form of major population differences: Caucasoid, African, Mongoloid, all of which are now breeding true in the British Isles or the United States.[1] These are the result of older, continental separations, on a grander scale, about whose origins we still know nothing. We shall, in fact, be asking how many such grand divisions may be represented in the total of Pacific peoples. But it is important to begin by looking at the kind of structure I have tried to describe: population complexes, over large areas, of local, naturally differing groups, and to renounce the search for faraway unmixed ancestors. The more we get down to cases, the less baggage we shall need in the form of preconceptions about race and races.

Science Ltd

Earlier, I talked pridefully about the accomplishments of present-day anthropology, comparing them to the work of older writers. But pride goeth before a fall, and the accomplishments of any age are incomplete. Our work today is still coarse-grained. The archaeologists have clearer dates and records, but their conclusions are subject to abrupt changes because of unexpected finds in unexpected places; and they have always a great deal of homework to do in the close comparison of styles, of stone-working techniques, or of pottery form and texture. Comparisons of these give them their answers, the hole in the ground being only the start. The linguists are still collecting languages intensively and going from one level of complexity to the next; now that the Pacific has been thoroughly explored one might think language study would be tapering off, but the opposite is true. Physical anthropology, which I shall be trying to use as a main witness, is especially unfulfilled. The total of actual information is miniscule compared to what might be had. So, while it is fine to have computers, they can give judicious answers only to judicious questions based on good data, and the gaps keep us from asking all those questions.

There are other questions to which we cannot give sure answers.

---

[1] If you try to go much further, you will begin to see the futilities of 'classification'. The US census classes Americans as White and Non-white, which is preposterous but probably good sense. Other official forms evidently have further boxes to check, like 'Oriental'. I am telephoned regularly by some frustrated clerk asking, 'What race is a person from India?'

As a safe thread to lead us back through the labyrinth of movements, contacts and migrations, we have no absolute proof that
physique remains the same, that the 'races' we see today are like
their direct ancestors a few thousand years ago – well within the
time of Pacific prehistory. Blood groups in particular are probably
quite untrustworthy as a guide to origins over any such period.
From all the signs, skulls and teeth are much more stable; the
burden of proof is on anyone who argues otherwise, though we
cannot say why cranial form should be persistent.

So I must warn the reader that some of the 'science' behind
reconstructions of Pacific history is still pretty soft, with plenty
of room for guesswork, or what is known professionally as 'constructing tentative working hypotheses'. I shall be cautious, but
not to the point of suffocation. Some who have tried to re-create
movements and migrations have grown old in the effort, and have
come to doubt that, for example, the origin of the Australians will
ever be known. Others feel reconstructing history is a pastime, not
real science, which should deal in basics.[1] That is true. Physical
anthropology should be concerned with fundamental aspects of
biological structure and change, as I could show, I would like to
think, from some tedious articles of my own. Archaeologists feel
their obligation, as social scientists, to study the ecology and social
patterns of bygone communities. Good. And to linguists, matters
like a Pacific argosy may be infradig, their mission being to view
language as expressing social patterns and cultural imperatives,
even the structuring of human consciousness – using linguistics as
a keyhole to peep at Psyche bare. Good.

But let us loosen our collars. Breathes there an anthropologist
with soul so dead as never to have asked: 'Where *did* the Polynesians come from?' I think an archaeologist's eye sparkles less over
a settlement pattern than over a striking new date or discovery.
Prehistoric reconstruction is history, after all, and if it happens
to be particularly good fun as well, let us not be puritanical.
I have enjoyed myself greatly in reconsidering the physical
anthropology of the Pacific. I have taken particular pleasure in
learning what I could from the surge of knowledge in archaeology
and linguistics in the last few years, above all in the broad and
imaginative interpretations lately put out by certain of my fellow
anthropologists. These are speculative to a degree, but their makers

[1] I am not creating straw men; these are virtual quotations.

8

know the basis of fact thoroughly from their own and others work, and do not mind finding later on that their speculations have been wrong in part. Their interpretations do the service of drawing attention to what the facts suggest, and this pushes study along a little faster in every field. It is also what puts excitement in it all. I shall try to do them justice; in any case I am in their debt.

2

Land,
people and culture

Oceania is an island world, its land surface dispersed by the waters of the Pacific. This creates special confinements of the movements and the contacts of its inhabitants, even when their boats command long distances like those separating the Polynesian archipelagos. Climatically it offers considerable contrast, as between the drenching monsoon of Java and the aridity of the Australian desert. Topographically also: New Guinea is an island, but its interior highland natives do not know this; they have no conception of the sea and no word for it, while an atoll dweller in Micronesia must be conscious of it each minute of his life.

Fortunately the variety, geographic and human, is strongly patterned, which makes it easier to describe and deal with. The traditional divisions serve almost all our purposes. Aside from Australia, we have Polynesia, the 'Many Islands', lying in widely separated groups east of the international date line. Just west of the line is Fiji, where the world's days begin; from here Melanesia (the 'Black Islands') extends westward through New Guinea. North of Melanesia lie the islets of Micronesia, most diminutive land areas of all. And west of both Melanesia and Micronesia are the major land masses of Indonesia, the Indies of former days. This does *not* mean simply the Republic of Indonesia. It does not include West Irian (the western half of New Guinea), which is anthropologically (and of course geographically) Melanesian, but it does include the Philippines and, again anthropologically and geographically, Formosa. (The Chinese citizens of Taiwan are to the aboriginal tribes of the island as the

'White' citizens of the United States are to the American Indians.

In the whole Southwest Pacific the land is actually continental in nature and area. Australia, the southern anchor, is a true continent. Part of Indonesia is likewise truly continental, with the islands of Sumatra, Java and Borneo sitting on the continental shelf of Southeast Asia. The straits lying between them, and separating them from the mainland, are narrow and shallow; and at various times in the Pleistocene when seas were lower, they were all part of Asia. That is how the typical large mammals of the mainland got into these islands, and how man himself, about a million years ago, first entered Java.

In Indonesia's eastern half the straits are narrow but often very deep, so that they did not join the western land mass. None the less, during the seventy million years of the Tertiary, radical rises and falls in this unstable zone allowed placental mammals ('our' kind) to penetrate from Asia, now here, now there, and even during the Pleistocene. Later than Java Man but probably long before recent man, perhaps 150,000 years ago, earlier human beings also got into many of these islands.

With the island of Timor this zone comes close (three hundred miles) to the northwest corner of Australia. Here again is a stable land mass, which includes New Guinea. But all along its edge deep waters have made an important barrier for land animals, which the placental mammals never crossed. Instead, New Guinea and Australia, also joined at times by lower seas, have been a refuge for other kinds of mammals, the marsupials and the monotremes, the last being the very peculiar egg-laying platypus and spiny anteater. New Guinea is more mountainous and more fertile than Australia, with ranges higher than 15,000 feet in both east and west. Australia has nothing half this height, its highest point being Mount Kosciusko, with an altitude of 7,328 feet.

Eastward from New Guinea, curving around to the south, the rest of Melanesia forms a broad arc of islands of respectable size, though they are small compared to New Guinea itself. These are also of continental character, in the varied rock types which compose them, and in the kind of faulting and mountain-building they show; at any rate they are neither volcanic nor coral in their primary nature. New Ireland, facing the open ocean on the north, looks like a pushed-up piece of coral, but it rests on igneous rocks; and its large southern neighbor in the Bismarck Archipelago,

New Britain, is mostly formed of granite. The Solomons make a double chain extending southeast from New Britain and pointing toward the New Hebrides and Fiji; Bougainville in the Solomons has recently been the scene of a major copper lode find. To the south of all lies New Caledonia, another large island, with a wealth in nickel ores, once more a 'continental' trait. Finally, well below the tropics, is New Zealand, exceptional in being so large an isolated land mass and in being originally populated not by Melanesians but by the Polynesian Maori.

All along the northern edge of this whole arc of islands runs the Andesite Line [242]. Beyond it lies the deep, quiet Pacific Basin with its widely separated islands which sit on the tops of volcanic mountains. The volcanoes are quiet: they pour out basaltic lava, building up great mounts from the sea floor of which many have become islands. Not so the volcanoes of the 'continental' islands and other areas outside the Andesite Line (which runs all around the Pacific on the north and down the Americas). These are violent and explosive and so are the earthquakes of this zone, especially from the Philippines through Japan and around the American west coasts. The Solomons likewise have earthquakes, and the town of Rabaul, at the volcanic north end of New Britain, has periodically had such deadly volcanic explosions and convulsions that, in spite of its beautiful harbor and hills, it has lost its former position as capital of the Territory of New Guinea. Going skyward every thirty years is too much for most administrations to stomach. By contrast, under comfortable Mauna Loa on the island of Hawaii, the goddess Pele fumes and spits discreetly: her occasional lava flows may burn down a little property but otherwise she is spectacular and harmless, perfect for tourism.

Opposite Melanesia, on the north side of the equator, are three festoons of the Micronesian islands. The first of them sits on a long ridge which runs from the west end of New Guinea north to Tokyo, following the Andesite Line and curving around the Philippine Sea: these island groups from south to north are Palau, Yap and the chain of the Marianas including Guam and Saipan. The second chain runs straight east from Yap: these are the Carolines, mostly coral atolls but with a few volcanic members surrounded by reefs, such as Truk, Ponape and Kusaie. The third crosses the end of the second on the east, where the Marshall Islands begin a long line running southeast through the Gilbert

Islands and the Ellice Islands (culturally Polynesian) to abut the Andesite Line between Fiji and Tonga.

East of the international date line, in the great empty half of the Pacific, are scattered the Polynesian groups. They lie in a great triangle with Tahiti at the center and with isolated angles at Hawaii in the north, Easter Island in the east and New Zealand in the southwest, each of these being at least twelve hundred miles from another inhabited Polynesian neighbor.

All (except New Zealand) are built on ocean volcanoes, rising from the bottom. For human habitation especially it is convenient to divide them into 'high' and 'low' islands. In the former, volcano-building has carried above sea level, perhaps well above, making good-sized fertile islands, often of dramatic shape. Low islands have formed when the mountain top does not now rise above the sea, but has done so in the past or else has been close enough for coral to grow on it, and so the visible material of the island is coral. Some Pacific atolls must have had extremely long histories of growth as the base sank: test drills on Eniwetok in the Micronesian Marshalls went down through over four thousand feet of coral and limestone before reaching volcanic rock.

Atolls are a typical development of such growth, and Charles Darwin first divined how they form. If coral grows up from a submerged top (which cannot be deeper than about a hundred and fifty feet at a maximum if coral is to grow at all), it will do better on the seaward side, since the polyps need water with salt near its natural concentration, as well as nutriment. Eventually this produces a ring enclosing a lagoon, which does not fill up because its waters support coral growth poorly; this is the ideal atoll. But all combinations of reef and island can occur. If a high island is submerging, reefs will grow around its shores: a fringing reef in contact with the beach and a barrier reef further out, again enclosing a lagoon. Contrariwise, when volcanic islands have more recently risen from the sea (for example the Marquesas Islands) such reefs may not have formed; the shores rise straight from the water without reef protection and navigation and fishing are more difficult.

Land Areas

To wax statistical for a moment, we may compare the actual land areas of the several regions, remembering that jagged mountains

and red deserts are not as habitable as healthy fertile valleys. The
following are the numbers of square miles:[1]

Australia	2,974,581
Indonesia	788,541
New Guinea	316,615
Island Melanesia	58,271
New Zealand	103,736
Island Polynesia	9,964
Micronesia	1,326

For comparative sizes, let us take Australia as 100.[2] On this
scale, Indonesia (*including* the Philippines and Formosa) is 26·5,
New Guinea is 10·6, Island Melanesia is 2·0, New Zealand is 3·5,
Island Polynesia is 0·3, and Micronesia is 0·04. Or, summing all
the land areas large and small, in Polynesia and Melanesia, we
have:

Melanesia	12·6
Polynesia	3·8
Micronesia	0·04

Evidently 'Micronesia' is a good name – its total area is slightly
greater than that of Samoa alone, which in turn is slightly larger
than the state of Rhode Island.

Aboriginal Population Numbers

Land areas are obviously no guide to numbers of people. The
Australian desert on one hand, and an island of favorable size with
fertile land and plenty of sea life around it on the other, are two
quite different bases of support for man. Human culture is the
second factor: if the inhabitants are pure extractors – hunters
and gatherers, as in Australia – even a fertile environment will not
provide what cultivators can wring from it.

The numbers actually living in various regions before Europeans
arrived is now hard to estimate, given the often violent impact of

[1] Sources used for area and populations include: Kennedy [137]; *Handbook
of Papua and New Guinea; Pacific Islands Monthly;* McArthur [163]; *Information
Please Almanac.*

[2] Including Tasmania. On the same scale the continental United States, not
including Alaska, would be 101·6.

the last two hundred years with diseases like measles and influenza, and the atrocious raiding for labor. The worst case of the latter was the carrying-off of the greater part of Easter Island's population to work in the mines of Peru, and that was by no means the only island to suffer. Some of these victims were eventually repatriated, but the repatriators often thought one island as good as another to dump their obligations on. And the fifteen survivors who got back to Easter Island brought smallpox.

So the common story has been one of population decline, followed by a low point in the late nineteenth century and a rise in the present one. In some cases the declines have been thought to be devastating; but that idea may be false, due simply to gross overestimates of the original population, perhaps four times the actual one. That is to say, a decline from 100,000 to 20,000 would be devastation itself; decline from 25,000 to 20,000 would merely be a decline. Early observers, including the hard-headed Captain Cook and his associates, seem always to have erred on the inflationary side, doing their reckoning for a given island group from crowds seen in one place, numbers of native canoes counted, or simply miles of coastline, whether or not the interior might have been equally thickly settled. Dr Norma McArthur, a leading student of population and its rises and falls, has reviewed [163] the whole known population history of a number of archipelagos and finds that deflated estimates of original numbers are sounder and more consistent.

Let us take Tahiti, which has been carefully considered by both McArthur and Oliver [183]. Tahiti was indeed subjected to invasions of venereal disease, dysentery, some kind of influenza virulent for the natives, smallpox, scarlet fever and whooping cough, at least; and also to the extra spin put on internal wars which was provided by missionaries christianizing some chiefs and so giving them one more thing to fight for. This is a formidable list: the glamorous view of that beautiful island and its beautiful people which prevailed in the drawing-rooms of Europe must have had a reverse side, the view seen by the Tahitians themselves.

At any rate, numbers counted in the seventy years up to 1900 (now including non-Tahitians) ran to about 8,000 to 10,000 souls. But naturalists on Cook's second visit – after Tahiti had apparently already had its first gift of some kind of influenza from a Spanish ship – figured the population in 1774 as 120,000. This they considered a moderate estimate, since from the breadfruit-carrying capacity of the island they thought the number might actually be between 170,000 and 204,000. Compare two later estimates cited by McArthur, both made in 1797. A pair of missionaries toured the island and reckoned 50,000 people; another man made the same tour a few days later, counting houses, and estimated 16,500.

McArthur herself concludes that, before the first contact in 1767, the population would have been under 35,000, and perhaps nearer 18,000 as a low figure, which is still actually a fairly large population. Oliver, however, from some detailed lists of localities, thinks 30,000 is actually the best estimate. Any of them suggests some caution when one reads that New Zealand and Hawaii might have had 250,000 inhabitants apiece (Cook's estimates), Hawaii perhaps as many as 400,000. The generally accepted figure for Hawaii at Cook's arrival is 300,000, though at the first actual count in 1823 it was under 135,000 and by 1853 was down to 70,000. Schmitt [207,275], the latest reviewer, estimates less than 250,000, perhaps as low as 200,000.

Even for Yap in Micronesia, with thirty-nine square miles of land, two competent anthropologists have been willing to accept old estimates of 40,000 or 50,000 respectively. The last would give a density of over 1,250 persons per square mile, which is manifestly suspicious;[1] more likely estimates would be between 7,500 and 10,000 – say 8,000 – and even that might be generous.

So we might look at some estimates for pre-contact numbers, loosely made on the basis of all this, but probably conservative.

In Australia, before the taking of land for farming and the sliding of considerable numbers of aboriginals into the slums of the cities of the southeast, the population has been figured at from 250,000 to 300,000. In such hunter-gatherer societies, social groupings tend to be of uniform size, while density fluctuates according to natural resources. Grossly, any Australian 'tribe' – that is to say, a group of bands speaking one language – is thought to have numbered about five hundred, its territory being larger in poor regions, smaller where natural food was better and more reliable. This

---

[1] Some present-day figures may approach such a density, to give a fair indication. For example, Kapingamarangi [161] is rated at 1,040 per square mile, having only 0·52 square miles, and this is extreme. On the other hand, existing densities in the Gilberts (432 p.s.m.) and the Ellice Islands (757) are described by the colony administration as constituting 'acute' population pressure (GEIC report for the years 1964 and 1965, published 1968).

would be a safer estimate than any juggling of densities and, given about five hundred languages, leads to the figure cited. Tasmania [134] had perhaps 4,000 aboriginals, also distributed unevenly, the mountainous rain forest being empty.

New Guinea, where the people had been expert horticulturalists for a long time, all over the island, was found to have a surprisingly dense population when the healthy and fertile highlands were entered by Europeans for the first time in the 1930s. The former Dutch half, now West Irian, was explored sooner and is rather less favorable. In any case large areas in both halves are still almost unaffected by outside contact. With the putting down of warfare and head-hunting, and control of such disease as there is (tuberculosis is a danger) the population has been increasing. But it can hardly have declined seriously at any time; it is exceptional among the 'primitive' areas of the world for its high numbers and its fairly dense occupation by a great many mutually isolated communities and languages. Having today well over 2,500,000 natives in the whole island, it very likely had a population of 2,000,000 in its recent aboriginal state.

Island Melanesia is difficult to assess. Among other diseases malaria and yaws were endemic. European contact was varied as to time but generally late; and these large islands were explored only gradually, some very recently indeed. Except for Fiji and New Caledonia the population is still overwhelmingly – almost entirely – indigenous, something hardly true of Hawaii or New Zealand in Polynesia. Numbers of the original stock have been increasing rapidly in recent decades: a rough total, from the Admiralties through Fiji, from various counts over the last ten years, amounts to something over 700,000.

Reckoning any distance into the past would be difficult. Distribution in the Solomons, for example, is spotty. Bougainville has a population of over 70,000, growing rapidly, and Malaita has more than 55,000: but other islands of similar size had far fewer. Choiseul, with under 8,000, is unpopulated in the middle, the cause being head hunters from New Georgia late in the last century (apparently this was a result of approaching civilization, steel axes having lightened life's burdens for the men of New Georgia so much that they found time hanging heavy and employed it in head taking). Similar effects from blackbirding–raiding by whites for profit, not by blacks for pleasure – are unmeasured.

New Caledonia is estimated to have had a population of 70,000 in 1850, but this sounds like the suspect figures I have described; the island had 36,670 Melanesians in 1958 and 43,300 in 1964. For Fiji – the only area taken in hand by McArthur – the first census, in 1879, counted 108,924 Fijians (with a few thousand missing). This was after an apparently disastrous measles epidemic, and various other estimates and counts suggest an original figure on the order of 130,000 to 140,000. Numbers declined continuously to 1921, when the census was 84,475 Fijians. Since then the Fijians have been outnumbered and outbred by the population imported from India; at the end of 1970 there were 266,189 Indians, but there were also 255,102 Fijians, and for the first time birth rates for the two had come together.

Such fluctuations and uncertainties make it impossible to see the center of the target, but with a likely original population for Fiji of 130,000, the total for Melanesia must have been over 300,000, and this could be conservative.

To come back to Polynesia and Micronesia, these have almost certainly been overvalued. McArthur believes that all the Polynesian groups whose population histories she reviewed (Tonga, Samoa, the Cooks, and French Polynesia, which runs from Tahiti eastward and includes the Marquesas) would have summed to a mere 100,000. This seems low indeed, especially since Oliver rates Tahiti higher than does McArthur; but I cannot guess by how much to increase the figure. Hawaii should have had much more than the 135,000 of the 1823 figure, but from what we have seen 300,000 would be too high. If Hawaii and New Zealand each had about 200,000, and Easter Island a few thousand, the whole of Polynesia might have had between 500,000 and 600,000.

Micronesia? Rapidly growing populations can be sustained by some areas at least: native Gilbertese rose from 29,923 in 1947 to 40,702 in 1963, but this is a doubtful guide. So is the 1964 population of the rest of Micronesia, Guam included: about 133,000 (Truk alone had 24,521). So an indigenous total for Micronesia, not up to date, is 174,000. To show how this represents recent increase, apparently just after a long decline from disease and cultural interference, compare totals for 1935–7, about 98,000; and 1947–9, about 107,000 [102]. Aboriginally, however, we must remember the limited resources, and the effect of periodic typhoons in chopping back group after group. Ulithi (pop. 1949, 421; 1960,

514) was struck, in November 1960, by a very severe typhoon [145], with inadequate Coast Guard warning (there would have been none at all in the old days). Two lives only were lost, both children drowned after being pinned down in a fallen house. A quarter of the houses were wrecked. But this kind of damage is not the point. Two-thirds of about fifty outrigger canoes were destroyed, and only two of the six ocean-going canoes survived undamaged. Two-thirds of the coconut trees were lost, and all coconuts blown down; banana plants and breadfruit trees were rendered temporarily useless; taro pits were filled with salt water and sand, and the taro lost; beaches were greatly eroded and changed. Ships arrived promptly from Guam with C rations and saved the population with this disgusting European food. Now imagine aboriginal times. No ship summoned by radio with food; almost no food except some rescued coconuts on the island; few canoes left for fishing off reshaped beaches; only two canoes to travel to Yap for possible help. The loss of life would not have been two small boys, but most of the population.

If, then, islands like Yap, Palau and Truk had populations running from 8,000 to 12,000, these being guesses, and if we allow something more generous for the Marianas, we might award Micronesia an aboriginal population of 80,000.

The following, then, are possible figures for the several parts of the pre-European Pacific. They are strictly my own totals, from the discussion above, and have no official or expert standing. It is almost an act of irresponsibility to try such tallies at all in the circumstances, and I do so simply to suggest orders of magnitude and as a comment on errors of the past. (I can suggest no figure for Indonesia, since its history had carried it into a civilized state, with a very heavy population, long before European arrival there).

Australia	250,000
New Guinea	2,000,000
Island Melanesia	300,000
Polynesia	550,000
Micronesia	80,000

Outlines of Culture

How the people live – what they eat and make, their social systems and religious ideas – follows the same conventional divisions. Not precisely, however: to suppose so would assume that the islanders had dropped from the clouds, without histories of movement, development and exchange. Also, excepting for the hunters of Australia, there are some general Oceanic items or ideas, though they may be differently emphasized. The base of domestic plants is one; the sacredness of human heads, going beyond mere trophy-taking, is another. And there are cross-cutting patterns of importance as well, such as a Polynesian development of aristocracy overlying a Melanesian social organization in Fiji or the Trobriands. Micronesia, we shall see, has 'mixtures' of ideas characteristic of Melanesia or Polynesia. By contrast Polynesia, though differing in material gear from west to east, has a highly unified social and economic structure, which was apparently developed early and adhered to with tenacity as new island groups were settled [168, 9].

Here are sketches of the cultures of each of the general Pacific areas as they were seen at the time of European arrival.

AUSTRALIA

The Australians and the Tasmanians were pure hunter-gatherers. The men were exceedingly skillful at hunting down a healthy diet of marsupials (kangaroo, opossum, etc.), lizards (especially the goanna), witchetty grubs and where possible birds and fish. The women were responsible for digging up and gathering wild plants, along with honey ants and other such small game as they came across. They used a simple grubbing stick and put their booty in an oval wooden bowl or a string net. The men, aided by the dingo, did their hunting with thrown spears or clubs. All this was pure hand work for, unlike settled peoples who may hunt a good deal in the woods around them, the Australians were without traps. They lived as constant nomads, camping where there was water, carrying everything with them – spears, spear-throwers, trays, bags and, last but not least, infant aboriginals. Costume for the men, always optional, was a bark or string belt and cord wrapped around greased hair (a good place to carry a supply of cord). Female apparel was rather less.

Their manufactures were limited to what the above implies. Stone knives and axes were well and simply made, if not technically impressive; they were hafted by a very strong gum which called for elaborate preparation. Hair, usually human, was used for cord and netting. Containers were made of bark or soft wood. With this small inventory of goods, and with any kind of a substantial hut a rarity, it can be seen that they would ordinarily have left very little cultural debris for the investigation of archaeologists. They did, it is true, make occasional milling stones, as well as bone points. We must also count sacred objects. Their churingas, engraved flattish stones, might survive, but the other things were highly perishable structures of feather, string and wood. For ceremonies their costumes consisted typically of glueing feathers and down in patterns to the body with their own blood as an adhesive, together with much use of paint.

/ Other ritualistic attention was paid to the body, but not by donning something – rather by mutilations, painful but certainly portable: circumcision; knocking out of some incisor teeth; and scarring the arms, chest and back in broad and heavy welts by making cuttings and filling the cuts with ashes. The tribal distributions of these things show that, as ideas, they have probably been diffusing for a long period over the continent from some original point or points. This gradual and rather regular transmission is something we might bear in mind in other Australian connections/

For all the wandering, the lack of cultural encumbrance, the close contact of nature and the human body, there was an astonishingly high degree of organization of society and of land. Nomadism was not absolute. A band, everywhere about thirty to thirty-five souls, moved after fresh game within its own territory where it knew the water-holes and the routes; it avoided on pain of conflict the territory of other bands, which of course had their own problems of water and precious supplies. If they were nomads, they were not like pioneers. The Yankee frontiersman took God with him when he moved, and of course the Devil as well./But in Australia, the totem spirits, the connection between man and nature, were intimately identified with each particular landscape, The myths, the aboriginal bible, were all about this rock, that ocher deposit, those trees and the totem heroes which each such thing commemorated. A horde, therefore, was held to its homeland by a supernatural bond, and not only by antipathy toward trespassers on the part of other hordes. So any change of location, even expansion into empty territory, would be slow, held in check by spiritual unfamiliarity with new country./

But this did not mean compartmentalizing and isolation of the population. Society was so thoroughly organized, on a totemic basis, that everyone knew whom he could or could not marry and who his 'relatives' were – such was the general elaboration of the classificatory system that it enforced intermarriage of bands, but also gave a means for extending classified relatives ever outward. So a man could travel, on peaceful intent or in the pursuit of connective totemic legends, and always find out how he stood in relation to some stranger host (and the host's womenfolk). Thus there was in fact a mechanism for the slow, peaceful transmission of ideas and culture, and of genes as well – a mechanism which was stable, with brakes against abrupt movements, changes or migrations. (Genes were also exchanged at occasional corroborrees, when a whole tribe met and normal bars were down.) All this is of importance to interpretation of micro-evolution, and also culture history; and it contrasts strongly with New Guinea. The pattern is probably of considerable antiquity. Perhaps the study of language will eventually help here, by revealing anything special about linguistic likenesses and transmission in the continent as a whole.

INDONESIA

By way of contrast with Australia's general simplicity, we may turn to Indonesia to see the great range of cultures which have entered the Pacific or paused at its brink.

As a meeting point of human and cultural currents the region (with Southeast Asia) is probably unique. If we look at it on the map we have no difficulty in understanding this for prehistoric times; and its known history is that of a zone of conflict among nations, among religions, and among cultural traditions. In the early sixteenth century it was the end of the line, so to speak, for the Spanish coming from America in the east and the Portuguese coming around Africa from the west. The Dutch replaced the Portuguese, and the French and British appeared, taking over Indo-China and part of Borneo respectively. The Spanish remained to christianize the Philippines, always troubled however by the Moros in the south – the 'Moors' – the northernmost spearhead of Islam coming via India from the Arab world across the Indian Ocean. Islam has been the most successful religion, even expanding recently at the western end of New Guinea. In Indonesia it overran Hinduism (except in Bali), which in turn had overcome the earlier spread of Buddhism. The Chinese made a colony of Formosa and were important traders further south a thousand years ago, particularly in Borneo, which still supplies birds' nests for soup. But the great external influence was that of India. The latter not only furnished three religions but also writing and the flavor of so much art and building. It also supplied the pattern of small states governed by rajahs and sultans, giving rise occasionally to important empires like that of Majapahit (Java) or Shrivishaya (Sumatra).

Thus civilization in Indonesia goes well back to the beginning of the Christian era, and then gives way rather abruptly to an archaeological past. This known history explains thè higher arts and politics. It is interesting for us mainly as demonstrating how its geography has placed it at the end of various channels of influence: from the mainland; down the east coast of Asia from China; and along the south of Asia from India.

Underneath the historical culture lies a simpler, pagan one. Various names, none very satisfactory, have been suggested for it, such as 'Proto-Malay'. It is the indigenous culture, masked by the long reign of civilized communities but still existing and having various features in common with the aboriginal tribes of Formosa and the Philippines right down to the Barrier Islands south of Sumatra. When I say the people live in autonomous rice-growing villages, this is widely true; when I say that they are head hunters I mean that they were such until colonial or independent governments could stop them. Not very old men still remember unpublicized head takings, and nobody could prove that they have actually ended everywhere.

The people tattoo themselves – gaudily in some parts, with restraint in others – and may file their teeth or in other ways deface them, perhaps removing the enamel in front so as to allow a dark stain to replace the white, which is despised (only animals, children and Europeans have white teeth). But their lives are not by any means as barbaric as this suggests. Villages are well built and well kept; the longhouse of Borneo is one of the most striking forms, but other substantial raised wooden houses are used, for example in Formosa. Communities are of moderately good size – a few hundred – and govern themselves as a rule by a head man and a council of elders. Ideas of law are well developed for people at such a culture stage. But religion is not. Spirits are minor beings, not the basis for much priestly ritual. Instead the approach to them is highly practical: they are desired either to keep away or to come on some specific errand of aid to the applicant. Small sacrifices serve as the incentive.

The staff of life is rice, and everyone has seen pictures of the admirable terraces built on hillsides by the Filipinos, to hold water for their paddies. But this practice is perhaps not the oldest, and many peoples, notably the Borneans, grow other varieties of rice less efficiently in dry gardens. Others grow millet; still others depend on yams, with the important recognition of coconuts, bananas or other fruits. Many are good hunters, using the blowgun, spear or bow, and they are excellent and ingenious trappers as well. Thus on a solid economic base they live settled and well-ordered lives, very different from the wandering Australians. Their arts and the impedimenta in their houses are in accord. They are good weavers and dyers (a few, however, make and use beaten bark like the tapa of Polynesia). They are good iron workers as well, and also do some work in brass for personal adornment. Basketry is good, pottery indifferent.

If we arbitrarily allocate the civilized bulk of Indonesia's population to the cosmopolitan world of China, India and Europe, then the people I have just described constitute the highest level of Pacific culture. They are not the primitive people of the region, for still other groups exist who are not village farmers but live as nomad hunters, moving from camp to camp in the forest. Such are the Shom Pen of the Nicobar Islands, the Kubu of Sumatra, the Toala of Celebes, the Punan of Borneo and the Negritos of the Philippines, the Semang of the Malay Peninsula and the natives of the Andamans. These are not a unit physically or culturally. The Andaman islanders are Negritos pure and simple, of pigmy stature and infantilized 'Negroid' traits of skin, hair and face. The Philippine Negritos look different, are not invariably small, and are doubtless somewhat mixed with other Philippine populations. In language the Andamanese are isolated from all other known peoples; Philippine Negritos speak Philippine languages. The other hunters are definitely not Negrito but basically resemble other Indonesian peoples. It is hard to say how much the condition of these latter may result simply from cultural impoverishment and how much it represents a real cultural layer of scattered interior remnants of pre-agricultural societies. (I think the first explanation is the more probable.) Only some Philippine Negritos and the Andamanese are shore living, adding sea food to their hunting-gathering diet. We may provisionally assume that the Negritos at least have not regressed culturally and that they are likely to represent an historically separate strain from the other groups mentioned.

MELANESIA

The other three areas, Melanesia, Polynesia and Micronesia, are each culturally more homogeneous, though differing. All are occupied by settled gardeners. None harbors nomadic peoples.

Melanesia begins with a rather ragged border at the west end of New Guinea. In that part of Indonesia there are some Papuan languages and Melanesian-looking people, while in New Guinea itself Indonesian influence has been fairly strong at that end, on both the north and south coasts. Bronze artefacts have been found at Lake Sentani behind Sukarnapura (the former Hollandia), well along the north shore, as one example of Indonesian trade and influence. Elsewhere in Melanesia there exist two major linguistic strata, of the Papuan and Austronesian languages, a fact which will not be neglected in later chapters.

The Melanesians, with their dark skins and 'Negroid' appearance, are of course different from the Indonesians, and in their often lavish dance or ritual costumes they give a more barbarous impression. But their economic life is the same, except that the staples are yams, sweet potato, taro and the banana-plantain family – no grain. They all raise pigs for meat, and New Guineans can hunt a few marsupials as well. Their cultivation is complex and skillful, and they are also fond of decorative plants, especially croton, in and around the village. Partly because of New Guinea's great size, more Melanesians live inland than on the water; but the shore dwellers know the uses of the sea, in fishing, in trading by canoe and, paralleling some Indonesians, in living in pile dwellings over the water for comfort and protection. There is rather more of an accent on secret societies and men's houses, some of which in New Guinea are of great size. But the people share various ideas with Indonesia, especially head trophies and religious beliefs, which turn on ghosts and spirits. The industrial arts put them on a lower plane: their excellent woodwork was formerly done entirely with stone tools, or shell and boar-tooth knives. Pottery, not of high quality, is made fairly widely, though only in special villages or islands. Mats and baskets are made by plaiting, and net string bags are important, especially in New Guinea. A principal interest is manufacturing special objects for prestige trade: shell money or bailer shell ornaments; boar-tusk armlets; feather 'doughnuts' the size of a large pudding; mats; axes.

POLYNESIA

Polynesian culture is like a further step in the same direction, though it has a strong stamp of its own. Foods which are secondary in Melanesia become primary here, breadfruit and coconut especially. Both of these can be eaten at somewhat different stages of ripeness, and the former can be stored by mashing down the meat in a pit. There can be little hunting for animal meat – there is little 'inland' in these smaller islands, and no native wild animals of value as food in places so distant from the continents. The one exception was the giant flightless bird of New Zealand, the moa, which the early Maoris soon hunted into extinction. Thus the pigs, chickens and dogs which the Polynesian explorers brought with them could be raised for feasts but hardly for daily consumption. Instead the Polynesians took fish and other sea life in great abundance and by a variety of skillful means and no one could complain of a diet poor in protein.

It is hardly necessary to insist here on their achievements in navigating ocean-going canoes. The best of these, sail powered, were very large and fast, and were put to sea on the basis of a considerable native science of wind, currents and star positions. Polynesians were in and out of boats of all sizes all their lives, and we need only recognize that without this development the islands could not have been settled. Castaways on a raft, even had they survived long voyages, would not have had the food plants or domestic animals to establish themselves on a landfall otherwise so poor in resources.

Culture in Polynesia had a uniformity (New Zealand providing certain exceptions) and a crispness which is striking beside the lands to the west. The great likeness in language was noted early. This was followed by the finding of wide correspondences in the myths and voyaging traditions of different island groups. These in turn were related to the religious aspects of chieftainships, especially in the east. The chief was a sacred, tabu person, deriving his sacredness from his directness of descent from the founding ancestors and beyond them the principal gods themselves. Such a political and religious structure was quite different in character from the simpler gods and chiefs in Indonesia or Melanesia. It widened the authority of a chief, and sometimes led to establishment (by war) of the rule of one man over a whole archipelago. This happened in Hawaii, in full view of the Europeans, where the king was so sacred that none could safely be his spouse except his own sister, until Kamehameha II removed the staggering burden from everyone by bravely decreeing the end of his own sanctity. The idea of mana, of inherent power in object or person, was a prominent one in Melanesia, but not to such a point as this.

These highly developed ideas were a special Polynesian efflorescence. In other ways the culture seems clear-cut. When Europeans came there was no pottery – containers were of wood or coconut shell, or simple basketry. Matting, however, and the use of decorative cord in lashing house parts and boats, were real artistic achievements. Except for a very crude cloth in New Zealand, virtually finger-woven from bark thread, there were no loom textiles; instead tapa – bark cloth made by beating the inner bark of the paper mulberry out into flexible sheets – was made in profusion and colored and painted handsomely; even the tapa now produced for tourists can be well made. Upper-class people on a gala occasion might wear large amounts of tapa elegantly arranged in full skirts, along with headdresses, flower wreaths or complicated hair arrangements. Polynesians tattooed themselves lavishly, but were most fastidious about constant washing, cleaning their teeth and oiling themselves, or using perfume and flowers when they felt like it. With their large and well-built houses, their stone temple platforms or maraes, their big decorated canoes (all these things exhibiting skilled carving of beautiful native woods), and their elegance of dress and general sense of beauty, it is little wonder that they appealed at once to the Europeans who first saw them.

MICRONESIA

Micronesia has a Polynesian flavor but lacks the Polynesian homogeneity. The basis of life was similar, with similar limitations. High islands had all the usual food plants; low islands had greater difficulty in growing them, taro needing special pits; and the only reliable food on the driest atolls, except for ubiquitous fishing, was coconut and pandanus. Tapa was not made: the paper mulberry could be grown in few places, and in any case the Micronesians had much better 'cloth'. True textiles were made in several islands, on a simple loom of Indonesian type, and in Kusaie an exceptionally sophisticated technique of dying segments of warp thread was used. Elsewhere – in Samoa too – plaited mats of such fine texture were made that they were pliable as cloth and were used as clothing.

Socially a good deal of variety obtained. Yap had a structure of nine social classes (these are an Indonesian trait) combined with the Polynesian kind of personal aristocracy as well. On Ponape another aristocracy existed of ranked titles, partly hereditary in basis but also achieved by success in yam growing for competitive display; here is a combination of ideas which are Polynesian and Melanesian in character respectively. The stone money of Yap – large and virtually immovable millstone-like objects – also recalls Melanesian ceremonial and reciprocal gift exchange. (The classic Melanesian example of this, made famous by Malinowski, is the kula 'ring' of the Trobriands and other islands off New Guinea, the ring being the circular prescribed route over which prestige-bearing shell ornaments move in a regular pattern.) Micronesian religion was generally in a minor key, with nothing like the Polynesian pantheon.

Altogether the local cultural individuality, though including themes common to Micronesia, Polynesia and Melanesia, suggests a matrix of ideas of some antiquity, from which the more homogeneous Polynesian culture might have budded as a single growth, and which might in fact have been a general importation of the Austronesian-speaking peoples. But, except for language, this is all I shall have to say about the living cultures of Oceania, for two reasons. One is respect for the subject of cultural and social anthropology: it has been the work of the great majority of students of the Pacific and a non-ethnologist like myself should not try to use it critically.[1]

The second reason is that I doubt whether living cultural forms are safe materials in historical reconstruction. Instead, I shall

---

[1] There are plenty of good books on culture, especially for Australia. Oliver's *The Pacific Islands* [181] is perhaps the most general.

describe the people themselves: how they look and how anthropologists assess them through blood and external features. But anthropologists have now realized that trying to work out prehistory from physical traits alone is little better than phrenology. So, after learned chapters on body form and blood, I shall plunder the wagon train of the linguists, whose brilliant work adds much more. If, after plundering, I seem like the Comanche who does not know how to put on the cuffs and corsets he has plundered, do not blame the linguists; I am not their responsibility. I shall then proceed with general examinations of major areas. Here it is the archaeologists who have the unanswerable facts, even though language and physique can tell them when and where to step carefully.

3

Outer differences: color, size and shape

The Pacific has people who are light brown and people who are almost black. It has Polynesians who are tall and run to corpulence, and New Guineans who are all muscle and bone and other New Guineans who are dwarf in size. How do these many populations differ? And why, when and how did they come to differ? The first question – how they differ – could be answered at great length, but out of mercy for the reader I shall be as economical as I can, partly with help from that new genie, the computer. The second question covers the whole work of physical anthropology; it is the story of recent human evolution. But it is not the story of this book.

Still, we must face the questions, if only superficially, because, if there is one thing we must not do, it is to be satisfied with that simple idea that some 'pure' ancient 'races' came out into the Pacific, and there mixed: end of story. Without doubt, populations which were physically quite different did arrive, and did mix in varying degrees. I shall be trying to trace this. But we have to remember that they may have changed after they came, just as they evolved before they came. It is known that people can change measurably in a new environment, in one generation, as did Japanese who migrated to Hawaii [210]. Such immediate change generally reflects nutrition, good or bad, and it seems to affect size, not shape, which is far more conservative [240]. So the Polynesians may have become relatively tall in the mid-Pacific rather than in their original home. Proportions in an underfed child or in a whole population appear more deep-seated. Tanner [239] has shown that among long-legged Olympic hurdlers, or short-legged

Olympic weight lifters, or ordinary-legged men in the street, US Blacks are consistently relatively longer-legged than their counterpart Whites (actually an old popular observation). Tall Africans (Tutsi) and short Africans (Hutu) both living in Rwanda have the same pattern of limb proportions as they grow up [111], a pattern differing from that of Europeans. All the same, these tall East Africans give evidence [202] that size is set largely by the inherited constitution of a population and is only partly a plaything of the environment: no child of Pygmies can expect to find himself at the oar of a Harvard crew. Therefore it can be difficult to judge how far a people's size is direct response, within its own genetic limits, to a good environment and diet, and how far it has resulted from natural selection over a longer period. We have at best some justification for thinking that many aspects of physique or shape of head and face are fairly persistent properties of a population.

We have almost no such factual research on Pacific peoples. We can only compare them descriptively, bearing in mind what has been learned elsewhere: how little we can say as to which features can be modified in a single generation, which ones may change in a few centuries as a response to the new and greatly varied kinds of Oceanic habitat, and which ones are so deep-seated that they may have changed hardly at all over thousands of years.

Skin and Hair

These most obvious human differences were naturally the first to be used in the attempt to classify races. Although in this post-Darwinian age we are absolutely obliged to accept the idea that skin color differs because of natural selection, it nevertheless remains a mystery after more than a century of anthropological and physiological study. It is all very well to note that dark skins are associated with the tropics, in Africa, India and the Pacific, where the sun is highest. This is a hint, not an answer. There are tropical peoples (American Indians, Malays) who have not developed very dark skins, and on the other hand many tropical habitats are greatly shaded by clouds or forests.

Unquestionably a densely pigmented skin is an efficient absorber of ultraviolet light and a protector of its own tissues. Australian aboriginals and African Negroes are virtually immune to skin cancers which occur frequently in Caucasoids in the same places exposed to equal amounts of sunlight. Blum [20], reviewing this, is not impressed, since skin cancers are seldom lethal, and occur too late in life for much effective action of natural selection. Loomis [149] has suggested that skin regulates the human synthesis of vitamin D, needed in bone formation and maintenance. Food is not a dependable source (except for fish livers), and in the cloudy northern winters a fair skin, even if only the cheek is exposed, will allow sufficient sunlight to penetrate to synthesize enough vitamin D to prevent rickets. In equatorial latitudes, however, too much vitamin D resulting from sunlight, says Loomis, will bring on calcification of soft tissues, kidney stones and death from kidney disease. Other explanations have called on heat regulation in the body in various ways, but have not been satisfactorily demonstrated from the point of view of selection. And it may well be a mistake to look for single causes. Skin as an organ has several functions, and so its color may also be a response in balance to several factors. The color itself is primarily a brown pigment, melanin, which is a basic property of vertebrates and not special to man. Such a resource is likely to have fulfilled more than one adaptive function, in man as in other animals.

In any case, all this does not appear to bear heavily on problems of the Pacific. As things stand there is no evident reason for the existing distribution – dark-skinned Australians and Melanesians, living both in glaring deserts and misty high mountains, surrounded by lighter-skinned tropical Indonesians, Micronesians and Polynesians – other than the obvious one that these all had their basic skin differences before they came to the Pacific. The main matter of interest is local distinction, above all the very black peoples of Bougainville and a few other places.

There is one intriguing point of a different nature. Melanin is produced in the skin by cells called melanocytes. Oddly, the number of these cells is generally alike in different races (though higher in American Indians than in Africans!), and it is the rate of production of melanin, not the cell number, which controls color; tanning results, even in dark skins, when sunlight stimulates greater production. Melanin is then distributed in the skin in the form of melanosomes, very small granules of the pigment. Recently Szabó and his associates have found [238] that, in a handful each of Caucasians, Chinese, Japanese and American Indians, the melanosomes are packaged, so to speak, or grouped in bunches

surrounded by a membrane. By contrast, in Negroes the melanosomes are longer and wider, and are not packaged but individually
dispersed. Now the melanosomes in Australian aboriginals are
also dispersed in this way. But in some Solomon Island natives of
Bougainville (Nasioi, who are actually particularly dark) and of
Malaita the melanosomes are packaged as in Caucasoids and
Mongoloids. It will be interesting when more is known about
these differences. But that is only one of the things we need to
know more about; we even lack good, systematic records of skin
color itself from most Oceanic peoples.

Hair has a few points of general interest. The variety of form is
great. Australian aboriginals have straight to very curly hair.
Polynesians have a range shifted from this a little in a curlier
direction, but with much hair showing only low waves. Micronesians show, in places, more frizzly hair, probably from Melanesian mixture. Melanesia is typically frizzly haired, or even woolly-
haired, though the average appears less woollied-up than African
hair. And there are even Melanesian localities where straight hair
is found, with wavy hair also, these being where admixture from
the Indonesia–Micronesia–Polynesia arc is a possibility, that is,
among island peoples. not those of central New Guinea.

On top of this, dark reddish hair occurs both in New Guinea
and the Solomons. And over large parts of Australia, especially
the center, children are very often blond-haired, something also
found in much of Melanesia and a few places in Micronesia. As to
hair form, that of Melanesians resembles that of Africans, but is
frizzlier and makes a more open mop, being less spiralled. Like
skin, hair differences have not been solidly explained in terms of
adaptation, but such a mop is certainly advantageous as an in-
sulating body against the sun and it also lets scalp perspiration
evaporate efficiently. A new study by a Harvard student [126]
measures several aspects of hair curl, finding considerable and
significant quantitative distinctions between Solomon Islanders
and Africans, especially in the greater irregularity of curl in the
former. This, with the melanosome difference described above,
argues that Melanesians and Africans are not related and, more
important, probably evolved their tropical adaptations (assuming
that is what they are) of skin and hair independently of one another.

A noticeable if superficial distinction is found in ears. The
characteristic short, squarish, slightly cupped external ear seen

normally in sub-Saharan Africans, including South African Bushmen, does not appear in Melanesians, whose ears are not discernibly different from those of Europeans, unless they are even narrower and longer.

Measurements of Body and Head

Information of this kind has been gathered systematically for a long time and in great amounts, as the standard currency of anthropology. Valuable as it is, you could look at average figures until doomsday without being able to put together more than an outline of likenesses and differences, let alone their meanings. I will not drench the reader with tables of figures. Instead, I have used a computer to simplify and relate them [123], and I will give here only an introductory review of what the measurements have shown.

The Polynesians are tall and large-bodied, with heights falling mostly around 170 to 173 cm (5 ft 7 in. to 5 ft 8 in.). This is tall for the world's populations, even if not for American college boys. Their heads are fairly large and their faces both broad and long (about 145 × 130 mm). For Oceanic peoples the nose is relatively long, though by European standards it is broad at the tip and low between the eyes. The nasal index, or ratio of the breadth to the length, is about 75 to 80, which is by no means a pinched nose.

In the shape of the head, however, there is a pattern of difference. The cephalic index (ratio of breadth to length) is low, i.e. the head is narrow, around the periphery, above all on Easter Island, which has turned in an average figure of 75. As we move toward the center from all directions it rises to about 79 to 81 (in Samoa, Tonga, the Marquesas, the Tuamotus) and reaches its highest level in the Society Islands, at about 85. Only Hawaii breaks the pattern, since although it is on the periphery of Polynesia, heads are as short and round as in Tahiti. Moving into Melanesia we come first to Fiji. In spite of their darker skins and frizzly hair, the Fijians have the measurements of Polynesians, and may individually be very large indeed, like occasional Polynesians. The average height is the same, as is the size of head and face. Only the nose is different, being both shorter and wider than in Polynesia, with a nasal index ten points higher. None of this is surprising in view of the close historic contacts between Fiji and both Samoa and Tonga, especially the latter. It is really the almost complete similarity in measurements which is surprising, and this is apparently somewhat less marked in the interior and west of Fiji.

Polynesian likenesses to Melanesia do not stop here. For example, the people of the southern islands of the New Hebrides, Tanna and Eromanga, approach Polynesians in dimensions of face and nose, though they are somewhat shorter and heads are smaller. As we shall see, the resemblance is probably no coincidence.

Southern New Caledonia also shows a partial likeness to Polynesians in stature and head size. But in northern New Caledonia we meet something quite different: a rather Australian appearance in many men is matched by a likeness in average measurements of height, head, face and nose. The same holds for the Loyalty Islands and for Tolai of northern New Britain (on a not too reliable set of records). In general the Tolai look more like other Melanesians, with entirely woolly hair.

Elsewhere in Melanesia and in New Guinea the impression prevails of disorganized variation, with no large area of uniformity either in appearance or in measurements. But short bodies are the general rule. In interior New Guinea, especially in mountainous areas, at widely separated points, people of truly pygmy stature are found. The shortest on record, forty men of a Tapiro village in West Irian, averaged 145 cm (4 ft 9 in.). Shore people are nearer 160 cm. Outside New Guinea, however, there are further spots of short people, again generally mountain-living: Baining of the Gazelle Peninsula of New Britain (neighbors of the Tolai), Nagovisi of Bougainville, and natives of western Espiritu Santo in the New Hebrides. But these differ among themselves in such things as nose and head measurements and ratios of the same. The rest of Melanesia varies in every kind of way in these same simple measurements; in the south and west of New Guinea men are long-headed, with a relatively delicate build and skull; the latter, with its sloping forehead and flat temples – not really a primitive look – has a graceful quality that has made it a collectors' item among Europeans and not only among the natives (though the latter of course do the basic processing). These same natives often have what has been called a 'Semitic' nose, because of its relative prominence and narrowness. The local heterogeneity, in measurements as in other traits, even in a single island like Bougainville, is quite extraordinary. Both Douglas Oliver and Jonathan Friedlaender, who have done broad surveys in the island, got impressions of marked differences in outward appearance. In a later analysis of Oliver's material [122] I could find no signs of simple local adaptation to environment; rather the variety seemed to reflect differences of old standing, which Friedlaender [66] ascribes to a high degree of local isolation fostered by social fragmentation.

This in miniature is a main problem of Melanesia itself and, beyond it, that of the whole Pacific. With such marked variety, how many different ancestral populations, original immigrants to the Pacific, should be allowed for? (Obviously, the fewer the better.) One might expect, from the observations I have been making, about four for Melanesia alone: Australoid, Melanesian (the ordinary negroid-looking kind), 'Papuan' (the narrow-nosed, high-skulled types) and 'Negrito', a true pygmy black. Just such a set has been commonly accepted in the past. How can we tell if these are realities? How can we tell if there are really boundaries, physical and genetic, between them? This is a main problem of my book; I will take it up in smaller pieces further on.

As to Australia, the skull form, with its particularly heavy brows, sets the aboriginals apart to some degree from Melanesians, though there are overlaps here. Stature is about medium (165 cm) or above, but Birdsell found a pocket of shortness near Cairns in Queensland, where in one locality men averaged only 155 cm. Birdsell sees other local distinctions, which we shall look at again; but on the whole Australian heads are long and narrow, and noses short and broad.

Micronesia has not been studied systematically, though we have a number of short lists of measurements. Some Micronesian populations seem like undersized Polynesians; others, in the west, perhaps more Indonesian; and in the center and west hair, skin and facial features suggest Melanesian connections. Under all this, measurements are less variable. Stature is modest, men averaging between 160 and 165 cm, usually closer to the first figure. Faces are narrower though not necessarily shorter than those in Polynesia, and noses are probably narrower.

Indonesia and Southeast Asia are more difficult to describe either broadly or in detail. There is a general but not pronounced

'Mongoloid' appearance, with straight black hair (sometimes wavy), and a moderate fold of skin over the inner canthus of the eye (causing the 'almond' eye of oriental beauty). These all seem to be a collection of populations distinct from Chinese or Japanese, both in the less 'Mongoloid' features and in a browner skin. Supposed types have often been referred to as Malay, Proto-Malay, Indonesian, etc., but without very specific or useful distinctions following from this. As to measurements, about all one can say is that stature is short (155 to 160 cm) throughout, heads are round (index 80 to 85) and noses, of medium breadth, are not protruding, but are in fact quite flat.

In addition there are 'Negrito' peoples in the Philippines and the interior of the Malay Peninsula who are ethnically quite distinct, with woolly hair and dark skins, sometimes being very short of stature. Certain other short people – the Sakai – do not fall in this category, although they may have mixed somewhat with Negritos. Their name signifies simply 'aboriginal' to the Malayans, and they do appear to be simply a short, nondescript population not fundamentally distinct from Southeast Asiatics generally.

Quoting such cursory descriptions of size and shape and trying to juggle figures on many groups at once has always been difficult and indigestible; and the more figures the worse the confusion has been. It has certainly not begun to solve the problem of 'how many kinds?' Let us now use measurements in a more objective analysis.

A Multivariate Analysis

This is based on finding 'generalized distances' between individuals or populations. Supposing you have two measurements (say, head length and head breadth) for two islands, A and B. You could say, from the figures, that A is four millimeters shorter in the head than B, but three millimeters wider than B. You can put this in a single number, if you want to compare the 'distance' not only of A and B but of a number of others as well. Suppose you plot A and B on graph paper, using head length as latitude and breadth as longitude. The length difference then becomes one side of a right-angled triangle, and the breadth difference the other side. By the old Pythagorean theorem, the hypotenuse (which is the straight line distance from A to B) is the square root of the sum of the squares of the sides, and the answer here is five. Now this is about the limit of the arithmetic I myself can do without a computer. But having one, and using the same kind of geometry, you can increase the number of dimensions, or measurements, that you use, adding stature, or face width, or any number; simply sum the squares of the differences of A and B and take the root and you have the single 'distance' in a multispace.

I assembled [123] average figures on 151 local populations (males only) of the Pacific (excluding Indonesia for the time being), for which the original authors had furnished all seven of the following measurements: stature, head length and breadth, face length and width, and nose height and breadth. Before using such measurements to compute distances, however, something else should be done: they should be transformed. Drawing head length and breadth on graph paper, as I have described, does not mean that the two measurements are really at right angles and independent (as the Pythagorean theorem demands), and so the computed distance might be misleading. One population which was very much like another in shape, but somewhat larger in size, would reflect the size difference in all the seven measurements and so give an unjustly increased estimate of total distance. The tendency of stature, head and face to vary together is called correlation. The computer removed this common element by a method known as principal component analysis, which takes all the information contained in the measurements and transforms it into an equal number of new scales. These have the vital property of being completely independent of each other, which means that, algebraically, they are all at right angles to one another. (Here you must imagine a space having seven dimensions, not three as in the ordinary world.) 'Orthogonal' is the posh word. With this, some or all can properly be used, like the sides of a right triangle, to compute the 'distances' among populations.

These components have another very useful property: they are ranked in importance according to the amount of information they carry over from the original measurements, and they describe themselves accordingly. If you must depend on the measurements in raw form, lacking this property, you are obliged to decide for yourself whether you think differences in body size tell more about relations among peoples than differences in head breadth, let us say, and you may be quite deceived in this. Here the first component, or factor, largely does express size differences among Pacific populations, also specifying that the size differences lie, above all, in the body height and the length and breadth of the *face* (among the measurements available). The same first factor shows that nose breadth is something almost entirely independent of body size, in the same population differences, an interesting if minor point. This first component accounts for fifty-three per cent of all the differences among the 151 populations, which are expressed in the seven measurements.

The second component, which carries almost twenty-four per cent more of the total difference, distinguishes between peoples having broad noses and long heads on the one hand (Australian aboriginals fall at this extreme) and narrower noses and broad heads on the other (central Polynesians are here). The third component, with a further 9·5 per cent of total difference, sorts out peoples who are, concordantly, relatively broad in head, face and nose (Fijians, or New Britain Bainings, two populations which otherwise share little in measured form) from those who are relatively narrow in the same respects (Caroline Islanders). The remaining four components together are associated with an aggregate of only 13·8 per cent of total difference and lack evident meaning of a coherent kind. After some trials I decided they could be dispensed with.

So the working information was virtually all compressed into three scales, explicit as to their meaning and as to their relative importance in distinguishing among 151 samples of Oceanic peoples, measured in the last seventy years at a cost of much labor by a large number of anthropologists. The computer, having devoted a number of seconds to doing the transformations, proceeded to spend the next minute or so figuring the 11,175 distances separating each population from every other. The final step, to make sense out of the whole, was a grouping process. The computer searched all the distances to find the smallest, thus picking the pair of populations closest to one another in physical form. It joined these two into one group with a single point in the middle to represent both. It next recomputed distances from this point to all other populations, searched the distances again, and picked the next closest pair. This went on, forming larger clusters toward the end, until all were united. A chart of the result is shown in Figure 1.

This suggests that the Oceanic peoples included here arrange

Fig. 1 Relationships of Pacific peoples by measurement

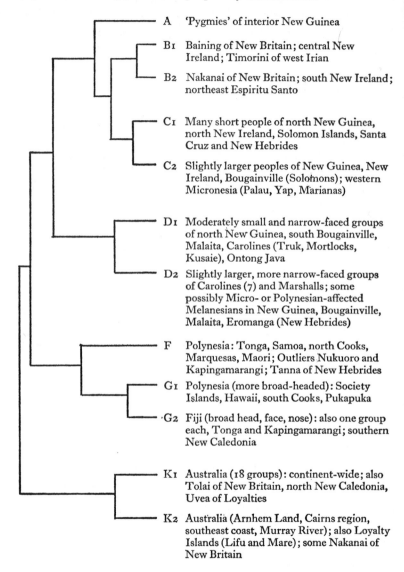

A   'Pygmies' of interior New Guinea

B1   Baining of New Britain; central New Ireland; Timorini of west Irian

B2   Nakanai of New Britain; south New Ireland; northeast Espiritu Santo

C1   Many short people of north New Guinea, north New Ireland, Solomon Islands, Santa Cruz and New Hebrides

C2   Slightly larger peoples of New Guinea, New Ireland, Bougainville (Solomons); western Micronesia (Palau, Yap, Marianas)

D1   Moderately small and narrow-faced groups of north New Guinea, south Bougainville, Malaita, Carolines (Truk, Mortlocks, Kusaie), Ontong Java

D2   Slightly larger, more narrow-faced groups of Carolines (7) and Marshalls; some possibly Micro- or Polynesian-affected Melanesians in New Guinea, Bougainville, Malaita, Eromanga (New Hebrides)

F   Polynesia: Tonga, Samoa, north Cooks, Marquesas, Maori; Outliers Nukuoro and Kapingamarangi; Tanna of New Hebrides

G1   Polynesia (more broad-headed): Society Islands, Hawaii, south Cooks, Pukapuka

·G2 Fiji (broad head, face, nose): also one group each, Tonga and Kapingamarangi; southern New Caledonia

K1   Australia (18 groups): continent-wide; also Tolai of New Britain, north New Caledonia, Uvea of Loyalties

K2   Australia (Arnhem Land, Cairns region, southeast coast, Murray River); also Loyalty Islands (Lifu and Mare); some Nakanai of New Britain themselves in three major branches: a complex and much varied Melanesian' grouping, with Micronesians attached thereto; followed by Polynesian and Australian main branches. The main joinings among these are actually of little significance as to their order. It is details of arrangement within the groups which are most informative. Within the Melanesian branch, five very small peoples of interior New Guinea form a first cluster A, characterized by short stature and small faces. The branches B and C include a broad spectrum of Melanesians, neither of these groups being specifically closer to the pygmy-like A branch, but only presenting some differences in pattern of body form. The people in B are almost all from the Bismark Islands of New Britain and New Ireland, and are marked by broadish heads, faces and nonses The C peoples by contrast run from interior New Guinea (some converging on the 'pygmies' in size as well as locale), through a series of coastal New Guinea populations, with some in New Britain and New Ireland, on out through the Solomons to the New Hebrides – a very protean collection, of moderate body size and no very characteristic features of head and face, though on the whole moderately broad of head and narrow of nose.

Another important-seeming inclusion in this amorphous C branch is that of three particular populations right at the west end of Micronesia, fringing the Philippine Sea: Palau, Yap and the Marianas (a Chamorro sample from Saipan). These speak languages separating them somewhat from other Micronesians, and have further special cultural aspects; this will come out in later chapters. The next branch, D, is composed of an overlapping mixture of Melanesian and Micronesian peoples, marked mainly by a tendency to general relative narrowness or length of head, face and nose. It is made up of two subgroups (in this analysis). One has this tendency especially pronounced, as well as another tendency, to slightly larger size (component 1), and includes most of the Caroline and the Marshall Islands of Micronesia; it also has a few Melanesian adherents, notably Eromanga in the New Hebrides and the Lau of Malaita. The other subgroup has a few of the Carolines and a number of other people in the Solomons (Malaita and Bougainville) as well as some from coastal New Guinea, almost all north coast. The entire grouping seems to reflect a sort of interdigitating between the Micronesians and some of the Melanesians in aspects of shape which can be measured. As a group it is only loosely attached to the more general Melanesian clusters and in fact, in other computer runs using more or fewer components, it is almost as likely to unite with the Polynesians.

The next clustering, F and G, is essentially Polynesian. The F branch is largely peripheral in the geographical sense, containing samples from Tonga, Samoa, New Zealand, the Marquesas, the northern Cook Islands, and the western outliers, Nukuoro and Kapingamarangi (also Tanna in the southern New Hebrides). Subgroup G_1 contains the Societies, southern Cooks and Hawaii, more consistently broad-headed, while subgroup G_2 is more generally broad in head, face and nose: it is Fijian, but also contains one sample each from Tonga and the outlier Kapingamarangi, and the southern end of New Caledonia. These divisions are in no sense absolute, and simply show some divergences within a group which is definitely Polynesian but which pulls in a few 'Melanesian' spots: Fiji, Tanna and southern New Caledonia.

The final branch, K, is quite uncomplicated: in this analysis it includes all the Australian samples used (numbering twenty-eight), and draws in northern New Caledonia and the Loyalty Islands as well as a few samples from western and northern New Britain. Some of these are peoples whose appearance or cranial form have previously suggested some degree of likeness to Australians, especially in the case of the northern New Caledonians.

Now there is nothing absolute about this statistical arrangement; it is approximative, but it is certainly informative. The picture as a whole is rather simple. It is based on a few measurements only, of course, but that cannot be the reason for simplicity. Major Polynesian and Australian clusters are well defined. For Melanesia the variation is much greater, as other lines of evidence have already suggested. If we had more to show for New Guinea we should probably find the variation still more fully exemplified. As it is, we see a diversity of form within a set of populations reaching from New Guinea to the New Hebrides; this diversity in turn appears to lie within a spectrum which approaches Polynesians at one point. Micronesians appear to lie in this part of the range, being close in turn to some northerly Melanesians, broadly speaking. At the other end are smallish people who become extremely small in parts of interior New Guinea, though without signs (in the clustering) of real evidence that they are isolated in physique from the other smallish populations of Bougainville and Santo, or from the generally wide range of size in New Guinea itself. This is a question to take up again later.

The Shapes of Skulls

Human skulls are another source of information for looking at different populations in a systematic way. Fortunately, in large areas of the Pacific, people have had a strong religious or magical feeling for heads, whether attached to necks or not. (In Polynesia particularly a head, above all a chief's head, has a tabu quality.) Again fortunately, many such communities have kept skulls in special houses. Still fortunately, early anthropologists following hard on the heels of missionaries collected large quantities of skulls from the skull racks as fast as the missionaries could convince the indigenes of their wicked paganism. Unfortunately the collections, large or small, are scattered all over Europe, some lost, some destroyed by war, and also often neglected by curators who have come to feel that skulls are *vieux jeu*, something for the nineteenth century. Perhaps; but such collections are irreplaceable; they will never be made again.

Skulls may be studied in much greater detail and more conveniently than living heads, and they make no demurrals. They differ in specific small features of bone formation, such as the presence or absence of certain little extra anomalous bones, and these have interesting population differences. And they allow a much wider employment of precise measurements of total size, of shape of facial parts, of angles and so on. For a long time anthropologists compared such sizes and ratios of Pacific skulls as they had done on the living; and here also, with only simple statistical methods to handle the results in a pre-computer age, they faced the hopeless job of mental juggling of many figures for small and uncertain results. This is what led quite naturally to a period of down-grading of work on crania.

What follows is an analysis of relationships I have done on populations of skulls [124]. The simplest form of the results is shown in Figures 2 and 3. These groupings may be looked at with the same eye as Figure 1 for the living, although the basis is different. For the living I gathered older averages, for seven measurements on 151 groups. The skulls, however, were prepared as a special diet for the computer. I measured them all myself, taking seventy

43

measurements and angles, on twenty-five different populations, each represented by about forty to fifty-five skulls of each sex. The statistics are a process like the previous one, though not an actual repeat: the seventy measurements were reduced to a much smaller number of new, independent scales known as discriminant functions.[1]

The result leads, as before, to 'distances', followed by a grouping analysis. The distances are much better estimates than in the case of the living, because the volume of information is very much broader and more subtle, and was obtained by the same worker. Unfortunately, good collections of crania representing a single population are hard to find, and so the peoples included are far fewer than what might be gathered on the living by one hardy anthropologist, moving at a good clip and taking only the seven measurements specified before.

Figure 2 is a first look at a world-wide selection of peoples; an attempt to cover the variety, in the skull, of living mankind as well as possible. The clustering is clear and unsurprising. Three sub-Saharan African Negro groups are joined, less closely, by Negritos of the Andaman Islands and South African Bushmen. This essentially African branch is linked, but actually only remotely, with the three available Southwest Pacific populations: two very closely related tribes forming a group for the lowermost Murray River in South Australia; surviving skulls of the aboriginal Tasmanians; and Tolais of northern New Britain. As appears in Figure 2, the Tasmanians are somewhat closer to the Melanesian Tolais than to Australians.

The other main division here falls neatly into a 'European' branch (including Middle Kingdom Egyptians) and a 'Mongoloid' branch, in which Hawaiians from the cemetery on Mokapu Peninsula, Oahu, are allied with two American Indian groups. Buriats of Siberia and Eskimos of the Inugsuk culture of Greenland, not closely related themselves, are also only loosely related to the previous group. This general arrangement of world peoples

---

[1] These will have more importance later on. Discriminant functions are a transformation differing from principal components in that the functions, or scales, result in the sharpest distinctions possible between populations. Their basic idea is to discriminate, and their primary application is to assign a doubtful specimen, on the basis of its transformed measurements, to its most probable membership in one of two or more known populations.

is quite stable when analyzed in ways other than the one shown here, and it holds in essential features for both sexes. It seems to say that Europeans, Hawaiians and American Indians are not very sharply distinguished cranially, and the actual 'distance' figures bear this out, especially for Europeans and Indians. The great human differences are found to lie on a triangle formed by the Buriats of Siberia, the Africans, and the Southwest Pacific peoples. The last two differ from the Mongoloid Buriats in shortness of the face and narrowness of the skull, especially its base; the Pacific group is further distinguished from the African by heaviness of the brow ridges over the eyes, and general prominence of the middle of the face, especially below the nose. Thus, although Melanesians appear to be 'negroid', like Africans, in some external features such as darkness of skin, bushiness of hair and

Fig. 2 Clustering of major populations based on multivariate analysis of skulls

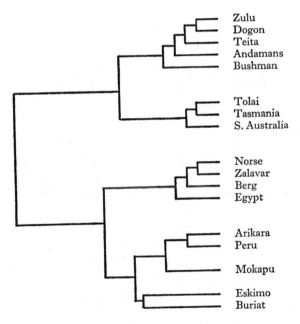

breadth of nose, they (and Australians) are decidedly different in the skull. This emphatic difference, not spelled out before, makes improbable any basic connection between Africans and Melanesians, as is also hinted by subtle differences in skin pigment and hair, described earlier in this chapter. An African–Oceanic connection has in the past been thought likely by some, including myself, though not by all anthropologists. In fact, while of course there are resemblances, such features as lip form, hairiness and overhanging brows in the Pacific peoples do constitute differences from Africans; and the nose, between the eyes, is not at all as flat as in Africans or, for that matter, as in Hawaiians or Asiatics.

Fig. 3 Clustering of circum-Pacific peoples based on multivariate analysis of skulls

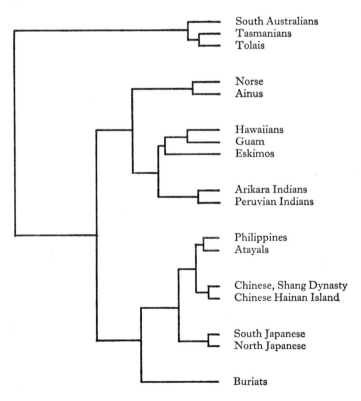

In Figure 3 the assemblage of populations is primarily circum-Pacific, bearing more directly on Oceania, although only a pre-contact series from Guam has been added from the Pacific itself. (Except for Polynesians and Australians, large collections for one place are rare.) Africans are omitted, but one representative European population is kept (medieval Norwegians), as are Greenland Eskimos for the sake of inspecting the 'Mongoloid' range.

Here, not unexpectedly, the trio Tolai–Australian–Tasmanian is far removed from all other groups, again by narrow skulls and low faces. Far Easterners make a tight cluster, in which three pairs are formed: (1) two Japanese series from opposite ends of the Empire (Hokkaido and Kyushu); (2) Chinese from Hainan Island, of recent date, and from the Shang Dynasty tombs at An Yang; and (3) aboriginals from Formosa (Atayal tribe) and a very general sample from the Philippines. Thus, grossly, there are pairs of Japanese, of Chinese, and of Indonesians, though this may be a little too neat – the analysis has not yet been carried very far. More reluctantly associated with all these are the Buriats of Siberia. Only slightly more removed is a third cluster, again with three pairs: Hawaiians and Guamanians, joined first by a pair of American Indian tribes (and by Eskimos, solo) and next by a coupling of Ainus and Norwegians. This seems to make 'Caucasoids' of the Ainus – it is almost surprising to see that the long-recognized European-like external features of the Ainus, though often under suspicion, are not in the end belied by the skulls.

The most important thing to say about this arrangement concerns the series from Guam. In the female skulls (the arrangement is not shown here) Guam goes with the Far Easterners, and in fact in the male skulls the minimum distances for Guam are also with the Far East. It is a trick of this rather simple statistical clustering that Guam pairs with Hawaii, apparently resulting from the still closer association of the Far East series, all of which form a first group whose central point comes to rest not quite so close to Guam as is the Hawaiian point. One other small difference: in the females the Norse–Ainu pair joins American Indians just before Hawaii does so rather than just after. The actual distance figures[1] correspond; the differences are not

[1] I will cite some of these figures further on where they are pertinent to particular problems; the full tabulation is somewhat too voluminous to give here.

great, and the disagreement in results between the sexes suggests that Hawaiians are no closer, cranially, to American Indians than are Europeans and Ainus, a fact we may take due note of here.[1]

Some Deductions

In this chapter I have tried to describe the ways Oceanic people vary in a few traditional anthropological, or racial, features, as well as in various factors that are better measured than judged by eye. To handle the latter I have used statistical methods which may seem dry, perhaps tedious, but which at least are able to handle strictly objective – as opposed to impressionistic – data in a purely objective way. In anthropology, this passes for relatively 'hard' science.

Purely as to physical likeness, then, this is what the results suggest:

1. Melanesians are a population which could have only a very remote connection, if any, with Africans; they are cranially distinct.

2. Melanesians and Australians have characters in common, especially cranially, but they are not a continuous or single population. Together, however, they are well differentiated from other populations, Pacific or otherwise.

3. Melanesians are a single basic population rather than composite, but a population of great genetic diversity. It has received spotty admixture from Polynesians in the east (as a first interpretation – what Fijians represent will be left until later).

---

[1] A more recent and more sophisticated clustering analysis from my skull distances was carried out by Dr Kenneth Kidd, who has kindly given me his results before publication. In this, the clustering starts at the trunk of the 'tree', not at the twigs as before; that is, the program makes an initial separation into two groups and then subdivides these further. Of 32,768 possible trees, many of nearly equal probability of best fit may result. Here, the best one of all is virtually identical with Figure 3, the only difference being that Eskimos join the American Indian/Guam–Hawaiian sets just after they have themselves joined, instead of just before. This trivial difference speaks well for the goodness of the result already described. Interestingly, in the 'second best' tree the Norse make a radical shift away from the Ainu to join the Melanesian–Australian branch (!). while the Ainu join the Guam–Hawaiian pair before Eskimos and American Indians do so. In doing so the Ainus behave as they do in other tests that I have done on the living (not described here). As to the Norse, they actually have certain cranial likeness to Australians which at least distinguish them from Mongoloids; also, they are introduced outside a natural context, so to speak, and their apparent instability is for this reason not so surprising.

It has undergone considerable local mutual admixture with Micronesia.

4. Polynesia is a fairly well-defined population, relative to Oceanic peoples generally.

5. Micronesia is varied (the material is not of the best), having some Polynesian resemblances but interdigitating with Melanesia to a considerable extent. Likenesses to Indonesians are not covered here.

6. Micronesia and Polynesia have a basically east Asiatic affiliation, but one which might be termed Proto-Mongoloid or sub-Mongoloid, to suggest greater likeness to such pre-Chinese Asiatic peoples as Formosan and Philippine aboriginals, Ainus and American Indians.

7. The irreducible number of basic populations entering the Pacific would appear to be no more than two, perhaps even if Indonesia is included. Fuller interpretation and reconstruction should be addressed to variety within these populations on entering the Pacific, and to differentiation within them since they arrived.

4

Inner differences:
enzymes, ear wax and
erythrocytes

Today almost anyone knows his own blood group: O, A, B, or AB. But the real meaning of these differences from person to person has barely begun to be solved. And the matter of interest to us, the different proportions from people to people, remains obscure for this reason.

It was in 1900 that Dr Karl Landsteiner first established the groups, by mixing blood samples from a number of his colleagues. More exactly, he mixed red blood cells from one person with the clear plasma on serum of another. In some cases the cells remained as they were; in others they promptly clumped, or agglutinated, so that they formed a non-functioning clot, which could be dangerous in the veins of a living person. This was in fact the mysterious danger which had been seen in blood transfusions tried before that time. The clumping was not haphazard: Landsteiner and his co-workers showed that people fall into four groups according to whether their erythrocytes (red cells) carry the A substance, the B substance, or both, or neither. Cells carrying one of these antigens cannot be put into a bloodstream which lacks it, because the serum of that bloodstream is 'immune' to it. This is a main system of defense against foreign bodies: the serum forms antibodies specific for that antigen; and the antibodies, as though with a docking mechanism, lock themselves to the antigens on two or more cells and so cause the clumping. The A and B substances are an unusual case, because they exist not only on the red cells but elsewhere in the body tissues and also in nature in other forms, so that everyone gets immunized very early in life to either antigen not present in his own blood.

Thus it is wise to know your blood group – if you are group O, for example, you cannot be transfused with blood containing cells with either A or B. And blood typing is a simple matter: drops of your blood are tested with two known sera, one anti-A and the other anti-B, to see what clumping, if any, takes place. But blood groups had extra dividends for anthropologists. Their discovery coincided with the rediscovery of Mendel's laws of inheritance and in due course became a prize example, easily studied, of those laws. The system has three kinds of gene: A, B and O. Obviously, you can have only two of them, one from either parent; and it is a flip of the coin which of your father's own pair of genes comes to you, and of your mother's pair likewise. If you get either A or B your blood shows it, and the effect is the same whether you are genetically AA or AO. If you are AB in blood type, you have to be AB in your genes; if you are O, you have to be OO in your genes. The beauty of the whole thing is that inheritance is completely understood, which is not true of previous tools of anthropology such as hair form or skull shape. And the proportions of the three genes in the gene pool of the whole population can be closely estimated, as soon as enough people have been typed.

That was the second boon to anthropologists. When medical work showed that populations differ in their gene proportions, a long and industrious survey of the world's peoples began, until at last no region of any importance remained unsampled. Hope burgeoned that more could be told about human history this way than the older anthropologists had managed with their measurements and photographs (which was not very much). To begin with, blood groups are right at the root of inheritance. In addition, a man's blood type cannot be affected by his life history, which might otherwise make him taller, or shorter, or rounder headed. And a lovely law, the Hardy–Weinberg principle, states mathematically that the proportions of genes in the population may be expected to stay the same, generation after generation. So the gypsies of southern Europe reveal their origins in India by the division of their blood types, which is that prevalent in India but not in Europe. And a mixed people will have proportions intermediate to their parent populations, suggesting just what the balance of mixture was. (That is to say, were you ruthlessly to breed Chinese, with twenty per cent of gene B, and Apaches, with no B at all, you would expect a new generation with ten per cent of the gene.) Hope indeed that, with enough reports in hand, many secrets of older migrations and mixtures might be read (although, as with earlier studies of race, the question of how parental populations and races came to differ in the first place was pretty much swept under the rug).

As the blood-takers came back from the bush a broad picture developed. Blood gene B was seen to be particularly high in central Asia and India, sloping off in all directions. In Africa A and B are about equal; elsewhere A tends to gain at the expense of B, and the latter is low in western Europe, especially on the fringes; it is essentially missing in the American Indians, the Australian aboriginals and the eastern Polynesians. Most American Indian tribes lack A as well, being completely of group O.

Selection and Drift

Does this map of the world, drawn in blood, somehow contain the history of human migration? It is an important question when we come to add many other blood systems to the picture, and study more strictly local patterns of distribution in the Pacific. How far into the past will a people's blood gene frequencies faithfully reflect those of their ancestors? How rapidly, on the other hand, might they change, and so lose such meaning? These are unknowns which have to be balanced; and they may, for all we know, be quite different for different kinds of blood system.

Keeping just now to the ABO groups, it was suggested long ago that gene B appeared late in man's development, in Asia and spread outward, catching up somewhat with A, which was still catching up with O. This is not possible: the Hardy–Weinberg principle says that blood genes do not simply spread like a wave just because they are new. An opposite view is the idea that Australians, Polynesians and some American tribes like the Blackfeet, all lacking B but with considerable levels of A, share a common ancestry, having been modified in outward appearance but not in the balance of blood genes. This, however, not only overloads the Hardy–Weinberg law; it also ignores the fact that such blood traits must respond to normal agencies of evolution and change.

The first agent is Darwinian selection. Great efforts have been made to detect selective advantages for one or the other of the ABO genes, with slender results. Individuals of group O are definitely but not overwhelmingly more prone to ulcers of stomach and duodenum, and those of group A to stomach cancer and certain other tumors. But these things seldom affect people of child-bearing age, which is the time during which selection does its work. Still, our ignorance does not mean that the ABO types are neutral, or put there by Satan simply to bedevil transfusions (which had no significance for human evolution). Rather, the very existence of such a polymorphism – meaning a set of alternative inherited conditions – signals 'selection' to evolutionists, since it is the classic way in which an animal population can adjust itself promptly if new conditions make one gene combination somewhat more favorable than that which is currently most common. This is especially so in the more complicated situation when the hete-rozygous, or mixed-pair, state is the most advantageous of all (for example, the possibility that people genetically AO have a slight advantage over those who are AA or OO). Therefore, though the truth is still unseen, it is likely that primitive populations have come under occasional but severe pressures from something, such as an epidemic or endemic disease, with certain blood types surviving best. So two peoples, neighbors or otherwise, may be alike in their blood proportions because they have had the same disease exposure, not because they share a common ancestor.

The second agent of change which I named earlier is genetic drift. The Hardy–Weinberg equilibrium holds best for large and cosmopolitan populations having great numbers in each genera-tion – one bucket of sand is very like another. In smaller groups an accidental shifting of proportions is more influential. The genes are less like grains of sand and more like cards in a deck. Surely nobody would play bridge or poker if every hand had exactly the expected luck in card values, and any bridge player must know that feeling of ennui on picking up a 4–3–3–3 hand with just the normal number of face cards. Fortunately the average deal departs markedly from the 'normal'. So, genetically, each small generation is not a perfect reproduction, a Hardy–Weinberg projection, of the one before it. There is a lottery of genes, and a wandering of proportions.

Especially important is Mayr's 'founder principle', a special case of drift. If a small band leaves home to settle elsewhere it may carry a biased stock of genes, untypical of the parent community. The migrants are apt to be a set of family groups, making the bias greater since a lineage is apt to have its own little biases from the population as a whole – after all, things do 'run in families'. And the Pacific, with small bands of founders reaching new islands, must have been the ideal setting.

For the real case, let us turn to New Guinea, where variation in blood traits is remarkable, compared to the rest of the world. In the Markham Valley, Giles [77] collected especially complete information on a number of villages. Three of them, the only speakers of the Waffa language, were found to be quite sharply isolated from each other as to intermarriage, as well as from speakers of other languages in the valley. The three villages must have had a common origin in the past, though the amount of time since then has not been estimated. Today they show clear differences in the ABO, MN and Rh systems: for gene B, in particular, the frequencies are 0·02, 0·14 and 0·27, a remarkable spread. The authors cannot disprove the action of natural selection in causing the differences, but are convinced that drift, especially the founder principle, is primarily responsible. 'Were fate now to reward any one main Waffa village with expansion at the expense of the other two, the genetic constitution of the resultant population would very likely be far removed from that extant in the people of the Waffa *Urstamm*'.

This suggests that figures for small communities are poor witnesses to ancestry. It also suggests that adding small communities to get average figures can be equally deceptive. And the same effects of drift can lead to total loss of some genes, a thing of special importance for Pacific populations.

Consider the case of Tench Island, a one-village atoll in the northwest corner of Island Melanesia, sixty miles north of Kavieng, New Ireland. Although isolated from contact until recently, it evidently has a Melanesian population affected in the past by Micronesian contact, and should be somewhat cosmopolitan in its characteristics. So the natives seem, in outward appearance. But its ABO groups are quite extraordinary: of fifty-four individuals, out of a total population of sixty-three [169] who could be blood-typed in 1963, fifty-two were group O and two were group B, with no A present at all. It is clear that accidental shifts in so tiny a population have caused the loss of A, with the B gene hanging on by its eyelashes. The two B individuals were a young woman and her widowed mother. The mother was unlikely, according to these reports, to have further children (who would in any case have only a fifty per cent chance of being group B, since the mother, like the daughter, is almost certainly OB in her genes, and so would pass the O gene, not the B, to half her children). The girl is the B gene's last hope. If she should leave the island, Tench would become a hundred per cent group O. If she stays and marries, the B gene has another flicker of hope. But (providing these now thoroughly missionized natives mind their morals and do not accept advances from B-carrying visitors) the gene is doomed anyhow: mathematical geneticists have shown that, at such low levels in a small population, chance alone, in the vast majority of cases, will eventually do away with it. If the population is larger, loss takes longer, that is all. Mutation might replace it, but mutations are so rare as to be extremely unlikely to happen here, and the end result would be the same. Tench is, in fact, a snapshot of a process drawn from theoretical genetics, where in small populations drift can overcome natural selection: we can say this even without knowing the relative 'fitness' of A and B in a place like Tench.

There is good evidence from other parts of the world of this tendency of a least frequent gene to disappear in small and isolated populations. On the other hand, satisfactory explanations exist [27] as to why it does not happen everywhere, in the large and crowded communities of the Old World continents. But this book is a history of the Pacific, not of blood, and I hope I have made the point. Perhaps blood types will point to ancestors and homelands; perhaps, and more likely, they are telling stories of trickling colonization of new places. For Polynesians the ABO figures say not where they came from or to whom they are related, but what has happened to them along the way. If, like American Indians and Australians, they lack gene B it means not that they never had it but that they have lost it, nothing more. In their migrations all these peoples must have had episodes of being reduced to small groups and, like Tench Island, losing B (and in some American cases A also). Each became, in a new territory, a large but B-less population; and that, not Pacific–American connections, is undoubtedly the meaning of the ABO testimony.

Evidence of the Erythrocytes

Long after Landsteiner's discovery – mostly after 1945 – other kinds of red cell antigen came to light. The delay was due to the absence, in these newer systems, of the universal antibodies of the ABO groups. Instead, antibodies were found only when a particularly sensitive patient had been immunized by perhaps repeated transfusions; even the Rh reaction, a severe one, follows only after sensitization of Rh-negative blood.

Not all these systems have been tested very widely, and, of course, reports continue to pour out. In hopes of being not entirely indigestible I shall, as with measurements, avoid tabulations and try to review what is best known and what seems to be significant, simplifying drastically in the process.

ABO

The O gene is present in every major human population and, outside the Americas, the A gene also. In Indonesia, particularly Java, the B gene is present in some strength, though lower than in much of Asia. At any rate it is about equal in frequency to A, usually slightly less but sometimes more. Gene frequencies are usually expressed as a proportion (e.g. 0·50) instead of a percentage (e.g. fifty per cent). In these terms the A gene in Indonesia runs upwards from about 0·20, and the B gene is slightly less. This carries over into Melanesia, although in New Guinea and New Britain there is a really great degree of fluctuation: in the Gazelle Peninsula of New Britain, the Papuan-speaking Baining are high in B and their Melanesian-speaking neighbors, the Tolai, are low. In the interior of western New Guinea tribes may show such a combination as A 0·18, B 0·38, though this is unusual; nevertheless A may vary from 0·04 to 0·40, and B from 0·03 to 0·39. In eastern New Guinea A begins to predominate, but this is a fragile rule. Two interior and rather remote peoples near the border of Papua and the Territory of New Guinea gave these results: the Kukukuku A 0·33 and B 0·03, and inhabitants of the Karimui plateau A 0·14 and B 0·21. (No such swing over short distances exists in regions like Europe or Japan.) However, values between these, with A higher, continue through the Solomon Islands to eastern Melanesia and down to New Caledonia; and in western Polynesia (Tonga and the Cook Islands) A is over 0·20, and B less than 0·10. But to the north, in Micronesia, the pattern, if there is one, runs the other way. Still in the northwest fringe of Polynesia, Samoa and the Ellice Islands are about equal in A and B. Next door, the Gilbert Islands are exceptionally high in both, while the Marshall Islands to the north are relatively low, though fluctuating from atoll to atoll. Westward in the center of the Carolines, Truk is intermediate, and equal in A and B, while on the western edge of Micronesia in Yap, Palau and the Marianas, both genes are low but A is distinctly predominant, especially among the Chamorros of the Marianas. In the same region the small atoll of Sonsorol is another instance of the absence of B (with high A). In general we must suppose that the small local populations of Micronesia would be especially subject to changes from drift or selection [103]: in other Caroline atolls, for example, B may be quite high (0·28 in Losap) or very low (0·03 in Satawal and Lamotrek, where A is low also).

As to Polynesia, B disappears in the center and in the margins in New Zealand, Tahiti, the Marquesas, Easter Island; and A may become very high, say 0·50 (meaning that seventy-five per cent of the population is group A, either AA or AO). In Australia B is present in the north but is lacking in the rest of the continent, and here again A may rise very high in some tribes.

In all this the patterns seem on the whole to be, not racial, but appropriate to local conditions. Indonesia is almost but not quite like eastern Asia, being lower in B. New Guinea has a heavy population, with local isolation, and the fluctuating B values seem to reflect this. The absence of B in Australia must be loss through drift and the founder principle, and the same for eastern Polynesia (unless these people, as Heyerdahl has suggested, are really American Indians, which I deny here and later).

MNSS

This system rests on two pairs of genes. One is M and N, so that you are type M (MM), type MN (MN), or type N (NN). Combined with these is either large or small S. Unfortunately there are fewer figures for this second pair of antigens, though they are interesting.

In much of the world the M and N genes are approximately equal in strength, i.e. 0·50 of each (although in the Americas M is high, sometimes very high). So they are in Indonesia, though M may predominate greatly among Malays, aboriginals, and Negritos, in the Malay Peninsula. But M slumps to low values in Island

Melanesia – the Baining of New Britain have almost none at all – and lower still in New Guinea – figures of 0·10 or less. It continues low across Australia, though fluctuating. Through most of Micronesia M is moderately low, especially in the east and west; but in the Marianas and some of the Carolines, and in Polynesia, it rises, apparently ranging around 0·50.

Thus if we suppose that the MN polymorphism is fairly stable over long periods, it might look as though a general early population of Melanesia and Australia had been particularly low in M and high in N. But we know nothing about rates and reasons of change in this system.

Big S seems absent for the whole of Australia, the known cases being suspected of having non-Australian ancestry. It is also missing among the Baining of New Britain and at least one of their neighbors. In New Guinea, however, it is found widely, at a low rate of occurrence and almost always associated with N; it has some wild local fluctuations, reaching 0·28 in the Western Highlands of eastern New Guinea, and 0·29 in a Mandobo sample from southern West Irlan, both high values. There is, in fact, a sort of ridge of high S running along the middle of the east central part of the island, a consistency which is interesting. In the rest of Melanesia and Polynesia, S is infrequent or absent: when present in Melanesia it is mostly associated with N, in Polynesia equally with M or N. Perhaps the chief importance of S is the distinction it makes between New Guinea and Australia.

Rh (CDE)

This is a most complex system: in its basic form it rests on three pairs of antigens, C/c, D/d and E/e, which are determined by corresponding gene clusters. (An 'Rh positive' person in the vernacular sense is one who has the big D part of the system, since this antigen gives rise to the strongest antigenic reactions; and a 'negative' person lacks it, having the small d on both chromosomes, usually with the gene arrangement cde/cde, the cde group being also denoted r.)

The 'negative' gene fluctuates around a frequency of 0·35 in western Europe, being remarkably high in the Basques of France and Spain. It is absent in the Pacific, where the overwhelmingly predominant gene is CDe (or R^1 in a shorthand notation). This combination stands at 0·85 to 1·00 in Indonesia, New Guinea and

Melanesia, with cDE, or R^2, taking second place, and with minute values of cDE, or R^0, and still more minute values of CDE, or R^z. (Other variants occur as rarities.) Only in Australia and Polynesia, and in the Gilberts and some of the Carolines, does R^1 fall, to the advantage of R^2, which rises to values of over 0·25: in eastern Polynesia and New Zealand R^2 may outweigh R^1, reaching 0·83 in a single Maori population. As to R^0, this is fairly strong in parts of northern Australia, rising to about 0·25 and surpassing R^2, as it does in the Negritos of Malaya. The R^z (CDE) gene is a world rarity, so that its appearance in many Pacific populations, and its rise to 0·08 in some Australian groups, are unusual. Taken altogether, the Rh system does not do much to distinguish among the Oceanic peoples, and in fact does more to unify them against the rest of the world.

DUFFY

Among those other systems not yet investigated very widely the Duffy may be important. It has two (known) genes, Fy^a and Fy^b. Fy^a has a frequency of about 0·42 in Europe and 0·05 in West Africa; Africans are unique in having a 'silent' gene, at a frequency of 0·90, which reacts to neither anti-a nor anti-b.

Fy^a seems to be the only gene in Australia, except for northeast Arnhem Land where Fy^b is definitely present. The same lack of Fy^b apparently holds for most of New Guinea and New Britain, though it is present at 0·30 in the 'Pygmies' of the Wissel Lake area in West Irian, for whatever that may mean. In Melanesian groups Fy^a is always 1·00 or nearly so, but in Polynesia it drops distinctly; though varying, figures run as low as about 0·50. This resembles American Indians and also Filipinos (0·75). By contrast, between the Philippines and Polynesia, the Micronesians appear to be almost always 1·00 (e.g. Truk and Palau), excepting for the Chamorros of the Marianas, with 0·88 to 0·92 and the Marshalls with 0·97. This is a clear difference between Micronesians and Polynesians, as far as either have been tested.

DIEGO

This antigen is characteristically American Indian, with moderate to low frequencies, but is also found at lower levels in Mongoloids of Asia (Chinese, Japanese, Filipinos and Dyaks of Borneo). It has been seen in no Oceanic population, covering Australians, New

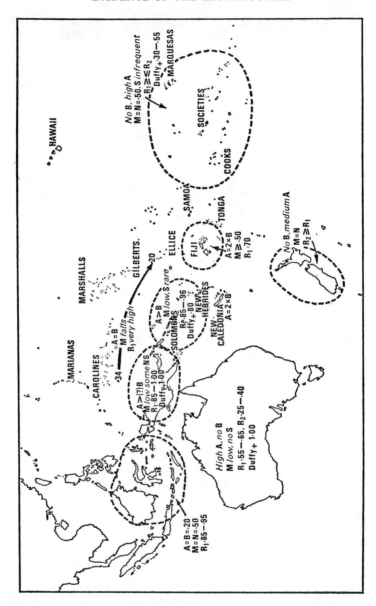

2 Blood types across the Pacific. This shows, in a general way only, characteristic gene frequencies for the main red blood cell systems in different main regions.

Guineans and a variety of Polynesians. There is one known exception: the fairly high frequency of 0·09 in the Marianas.[1] This might be laid at the door of early Mexicans and Filipinos accompanying the Spanish conquerors, but the explanation is not very satisfying, since something else, like drift, would have been needed to push the value this high [195].

Can the information so far be added together, to make something better than the sum of its parts? It has been attempted: several times over 'blood group races' have been drawn up. W. C. Boyd [24] found thirteen such genetic races of man, four being Pacific, as follows (the characterizations not necessarily the same as those I have made based on the most recent data):

Indonesian race A and B high, M = 0·6 to 0·4. R^1 dominant in Rh.

Melanesian race A and B higher than Indonesia. M low. R^1 high. Micronesians are similar.

Polynesian race B almost negligible. M above normal. S with N. $R^1 = R^2$. $Fy^a = 0·5$ to 0·7.

Australian race Absence of B, high A, M low, S almost lacking. R^z at its highest.

All these he puts in a Pacific group, which does reflect a certain community in the genes involved. Another fact should be mentioned: there is a subgroup of the A type (A_2, detectable only by a special serum) which is present in a small but persistent proportion of the A values everywhere in Europe, Africa and much of Asia. It is lacking in the Americas, apparently, and also in aboriginal populations around the fringe of Asia: Andaman Islanders, Thais, Ainus. It is missing in the whole Pacific, including Indonesia.

But the idea of such 'races', I think, rests on the innocent notion of ancient 'pure' strains, which could have mixed to produce the proportions we record today. We should look at different blood systems separately, and remember what can happen. I will give two more, rather extreme examples.

A small and isolated population of aborigines lives on Bentinck Island in the Gulf of Carpentaria, off that part of northern Australia where some B of the ABO system is present. These

---

[1] Sampling has been fairly good for Polynesia but not for Micronesia; such places as Palau and Yap are not yet known to lack it.

islanders possess only B and O, an extraordinarily high frequency of the R^0 gene (0·43), a particularly high value of the haptoglobin gene Hp^1 and a totally exceptional figure of 0·91 for the Gm^{ab} serum factor, missing in most of the continent. Tindale and others [216] believe the group to have been unaffected by outside contact for a long time. No other population, known or imagined, could have provided such a pattern, either by direct descent or by mixture. It can only be a case of drift, moving radically away from more typical Australian figures.

The islands of Rennell and Bellona, south of the Solomons, constitute one of the Polynesian Outliers, a westward colonization from Polynesia after settlement of the latter, certainly not more than two thousand years ago. Instead of high A and little B, they have a B frequency of 0·34 and almost no A at all, which is totally different from Polynesia and like nothing else in the whole Pacific (except Bentinck!). They also have the exceptional proportion of 0·70 for M, and no S. What 'race' gave rise to them? For ultimate effects of drift, imagine the result if Polynesia had been colonized from Rennell and Bellona instead of the other way around.

Serum Proteins

A newer field of study involves not the red cells, but the globulins of the blood serum. The technique to read them is usually electrophoresis, using an electric current to cause the components of one of these proteins to spread themselves along a background according to their specific electric charges.

HAPTOGLOBINS

These are alpha-globulins whose function is to pick up free hemoglobin released by the breakdown of old red cells, and so to keep it from loading the kidneys. Primarily, there are three visible forms of haptoglobin controlled by two genes, Hp^1 and Hp^2. For Hp^1, Europeans range around a frequency of 0·40; Asiatics appear to be lower, and Africans and American Indians higher. In the Pacific, Australians are rather low, especially in the extreme north (north Queensland, northeast Arnhem Land 0·10 to 0·18), the center and the Western Desert (0·15 or lower); elsewhere, in the northwest or south of the Gulf of Carpentaria figures are about 0·22 to 0·30. By contrast, New Guinea and New Britain are often as high as Africa or America (0·62 to 0·84), though there is great variety, clans of a single New Guinea tribe varying from 0·28 to 0·84 [19]. Still limited figures for Polynesia and Micronesia suggest a gradient, with high Hp[1] values to the east: Cook Islands 0·71 and 0·65; Samoa, Tonga and the Marshalls 0·50 to 0·60; Ellice Islands 0·49; Gilberts 0·45; Truk, the Mortlocks, and some other Micronesian atolls about 0·40; Yap 0·36.

These are rather marked differences, but they are difficult to interpret. It is not safe to infer anything as to simple migration and mixture, because, again, genetic drift is very probably involved, and it has also been suspected that the gene is subject to selection by relative resistance to malaria.

TRANSFERRINS

These are beta-globulins whose function is the transport of iron. There are different types, controlled by a single set of several genes. The commonest gene is TfC, and for convenience comparisons have been made of the next most common, TfD. Most world-wide frequency values of this fall under 0·10 (except in Africa, well under), so that the southwest Pacific seems to be unusually high. In eastern New Guinea the average value of a number of tribes is 0·12, and in New Britain 0·14. (There are no discernible differences between Papuan-speakers and Austronesian-speakers.) Australia is higher still: in the north about 0·13 to 0·17; in the south and in the western desert 0·20 or even higher. But in eastern Melanesia (at least in Fiji and the New Hebrides) values fall to about 0·02, and in the Marshalls, Gilberts, Ellice, Samoan and Tongan groups no TfD has been found. It is, however, present in Yap (0·01).

Is this gene a marker of early southwest Pacific populations of both Australia and Melanesia? It does exhibit something of a pattern, with a possible high focus in southern Australia [138, 139, 140]. It seems less random than that which drift might be expected to give, and lacks clues as to how selection might account for it. But all this is mere suspicion.

Gm SERUM FACTORS

These antigens of the serum gamma globulins may turn out to be the most complex system of all. It already rivals the CDE types, and gives striking distinctions between major populations. It came to light in 1956 in the course of technical manipulations of specially prepared red cells; an agglutination reaction being tested was found to take place normally in the presence of serum from certain individuals, but to be inhibited by the serum of others. A simple either/or, two-gene affair? No; resembling the Rh system, fourteen currently testable variations have been found, forming groups, as though one 'gene' or tightly bunched section of a chromosome can determine the presence of a number of antigens. For example, what I shall denote as Gm^{ab} (following Dr Melvin Schanfield) is actually, in the Pacific, a 'gene' determining at least these antigens: a, z, b^0, b^1, b^3 and probably b^5.

Developments have been so recent and rapid that older results are hard to compare with later ones which tested for more of the antigens, and information for the Pacific is extremely incomplete. Europeans (and also apparently Pakistanis, Indians and Ceylonese) are primarily *fb* in gene frequency (about seventy per cent, with some subdistinctions, such as the presence or absence of factor *n*), the rest being *ag* and *axg*, two widespread combinations. Africans by contrast are *ab* (about fifty-five per cent, covering the universal presence of *z* and some rare *x*, etc.), with *abc* constituting a second major 'gene' combination. Mongoloids vary, but have *afbn* and *abst* combinations not found elsewhere, except for the latter, which is found in Eskimos and North American and Mexican Indians but not South American. It has not been found in Oceania.

These combinations have been called phenogroups, haplotypes, allotypes and allogroups by different workers, who also differ in ways of denoting them. While the dust is settling I shall unwarily call the combinations 'genes' and, for the Pacific, I shall simplify ruthlessly and use the data only to put what light may be possible on one or two problems. Instead of giving estimated 'gene' frequencies, I will tabulate the results thus:

absent (frequency = 0)	—
low frequency 0·01 to 0·09	+
moderate frequency 0·10 to 0·20	+ +
medium frequency 0·20 to 0·45	+ + +
high frequency 0·45 to 0·70	+ + + +
very high frequency 0·70 to 1·00	+ + + + +

In addition I shall distinguish between groups speaking Austronesian and Papuan languages by designating them AUS and PAP respectively. Linguistic matters will figure prominently later on; the distinction is made here only because workers with the Gm factors have looked for evidence that the two language groups might represent two different migrations into Melanesia.[1]

TABLE I

Gm frequencies in Australia and Asia

	ag	axg	ab	afb	xg	abst
Australia						
center and western						
desert	+++++	+++	−	−	−	−
north	++++	+++	++	−	−	−
New Guinea (PAP)						
Fly River	+++	+	+++++	−	−	−
Asmat	++	+	+++++	−	−	−
Enga (W. Highlands)	+++++	+	++	−	−	−
Motu (AUS)	+	−	++	+++++	−	−
Thailand						
General Thai	+	+	−	+++++	−	+
Karen tribe	+	+	−	+++++	−	+
Meo tribe	+++	+	−	+++++	−	+
Taiwan aboriginals						
Ami	+	+	−	+++++	−	− ?
Atayal	++	+	−	+++++	−	− ?
China						
South	++	+	−	+++++	−	+
Central	+++	++	−	+++	−	+
North	++++	++	−	+++	−	++
Korea	++++	+++	−	++	−	++
Japan						
General	++++	++	−	+	−	+++
Okinawa	++++	++	−	+	−	+++
Ainu	++++	− ?	−	− ?	++	?*

* *Unknown; not yet tested.*

[1] Figures relating to this are taken from publications by Steinberg, Giles, Friedlaender and Schanfield, especially the last; I am indebted to Dr Schanfield for other comments and advice as well.

The first tabulation includes a number of east Asiatic peoples, mostly taken from Schanfield [205], who tested them. Certain south–north trends are visible: a rise in *ag* (and *axg*), a fall in *afb*, and a rise in *abst*. Schanfield views this as concordant with the existence of two major population groups, a northern and a southern, within the whole Mongoloid complex. This idea has been put forward before, on archaeological, linguistic and physical grounds, and is something we shall look at again in a few pages.

For Oceania, we may first consider Australian connections on the basis of the few figures now available. Aboriginals of the center and the western desert are unusual in the high frequencies of *ag*; they are also lacking in *ab*, which contrasts them above all with PAP peoples of the south of New Guinea, who are unusual in their own distributions (very high *ab*). Since north Australians have this last 'gene', they might be thought of (as other blood evidence suggests) as moving somewhat in the direction of New Guinea peoples serologically. Other Australian connections are not obvious. One frequently suggested is with the Ainu, who indeed lack *ab* and are high in *ag* frequency like other east Asiatic peoples. But Steinberg [233] suspects that pure Ainu populations (which do not really exist now) would lack *axg* and *afb*, and he ascribes the small amounts present in Ainus to Japanese admixture. In addition, Ainus have a low but sensible frequency of *xg*, a gene which has been found in no other population. In fact, Japanese would make a better match for Australians than Ainus. (Ainus, Australians and Europeans are all mutually distinguishable in this system, since Europeans have high frequencies of *fb*). Study of surviving hybrids of the extinct Tasmanian natives with Europeans might be rewarding, particularly for the presence or absence of *ab*, since this gene is lacking both in Europeans and in Australians of the main part of the continent, while it is common in New Guinea.

A second problem is that of distinguishing between PAP and AUS speakers, especially within Melanesia. The possibility of such a general difference – to be interpreted as resulting from separate migrations – appeared from Giles' early figures from the Markham Valley in New Guinea (see Table 2). Further results, however, have not borne this out. Instead, there is a geographical distinction between New Guinea and Island Melanesia, the first being high in *ab*, the second in *afb*. (Dr Schanfield suggests the difference lies in the *f* and *z* factors, which seem to substitute for

TABLE 2

Gm frequencies in PAP and AUS speakers

	ag	axg	ab	afb
PAP				
New Guinea				
South (Papua)				
Asmat	+ +	+	+ + + + +	—
Fly River	+ + +	+	+ + + + +	—
Balimo (Fly River)	+	—	+ + + + +	—
North (Terr. N.G.)				
Waffa (Markham V.)	+ + + +	+ +	+ + +	+
Minj (Wahgi Val.)	+ + + + +	+	+ +	+
Enga (W. Highlands)	+ + + + +	+	+ +	—
New Britain				
Baining	+ + +	+ + + +	—	+ + +
Sulka	+ +	+ +	+	+ + + +
Solomons				
Bougainville, north				
Aita	+	+ +	—	+ + + + +
Rotokas	+ + + +	—	—	+ + + +
Eivo (five villages)	— to + +	+	—	+ + + + +
Bougainville, south				
Nasioi (four villages)	— to + +	+	—	+ + + + +
Siuai (three villages)	— to + +	+	—	+ + + + +
AUS				
New Guinea				
Markham Valley (Atsera)	+ +	—	+ + + +	+ + +
Motu	+	—	+ +	+ + + + +
New Britain				
Tolai (nine villages)	+ to + + +	+ + to + + +	— to +	+ + + to + + + + +
Kilenge	+ +	—	—	+ + + + +
Solomons				
Bougainville	+	+	—	+ + + + +
Malaita				
Kwaio	+	+	—	+ + + + +
Lau	+ +	+	—	+ + + + +
Baegu	+ +	+	—	+ + + + +
Fiji				
Viti Levu	+ + + +	+ +	+	+ + +
Lau Islands	+ + +	+ +	—	+ + + +
Carolines				
West Truk	+ + +	+ +	—	+ + + +

one another – in their own particular fraction of the globulin molecule? The *z* is always combined with the *ab*, *ag* and *axg* combinations here.) Thus there seem to be three contrasting main groups: Australia, New Guinea and Island Melanesia. Does this mean three migrations, or does it mean three areas of selective differentiation? In any case, the fit to Papuan *vs.* Austronesian language distributions is not very satisfying.[1]

There is local fluctuation in both the PAP and the AUS speakers when small groups or villages are inspected (in New Britain or Bougainville), which is suggestive of genetic drift as in other systems; but the degree is actually only moderate, not disturbing the pattern typical of the locale except for the Rotokas in northern Bougainville. Even with such deviations, the differences lie within the same group of 'genes', a group which does not include combinations characteristic of Asiatic populations, to say nothing of those typical in Africans or Europeans. Perhaps the argument for long-term differentiation by drift or selection, even though the degree is extreme, looks best.

The one sample shown from Micronesia (West Truk) has a pattern generally like Island Melanesia, and particularly Fiji. Since Fiji doubtless has a major Polynesian component it will be interesting to see if this pattern obtains in Polynesian populations also. It approximates to the pattern of central China, except for the presence of *abst* in the latter; taking this fact into account, perhaps Formosan aboriginals like the Atayal may be looked at.

Enzymes

Enzymes of the red blood cells also lend themselves to the study

[1] Jeffrey Froelich, a Harvard graduate student, suggests to me an argument that the New Guinea Austronesian-speakers (Markham Valley, Motu) are intermediate in their Gm values between the New Guinea Papuan-speakers on one hand and Island Melanesia Papuan-speakers on the other. This could imply ancient separation and drift distinguishing the Papuan-speaking populations, as well as some hybridizing with each of them by the Austronesian-speakers, coming from another source themselves. This would also fit Schanfield's very generalized result, in Figure 4 on page 76. Just the same set of relationships has now been found by Froelich, in his final doctoral research, in features of finger and palm prints. In what seems to me to be the first fully satisfying use of such features in population comparisons, Froelich has used prints collected by himself and my wife on Solomon villages visited by the Harvard Solomon Islands expeditions, and by Eugene Giles from New Guinea villages. Applying, for the first time, discriminant functions (see Chapter 3) to finger print data, he arranges the villages in three dimensions. The result is highly consistent, putting Austronesian-speaking villages in New Guinea and the Solomons between the two more widely separated Papuan-speakers of the two areas. Neither Froelich nor I would view this as reflecting a 'wave of migration' rather than as gradual diversification among the Papuan-speakers together with latter-day movements of Melanesian peoples who had acquired Austronesian languages.

of genetic variation by the same technique used for serum proteins: separating their components according to their different
electric charges (electrophoresis). Once more, because blood is
easy to collect and, within reason, to transport, new differences are
coming to light. Unfortunately for the immediate present, too
little has been done, especially on Pacific peoples, to say anything
of consequence.

ACID PHOSPHATASE

This has six distinct types caused by combinations of three genes,
PHs^a, PHs^b and PHs^c. The last is very infrequent and the second
is everywhere the most common; therefore it is easiest to state
population differences in terms of PHs^a. This is the general world
picture:

> Europeans, frequencies between 0·30 and 0·40; PHs^c about 0·03
> to 0·10.
> Africans: several US Negro samples averaged 0·22, with PHs^c
> at 0·02.
> East Asia: PHs^c absent or very rare; PHs^a in Chinese apparently
> near 0·20, Japanese and Ainu both near 0·40, and samples of
> North Vietnamese 0·26 and Malay 0·34.

The few Pacific figures are interesting because they are mostly
low:

> New Guinea: three northern groups, all Papuan-speaking, gave
> conventional values of 0·26 to 0·38, with rare PHs^c.
> New Britain: four Baining groups (PAP) 0·10 to 0·20.
> Trobriand Islands (AUS) 0·20.
> Bougainville: seven villages of the northern PAP stock 0·21 to
> 0·30; six villages of the different southern PAP stock 0·02 to
> 0·18, thus not overlapping with the northern lot. (No PHs^c).
> Australia: very low figures for PHs^a in the north: (Bathurst
> Island, around Darwin, and near Cairns in Queensland) all
> under 0·05; elsewhere none at all has been found, popu-
> lations of the center being all PHs^b. Only more figures will
> suggest if the other genes have been lost by genetic drift, or
> whether PHs^a was low or absent among the earliest Australo–
> Melanesian migrants in general.
> Micronesia: Yap 0·26 (No PHs^c). This is like Asiatic figures.

PHOSPHOGLUCOMUTASE

Except for rare variants this occurs in three forms, determined by two genes.[1] There is little to say now. Most world populations range in gene PGM[1] from 0·70 to 0·80, with a few oddities running lower (Lapps, Habbanite Jews). American Indians are 0·80 to 0·90.

For the Pacific, an Indonesian sample has given a conventional 0·76. Elsewhere, values are the highest known. Five clans of the Enga-speakers of New Guinea range from 0·92 to 0·94; and in Australia ten tribes of the north and center run from 0·84 to 0·95. Highest values seem to be the most northern, and Elcho Island (off Arnhem Land) is a hundred per cent gene PGM[1]. Again, gene loss by drift comes to mind. (Recently [217] a third gene, PGM[3], has been found throughout New Guinea, at levels higher than PGM[2], or from 0·05 to 0·10; this gene has been noted elsewhere only as a rarity.)

Ear Wax

This is one of Fisher's [61] 'honorary blood groups', or physical traits which reasonably obey Mendel's laws on inheritance, and so I include it here. Cerumen, the waxy substance secreted in the ear canal, comes in two kinds, usually readily distinguished. One is soft, sticky and brownish; the Japanese call it 'honey ear wax' or 'oily ear wax'. The other is dry, flaky and grayish; the Japanese call it 'rice-bran ear wax'. 'Wet' and 'dry' are the simple terms. Japanese workers have made records on it for many years and have concluded that transmission is classically Mendelian: there are two genes, for wet and dry, and wet is dominant, so that the wet–dry gene combination makes ear wax just as wet as the wet–wet combination.

As to the reasons, McCullough and Giles [165] have suggested that wet wax, simply by being a more efficient coating, resists infections of and through the ear canal, which are common in hot, moist climates. But it is a fact that otitis is also common in the arctic. Petrakis [192] finds a degree of association between wet wax and breast cancer in women, both within a particular Japanese group and across different populations from the Far East to Europe.

---

[1] There are actually three completely different sets of genes causing variations in this enzyme, i.e. at different chromosome locations. The figures here refer to only one, designated PGM$_1$.

These possibilities for the operation of selection are not in conflict, since the mammary glands and those producing ear wax are parts of the apocrine gland system. This is also responsible for the odor of perspiration, which Orientals in particular find so offensive in Europeans and Africans. Japanese writers have shown the very close association – though not an absolute one in every individual – between wet wax and discernible body odor. The latter is rare in north Asiatics, who usually have dry wax: the Tungus, as Table 3 shows, have a very low proportion of individuals with wet wax and, out of 646 individuals examined, not a single malodorous Tungus was found [5].

The whole truth about this interesting trait is not known, but it does seem likely that population differences have persisted over a long time (it also occurs in chimpanzees). The reason for the Japanese head start in its investigation is not far to seek: their own population has significant degrees of both kinds of wax. Not so the Europeans, in whom dry wax is rare, or the Africans, in whom it is probably entirely absent; it was therefore slower to come to European notice. The prevalence of wet wax decreases somewhat as one goes east from Europe, falling to about sixty-five per cent of people in India.

TABLE 3

Ear Wax in East Asia

Percentage of wet wax

North Asia	
Tungus (four groups)	5 to 14
Mongols	12
North Chinese	4
Koreans	8
Japanese	
General	16
Kyushu	
Amakusa	20
Fukuoka	17
Oita	18
Kumamoto	16
Kagoshima	9
Ryukyu Islands	
Amami Oshima	41
Okinawa	34
Yonaguni Jima	35

Ainu[1]	
Shiraoi (Iburi)	87
Fushiko (Tokachi)	22
Southern Chinese	
Fukien Hoklo (Formosa)	31
Fukien other (Formosa)	21
Cantonese (Formosa)	35
Tan-ka (Canton)	20
Hainan Chinese	45
Moslems (San-ya, Hainan)	35
Southern non-Chinese	
Formosan aboriginals	
Ami	75
Puyuma	66
Atayal, Ami, Bunun[2]	40
Plains tribes	
Lo-tung	45
Wu-niu-lan	48
Wan-luan	37
Hainan, Li tribe	55
Malaya	
Malays	73
Aboriginals	93

[1] Ainu figures are ambiguous. Both samples are small (thirty and forty!). Only the Shiraoi sample has been generally cited, and this gives an impression of great contrast with Japanese. Adachi [5] considered the sample fairly pure, and the Fushiko village sample 'strongly mixed'. I have been told by both Professor Sakuzaemon Kodama and his son, Professor George Kodama, that Fushiko village was a relatively unmixed community, in a relatively remote and unaffected Ainu area, until recent times (see, for example, S. Kodama [141], p. 90) and so it is hard to see why Adachi's sample should have been much mixed when it was recorded many years ago. Shiraoi, on the other hand, while it still has credible Ainus for tourist display, is on the south coast of Hokkaido near Muroran, and would have been in earlier contact with Japanese immigrants and traders. The great difference between the two samples in ear wax may be due to errors of sampling. Adachi may have been correct as to mixture in the Fushiko individuals involved, and if the two groups were pooled, Ainu figures for wet wax would still considerably exceed those for Japanese. Unfortunately it would now be difficult to collect reliable data on pedigreed Ainu because of the rapid assimilation which has taken place.

[2] This sample is relatively small (seventy-nine), and a potpourri of quite different tribes.

Only an extremely modest amount of poking and peeking in Pacific ears has gone on. In Table 3 I have listed all the figures known to me for east Asia because they are suggestive in themselves and because they make a background for what Pacific information exists. It shows a very high incidence of dry wax in northern Asia. (Though not listed here, American Indians vary considerably in the trait, tending to about fifty-five or sixty per cent of wet wax but ranging, over all known tribes, from about thirty per cent to nearly a hundred.) As in the case of the Gm Factors, the immediate impression is of two 'Mongoloid' population groups, a northern and a southern, grading into one another because of an expansion from the northern center, on the conventional interpretation. Here again, perhaps the Ainu are exceptional among northern peoples.

In the north there is a high proportion of dry wax, extending into Japan. Okinawans, however, appear distinct from homeland Japanese, which they are not in the Gm factors. Such a fact might suggest an environmental effect of selection. However, Chinese populations in the south also exhibit a rise in wet wax, sufficiently irregularly to suggest migration and mixture with earlier peoples having high wet values, rather than climatic selection.

Aboriginal peoples are clearly at a higher level of wet wax, probably starting with the Ainu (though we may have reservations as to the data on the latter). In Formosa the mountain natives have higher figures than those of the western plains, who are more likely to have Chinese admixture, intergrading so to speak with southern Chinese, themselves probably mixed. Altogether the signs are that southern Mongoloids ranged aboriginally upward from fifty-five or sixty per cent of wet wax, reaching very high values in the Malayan far south. Altogether, it seems possible that dry wax is an ancient Mongoloid marker, already present in southern populations (and quite possibly reinforced by selection), increased by further migration from the north.

As to Oceania, shown in Table 4, it appears that, as we move from western Indonesia (Sumatra) into Melanesia, wet wax rises toward a hundred per cent. One might on this slender evidence argue for a linguistic difference in the trait, with Papuan-speakers being virtually all wet and Austronesian-speaking invaders possessed of dry genes to a significant degree. In the Markham Valley of eastern New Guinea, two sizable samples show

TABLE 4

Ear Wax in Oceania

Percentage of wet wax

Indonesia	
Achinese, Sumatra	52
Ambonese, Ceram	62
Western New Guinea	
Geelvink Bay (all AUS)	
Biak Island	76
Japen Island	72
Wandaman	58
Eastern New Guinea	
Markham Valley	
Onga (AUS)	92
Waffa (PAP)	100
Solomon Islands	
Bougainville	
Aita (PAP)	99·5 ?[1]
Nagovisi (PAP)	98·2 ?[1]
Ulawa (AUS)	99·8
Micronesia	
Ponape	72
Truk	54
Yap	61
Polynesian Outlier	
Ontong Java[2]	85

[1] The observer, D. Hrdy (with the Harvard Solomon Islands Expedition), could detect no wax at all in ten per cent and fourteen per cent of these series, respectively; the figures shown are obtained by subtracting the very small numbers of cases of dry wax.

[2] Recorded by the Harvard Solomon Islands Expedition. Ontong Java is linguistically a Polynesian Outlier but appears to be more Micronesian in general physique and is apparently intermediate in blood type frequencies.

a distinction which would conform nicely to the hypothesis. The only other Oceanic data are Micronesian. All that can be said is that they seem to be at a level which matches such non-Chinese aboriginals, i.e. Austronesian-speakers, as the Formosan hill tribes. Beyond this, useful things might be learned from variation of local samples and, of course, from information from Polynesia and Australia.

A Bewilderment of Figures

It easy to feel that the more we learn the less we know. Nevertheless all this genetic information is very important, especially if we can begin to judge what is meaningful, and how, and what is treacherous, and why. Partly from ignorance of these things I have not tried any clusterings like those from measurements in the last chapter; and in any case the unevenness of the information makes it difficult. A few others have done so by keeping to safe limits, i.e. by using uniform data and, generally, restricted information (see Friedlaender, below). I will give a rather striking example by Schanfield [205] shown in Figure 4 for some broad relationships, which has been carefully constructed. In doing so, I must point out on Dr Schanfield's behalf that it is preliminary (he is expanding his Pacific studies), that it is one of several combinations of peoples and of traits, and that it lumps some internally varying sets of populations (Japanese, and especially the two Melanesian linguistic groupings). It is nevertheless a satisfying result.

It is based on five blood group systems, but is known to be dominated by the Gm factors. The 'minimum evolution' form of analysis specifies the most likely genetic 'distance' traveled by each group on the supposition that all started from the common origin point, and by each group since it separated from another, so that the total line joining any two is a suggestion of their mutual genetic closeness. (In such a scheme, of course, no allowance is made for mixture, though this may be read into it.) It is easy to see three principal population distinctions: Japan (or north Aisa again), the hill peoples of Thailand, and Papuans of Melanesia.

To repeat, this leans on the Gm factors. From other blood traits, especially the more familiar red cell antigens, patterns have been less systematic, as we saw. Geneticists are still hopeful, but a number of anthropologists have lately concluded that the search for ancestral or continental connections from such data must be down-graded. Of all parts of the world, the Pacific is most inimical to the Hardy–Weinberg equilibrium – the persistence of gene proportions.[1] One familiar suggestion of a connection is that of

[1] To quote an informed worker, Professor Jane Underwood [103]: 'A persist-

Fig. 4. 'Minimum evolution' tree of Asian and Oceanic peoples based on five blood systems.

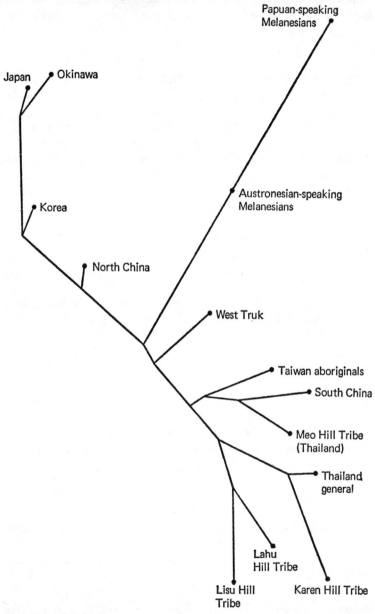

From Schanfield [205]

Ainus and Australians; blood data, with high B in the Ainus, and the unique or very rare genes Gm^{xg} and cdE, detract from the idea even more than the measurements of the previous chapter. On the other hand, the American Indian–Polynesian connection bears up well, there being general resemblances (with North America) in many systems, with only the Diego and possibly the Gm factors arguing the other way. But I do not feel either case is more significant than the other.

Rather, we should give our attention to matters internal to the Pacific. For one thing, as Boyd [24] noted, there is some consistency throughout Oceania in the genes involved (examples are the Rh and Gm systems, and the absence of A_2), in spite of the variation in frequencies: the peoples play different tunes but on the same strings; and departures from either Europe or Africa are very considerable, with greater likeness to east Asia. Also, ethnic and blood group boundaries within the Pacific do not fully coincide: you can set up well-defined Polynesian and Australian 'blood races', but you must exclude western Polynesia and northern Australia respectively. You are also, I believe, in danger of deluding yourself. Far more useful would be examining other phenomena, of which the following strike me:

1. Australia, except for the north, seems marked by gene impoverishment, that is, the loss or fall in several genes common elsewhere: B; S of the MN system; Fy^b; PHs^a and PHs^c; and perhaps Gm^{ab}; all missing. This, and unusual figures for some other genes, probably reflect both early settlement and long isolation. The absence of greater local variation would be partly a result of these losses: that is to say, if Fy^a is the only gene present, local differences in the Duffy system become impossible. However, the low but constant rate of intergroup marriage may also reduce local variation in other genes.

At any rate it is clear that the bloodhounds may stop looking in far distant regions for Australian 'ancestors'.

2. Across northernmost Australia genes absent to the south do appear: B, Fy^b, Gm^{ab}, PHs^a. This automatically suggests intro-

---

ing disregard for the conditioning effect of population characteristics will continue to adversely affect interpretations of human evolution: similarities in gene frequencies may be, in part, the product of like population histories, while, conversely, dissimilarities in gene frequencies do not, *per se*, demonstrate different racial origins'.

duction from New Guinea. Still, it is conceivable that the situation carries over from the Pleistocene, when broad land connections existed, and northern Australia might have had closer climatic and cultural affiliations with New Guinea than with the rest of Australia. A few other blood likenesses, not cited, would support this.

3. New Guinea differs markedly from Australia, not only in characteristic genes but also in the great local fluctuations in gene frequencies. This last would accord with the different population structure, marked by larger communities and larger numbers generally, but with warfare and mutual isolation of communities giving greater play to genetic drift over long periods. It probably supports what language and archaeology also suggest: early settlement and a long history of proliferation of local groups by splitting, as agriculture penetrated the interior, all in a setting of mutual hostility.

4. The same early settlement and history might explain a similar situation in the western part of Island Melanesia (the Bismarck Archipelago, and at least Bougainville of the Solomons). Otherwise Island Melanesia differs from New Guinea principally in the Gm factors.

In distinction from Australia, and in internal diversity, the Melanesian blood evidence agrees generally with the physical evidence of the last chapter.

5. As far as it is known, Island Melanesia displays no marked trends or characteristic features when taken as a whole. One important point: so far, no systematic or convincing differences have been found between Austronesian and Papuan language communities, such as would support two distinct populations and migrations (though the Gm and ear wax data give some such indications). Instead, on Bougainville [67] two distinct stocks of *Papuan* languages, a northern and a southern, can be well separated in blood terms, their several villages showing no overlap in the frequencies of PHs[a] (see above), nor in S of the MN system. This is one example of the importance of fine-grained studies. The results, and a cluster analysis, seem once more to suggest early arrival and long time mutual isolation of two populations, representing distinct Papuan lingustic stocks.

6. Eastern Polynesia strongly suggests drift and the founder principle hard at work during the period of migration and settlement; let us not review this again. Western Polynesia (Samoa,

Tonga) is less distinguished, grading into Melanesia and Micronesia in general frequencies, in the possession of gene B and so forth. All too readily this might suggest Melanesian intrusion and admixture into 'pure' Polynesians typified by those of the east. While some mixture in the west is quite likely, the whole picture is probably wrong. As in Australia, impoverishment has probably taken place, and the eastern Polynesians are neither 'pure' nor 'typical', in this misleading sense. In fact, the western Polynesians would be closer to the sort of population, as far as blood goes, from which the easterners were derived by emigration and isolation.

This does not imply that they emerged from an undifferentiated Melanesian–Polynesian parental community by segregation in all features, that is, by a sort of reversal of the melting-pot process. We are speaking of blood. I mean only that their blood distributions were originally more general and like those of the rest of the Pacific, and that change has been rapid.

7. Micronesia might be the matrix from which the Polynesia combinations came, if only because it has the variety in blood genes. This marked internal variation is not at all surprising in view of the small, dispersed populations, which however, unlike eastern Polynesia, were probably not all from one migration, and were stringently isolated afterwards.

Micronesian gene frequencies are indeed disparate. The Gilberts and the Marshalls give, respectively, these summary frequencies: B 0·26 $vs.$ 0·12; M 0·37 $vs.$ 0·20; R^2 0·25 $vs.$ 0·03. In general, the M gene is lowered (if not as far as in Melanesia) in the east and in the west (Yap, Palau), but rises in the Marianas and the western Carolines to 0·50 and above, as in Polynesia. Accordingly it is unsafe to see any trends at all, or even general distinctions between Micronesia and either Melanesia or Polynesia. There may turn out to be much useful information in Micronesian frequencies, for example relating to special distinctions in Yap, or Palau, or the Marianas, to supplement the presence of the Diego factor in the last. It is too early to tell.

8. Returning to results of the last chapter, a final question may be asked: whether any general blood distinctions are to be found between the Southwest Pacific (Melanesian and Australian) peoples, and those often referred to as 'Mongoloid' (Micronesians and Polynesians together). At the moment, the answer would be no. But many new tests remain to be made.

5

Language

Interest in Oceanic linguistics has expanded remarkably since World War II, continuing the work of earlier students, such as Capell. The number of trained linguists is much larger; they have worked very hard at collecting records of a great many languages; and the use of computers has allowed one school to make broad comparisons of the records. If we are awed by what they have accomplished, they themselves are awed by what remains to be done. Their results are already illuminating, sharpening the picture of movements in the Pacific – a picture which gives little comfort to traditional ideas. But there is plenty of controversy.

The major pattern is already known. In a single great arc, including Indonesia, Micronesia, Polynesia and much of Melanesia (especially coastal parts), all the languages are related in the Austronesian stock; it is estimated that if they were completely counted they would number over five hundred. (This was formerly known as the Malayo–Polynesian family; let no unwary reader detect a reference to Australia in the new name.) Enclosed within this arc, in Australia and in parts of interior Melanesia, is another, highly diverse set of languages, entirely distinct from the first. If all were counted, it is thought they would number over fifteen hundred (that is, about five hundred for Australia[1] and a thousand for New Guinea and elsewhere). Only recently have linguists begun to group those found in Melanesia into stocks or larger 'phyla', and to find possible signs of a very remote relation among all of them. They were originally called 'Papuan', but this suggested a recognizable unit of some kind, and was replaced by the more aseptic 'non-Austronesian'. However, such a term also covers English and Iroquois, and with the growing feeling that

[1] Perhaps depending on how they are counted: Grace [96] says 'over two hundred' is the number estimated.

these so-called non-Austronesian languages probably have some basic community, 'Papuan', as specific and unambiguous, is now again considered respectable by respectable students. I shall use it here in the same sense where convenient: that is, for non-Austronesian languages of New Guinea and Island Melanesia.

Geographically, the pattern is as if the island map had been picked up by its Australian corner and briefly and carelessly dipped in Austronesian. In Indonesia the effect was virtually complete – there are a few Papuan languages only in the east, near New Guinea, though the fact is important. In Polynesia and Micronesia (islands of small size) the dye also took completely. But no Austronesian languages exist in Australia, and the larger islands of western Melanesia were affected mainly on the coast (New Guinea, Bougainville) or irregularly (almost all of New Ireland, but New Britain largely in the northeast).

Language Changes

Languages, like blood group proportions, change as the result of certain processes or agents. This comparison is an analogy only: ethnic groups have adopted new languages in a few generations, and Chinese children may be brought up in American families with television English as their only speech, accompanied in neither case by an alteration in blood genes or in facial features.

One process gives a simple model of gradual change, something like genetic drift, though it is more systematic. Two languages, once the same, drift apart. A single language changes over time (Chaucerian to modern English), and two separated communities starting with one language follow separate lines of change. First their languages become different dialects, which in linguistic study does not mean a 'southern accent', or an unwritten language, or a provincial one differing from the official form. Rather, it signifies the appearance of distinct differences which the speakers of each dialect know how to disregard so that they are still mutually intelligible. For example a Scot says 'lass' when we Sassenachs say 'girl', each having chosen to make everyday use out of different words both present in Middle English.[1] Finally the two become

[1] British and American English probably differ largely in new inventions: lift *vs.* elevator, petrol *vs.* gas. But there may be something stylistic or psychological: what an MP would call a 'barracks', a Congressman is all too apt to call a 'temporary military dormitory facility'.

different languages, mutually unintelligible. But a linguist easily sees that the grammatical structure of the two is much the same. The vocabulary is also really much the same, although words of common origin also begin to take on different meanings, and substitutions for the original meaning occur. 'Lass' and 'girl' are not of common origin, but English 'maiden' and German 'Mädchen' are, although 'maiden' now translates as 'Jungfrau', and 'Mädchen' translates as 'girl'. In general, English, Swedish, Dutch and German (and others) share a great bulk of common, cognate words: hound, hund, hond, Hund; head, huvud, hoofd, Haupt; these are examples. But actually, 'hound' and 'Haupt' have begun to drift relative to their mates. We say 'dog', which in other languages means specifically a mastiff or bulldog, while we use a hound strictly to hunt with. And the Germans say 'Kopf' for head (except in Wagnerian operas), although they still use 'Haupt' for a lot of head-things, like 'Hauptstadt', a capital city. But the Romance languages have different sets of cognate words: Italian and French 'cane' and 'chien', 'testa' and 'tête'. This reflects the fact that Germanic and Romance languages are different main branches resulting from the earlier split of Latin and an older Germanic. Such more distantly related branches together make up a family, or a stock, containing all those languages which can be seen to have a relationship at all. These studies in fact began with the realization almost two hundred years ago that broad connections existed within both the Indo–European and the Malayo–Polynesian families. The last was established in the 1780s by the Spanish linguist Hervas y Panduro.

The above refers essentially to vocabulary. Language also shifts in the sound systems it uses. Modern German and Dutch have different sounds and so common words are not mutually comprehensible, but one who knows English and German, and can mentally make a few 'corrections' in spelling, is able to read Dutch without great difficulty. Sound shifts are typically quite systematic. In Polynesia, vowels are very constant, but certain consonants have shifted in different local patterns. For example, major islands in the Samoan and Hawaiian groups actually have the same name: Savai'i and Hawai'i. If the name existed in Proto-Polynesian (the parent, 2,500 years ago, of all Polynesian languages), this would have been Sawaiki, by a process of reconstruction which is relatively simple for the Polynesian languages. But modern

Samoan has dropped the 'k', replacing it with a glottal stop (the soundless halt which a Scot uses instead of 't' when he says 'bottle'). Quite independently the same shift took place in modern Hawaiian. Samoan kept the 's'; Hawaiian has changed 's' in such positions to 'h'. Hawaiian kept the 'w'; Samoan changed such 'w's' to 'v'. While dropping 'k' in the same places as Samoan, Hawaiian has used 'k' to replace 't' in a lot of other places: the original 'tapu' (vulgarly and incorrectly spelt 'taboo' by us) remains the same in Samoan but is 'kapu' in Hawaiian. The sea god Tangaroa (his central Polynesian name) hangs on to his vowels only: in Samoa, as originally, he is Tangaloa; in the Societies, Ta'aroa; and in the Marquesas, Tana'oa.

Grammatical rules – and Oceanic languages, like other non-Indo-European stocks, may have grammatical devices undreamed of by ourselves – are another field of conservatism and change. Now these several aspects of language, vocabulary meanings, sound shifts and grammar, may alter differently and at different rates, though little is now known about such comparisons. So linguists who stress different kinds of evidence may come out with different answers and arguments.

Furthermore, the above model – called in fact the 'genetic' or family tree model – can exist only in a vacuum. Languages do not get a chance to change in this laboratory way. They spread, and run into each other. In spreading, they have often replaced others widely or completely. Celtic Irish has almost totally given way to Germanic English in a century or two, as Celtic had much earlier yielded to Anglo-Saxon in England, without the annihilation of the Irish people (or even of the English language). If nothing had ever taken place except the slow differentiation of languages, in the genetic model, the primitive world would exhibit a myriad of very distant tongues. But we see large areas where languages are now closely related, though spoken by rather different peoples, as in the cases both of Indo-European and Austronesian. These families are certainly some thousands of years old in themselves, but equally certainly they do not go back to the dawn of mankind, or anything like it. A later language may spread, replacing a checkerboard of older, highly differentiated ones, giving rise to a 'new' language family as it in turn undergoes differentiation. People of European physique have occupied the west of that continent for 30,000 years, but Indo-European has swept away all previous languages except Basque, in the last five thousand years, and has in turn been invaded in spots by the Ural–Altaic languages Hungarian and Finnish. In this way Austronesian has evidently both occupied new territory, in Polynesia, and submerged older languages in Indonesia and parts of Melanesia.

In colliding, languages will borrow features of any kind, whether or not one language replaces the other. Norman French failed to replace Saxon English in the British Isles, but anyone can see the debt of English to French, a member of a quite different branch of Indo-European. (It is hard to write much in English without drawing from that side; you will see that I fail with the last word in this sentence.) Such borrowing can be detected by a linguist familiar with the languages and it is informative in the Pacific. A more radical result of contact is mixing, producing a language considerably changed from either parent because of the intimacy of contact; some would consider English actually to be a mixed language, though it is identifiable as basically Germanic. This, as we shall see, has caused a special divergence of views among Oceanic linguists.[1]

These students, in addition to searching for general principles of human language, are on the trail of correct connections among languages, and thus of Pacific history. In the quest, the traditional approach takes account of the various factors I have described, with all the room for disagreement which they allow, to see if a common ancestry can be shown for two or more languages, as well as to reconstruct the common ancestor. This leads to a natural hierarchy of languages, branches and families.

A different approach is the more recent one of lexicostatistics. When languages, in some general area such as the Pacific, are very numerous and varied, an attempt may be made to group them by comparing them in carefully selected word lists, to determine the number of words they share which are believed to have a common origin and meaning. This rates numerically the amount of voca-

---

[1] Leading modern students whose results and opinions I am particularly citing are Capell, Dyen and Grace, especially from articles and comments published in *Current Anthropology* from 1962 to 1966. For important aspects of interpretation and further data I am particularly indebted to my longtime Wisconsin and Harvard colleague Einar Haugen, who has been most helpful with advice and cautions, and to Andrew Pawley of the University of Auckland, who has done the same and has also let me read manuscripts which had not yet appeared in print.

bulary they still hold in common as compared with the amount of vocabulary for which substitutes have come into use at some stage. To do this on a grand scale – to take a list of something like a hundred and fifty standard words and compare each one with every other in 371 different Austronesian languages, as was done by Dyen [54, 56] – may lead to many millions of individual comparisons. That is where the computers come in.

This statistical classification, like the traditional one, endeavors to seek out a framework of relationships. There are two differences to notice. In the first place, lexicostatistics neglects grammar and structure and uses only vocabulary; it is therefore more susceptible than the other method to the factor of word-borrowing among peoples in contact, which may lead to false likenesses and groupings. Second, although the end result is indeed a hierarchical family tree, the statistical nature of the method puts all languages on a scale of gradually increasing distances among them, instead of proceeding by groupings for which there is also structural evidence for recent or remote common ancestry. So the word difference between languages is stressed, and the boundaries of the categories of classification become arbitrary, not the other way around as in the traditional approach to classification. In the lexicostatistical system of Swadesh, the hierarchy rests on the percentage of shared cognates (the distance between two languages increasing as the percentage of shared vocabulary falls), with the groupings changing to broader ones at chosen limits. These are the groupings suggested by Swadesh:

> *Dialects* of one language share eighty-one to a hundred per cent of cognates;
> *Languages* of one family share twenty-eight to eighty-one per cent of cognates;
> *Families* of one stock share twelve to twenty-eight per cent of cognates;
> *Stocks* of one phylum share four to twelve per cent of cognates.

As I have said, these limits are necessarily arbitrary. As Wurm and Laycock [260] point out, Dutch and High German share eighty-four per cent of cognates but are not mutually intelligible and thus are not properly speaking dialects; and yet in New Guinea languages with a smaller mutual vocabulary may be mutually intelligible.

Glottochronology is lexicostatistics in another guise, attempting a direct measure of time since two languages separated. It assumes a regular rate of the replacement of cognate words, so that this can be translated into a time scale. It tries to avoid the bogey of word-borrowing by choosing a standard list of basic words (parts of the body, etc.) which are seldom borrowed, being subject only to the slow substitution described. A few comparisons among historically known languages have indicated that about eighty-one per cent of the basic vocabulary of a single language will survive in the face of such substitutions at the end of a thousand years. Thus two languages being compared might be expected to correspond in only sixty-six per cent at the end of that time (each would not retain the same eighty-one per cent, so that the expectation would be eighty-one per cent of eighty-one per cent which is sixty-six per cent). So the categories shown above have been given time values: a sharing of twenty-eight per cent suggests a time lapse of three thousand years, and one of twelve per cent a lapse of five thousand years, according to the computed time scale.

But the limits of error are wide. The method has been shown to have fallacies, and many linguists question whether it can give such precise dates as it suggests; they also doubt that lexico-statistics can give accurate measures of relationship when the necessary qualifications are kept in mind.[1] None the less glotto-chronology does give some idea of time since the break-up of a proto-language, parental to a major or minor grouping; and for anthropologists, some idea is much better than nothing. Also, since lexicostatistics is quantitative, the method can use computers to digest enormous amounts of information and thus it can be very comprehensive, as Dyen's study, given below, will demonstrate.

Austronesian Languages in General

Let us therefore first review Pacific languages in Dyen's terms, turning to the work of others for help with interpretation in special areas. Dyen, who is continuing his analyses, has published [56] a massive lexicostatistical study covering 245 Austronesian lan-guages, probably half the total number. Before actual publication Murdock [177] abstracted and interpreted the report, providing a rearranged summary classification in which he used his own

[1] For one discussion, see Hockett [114] from whom the dating estimates are also taken: for a more specific and critical evaluation, see Grace [94].

categories of relationship, which have a more 'familial' connotation. I give below a further rearranged and reduced version of Murdock's list, with many omissions, in the hope of showing the

Stock[1]: Austronesian

I Malayo-Polynesian FAMILY[2]
  A. Heonesian SUBFAMILY
      BRANCHES
      1. New Hebridean (Efate; Murdock suspects others are eligible)
      2. Fijian
      3. Rotuman
      4. Polynesian
          a. East Polynesian cluster (Easter, Hawaii, Marquesas, Tahiti, South Cooks, Mangareva, Tuamotus)
          b. Maori
          c. West Polynesian cluster (Samoa, Tonga, etc., including Ellice, Ontong Java, Fila-Futuna of New Hebrides, Rennell I.)
          d. Nukuoro, Outlier
          e. Kapingamarangi, Outlier
      5. Mota, Banks Islands
      6. Gilbertese
      7. Carolinian (including Kusaie, Marshalls, Truk, Ponape – all except Yap, Palau) (put here by Murdock; Dyen only suspects Heonesian affiliation)
      8. Southeast Solomons (some languages of Ysabel, Malaita, Guadalcanal, San Cristoval)
      9. West Melanesian (a possible branch in Bismarcks and northeast New Guinea)
      10. Motuan (Port Moresby region of New Guinea)
  B. Chamorro, Marianas Islands SUBFAMILY
  C. Palauan SUBFAMILY
  D. Hesperonesian SUBFAMILY
      BRANCHES
      1. Celebes, two clusters: Bareic (Toradja) and Bugic
      2. Totemboan of north Celebes (isolated language)
      3. Sangir (between Celebes and Mindanao)
      4. Northwest, three clusters in Celebes and Philippines (most languages of the latter islands, some of Borneo)
      5. Sentah, Borneo
      6. Malagasy of Madagascar (including Maanyan of Borneo)
      7. West Indonesian, three clusters, from Bali west to Vietnam: Sundic includes *inter alia* Balinese, Javanese, Sundanese, Malay; Batak; Cru of Vietnam
  E. Formosan SUBFAMILY
      BRANCHES
      1. Central Formosan (including Ami, Bunun, Paiwan, Thao)
      2. Ataylic? (so removed from Central languages as to be possibly

       independent; see XI below)

F. Moluccan SUBFAMILY
    BRANCHES
1. Kuiwai, Southwest New Guinea
2. Sekar, West New Guinea
3. Ambic, of Ambon and Ceram
4. Buru
5. Fordatic, of Kei and Tanimbar (south of New Guinea)
6. Letic, of Kisar and Leti
7. Tettum, of Timor
8. Sikkic, of Solor and Flores
9. Endeh, of Flores
10. Sumba

II North coast of West New Guinea[3]

III Northeast New Guinea. Three isolated languages, also two possibly related to Malayo-Polynesian

IV Papua and Massim area.

V Bismarck Archipelago. Some isolated languages; some with possible relations to Malayo-Polynesian

VI Solomon Islands. Three groups; three isolated languages

VII New Hebrides. One isolated, three possibly connected with Malayo-Polynesian

VIII New Caledonia and Loyalties. Three groups: South N. C.; North N. C.; Loyalties

IX Micronesia. Two isolated languages, Yap and Nauru

X Indonesia. Enggano, south of Sumatra (this might belong to West Indonesian, I-D-7 above

XI Formosa. Atayalic, which is distant from other Formosan languages in I-E above, but may as Dyen thinks belong to that group

---

[1] Murdock makes Austronesian a *phylum* rather than a *stock*, which last is Swadesh's category to include related families with languages sharing twelve to twenty-eight per cent of cognates. Some of the pairs fall below the minimum figure, but not many. Semantically, 'phylum' seems to me to connote a group in which vocabulary sharing of the member stocks has almost disappeared, but which has common structural and grammatical features. This appears to be the way in which it is applied by Wurm and others to the Papuan languages of New Guinea.

[2] This is a new and restricted use of 'Malayo-Polynesian'. Within this family Murdock does not call a group with a single language (e.g. Chamorro) a 'subfamily'. I do so here, to indicate rank, as in zoology, when a major group such as a family may have only a single known species, but is given family status to recognize its individuality, suggesting a long evolutionary isolation.

[3] Murdock lists this and the following groups as 'Divergent languages and groups (each is at least potentially an independent family co-ordinate with Malayo-Polynesian)'. I am taking him at slightly more than his word, modifying his listing by giving each a Roman numeral to suggest this degree of equal rank with Malayo-Polynesian. These are the language groups which in a large number of cases, according to Dyen, share cognates with others outside their groups at a rate of about twelve to twenty per cent, in a few cases less. However, they are also groups which are much more incompletely known than Malayo-Polynesian, so that rank and internal structure cannot now be stated in the same way.

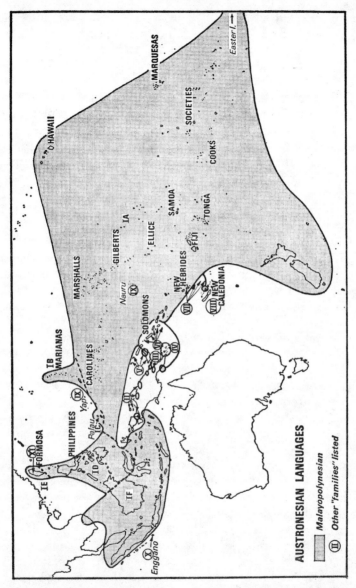

3 Austronesian language distribution. (Following Dyen and Murdock).
This contrasts the wide spread of Dyen's Malayo–Polynesian family
and its divisions with the restricted areas of the other more isolated
and divergent 'families' (II to XI).

skeleton to best advantage. Doing so doubtless compounds any distortions and simplifications which might exist in Murdock's rendering, and I apologize both to him and Dyen.

I have presented the above, resulting from Dyen's first major exposition of his analysis – not to be his last – to serve as an organization of the Austronesian languages. In doctoring Murdock's arrangement of it, my most probable fault is perhaps in making it look too much like a family tree rather than a purely statistical study, which is what it is. Of course, in all this a pattern of descent is the aim: indeed, Grace [94] talks about 'family trees' and Dyen's current work is toward a 'genetic classification', meaning the same thing. But I feel that, although linguists agree fairly broadly as to many of their groupings, none is really ready to say that a general tree can yet be drawn up.

As an innocent bystander I have no intention of even suggesting one. I shall only inspect some of the evidence useful to our interests in the several geographical regions. First, however, by way of anticipation, let us look at the gist of the whole, as well as I can present it. This should be done from two different perspectives, I think, because the difference between them does much to explain why ideas of migration and relationship remain in conflict.

A Difference of Viewpoints
THE VIEW FROM LEXICOSTATISTICS

Dyen's pattern, depending entirely on vocabulary, assumes a steady rate of divergence among languages so that ideally (of course not practically) the classification arrived at is inevitable.[1] What is the result? A broad band of the Malayo–Polynesian family, starting at Timor, sweeps clockwise throughout Indonesia and via Micronesia into eastern Melanesia and Polynesia, though having a few spots in western Melanesia north and south of New Guinea. Here and there within this arc or on its fringes – the barrier islands south of Sumatra; Formosa; Yap and Nauru in Micronesia – are languages not included in Malayo–Polynesian, being more isolated and distinct, while a much larger cluster of such diverse languages lies, ringed by the arc, in Melanesia. (As Grace pointed out, of

[1] Grace [94] quite rightly points out that the connections of Dyen's groups, where they would join the trunk of the tree (where the percentage of shared cognates is low, but where major groups come together), are arbitrary, and could be made in different ways by using minor corrections or slightly different figures.

forty 'branches' of Austronesian originally specified by Dyen, some of which I have promoted herein to 'families', thirty-three are found *only* in Melanesia.) Particular diversity exists in New Britain and adjoining New Guinea, around Cape Cretin, and in the New Hebrides, at the other end of Melanesia.

To Dyen, this and other considerations imply an origin for the entire Austronesian stock in the New Britain–New Guinea area followed by very early migrations to other parts of Melanesia, the New Hebrides being one. Secondary dispersals later (but before 2500 BC) spread the Malayo–Polynesian languages outward to Polynesia, Micronesia and Indonesia (and within Melanesia). While these, he thinks, took different routes, he considers as one possibility that Malayo–Polynesian as a whole stems from the New Hebrides.[1]

THE VIEW FROM STRUCTURE

Various other linguists consider that the limited base of lexico-statistics makes it one-sided. Grace notes [96] that Melanesian languages, though lexically diverse, are relatively uniform in grammar. Students in this school would subscribe to a quite different, less complicated history for Austronesian, and to a classification differing from Dyen's primarily in distinguishing between Indonesian languages on one hand and Oceanic (or eastern Austronesian) on the other. In general, they would imagine the existence of an original Austronesian great-grandparent some time before 3000 BC, which broke up to produce one or more Proto-Indonesian languages (and perhaps a Proto-Formosan) as well as a Proto-Oceanic). As descendants of the last, they would put into the Oceanic group almost all the Austronesian languages of Melanesia, Polynesia and Micronesia, excepting Chamorro and Palauan. This Proto-Oceanic later dissolved into smaller groups, some more diverse, some less. One of particular importance to us is Eastern Oceanic, which centers on eastern Melanesia and gave rise to some languages there and to Polynesian as well.

These writers do not deny the diversity seen among many Melanesian languages, but they suggest that some languages of

---

[1] Edward Sapir's 'age-area' principle has become an axiom for linguists, meaning that a region of high diversity within a given linguistic group or family should be taken as the prime candidate for that group's ancestral seat; and that broad areas with more closely related members should represent more recent spreads outward from such an ancestral home.

Melanesia may have changed more rapidly than others, and that all may be included in the general Oceanic group, distinguished from Indonesian languages. The pattern they see would call for less complex and comprehensive sweeps and movements than does Dyen's interpretation.

Things get more complicated when we go to details, but that is where the information is. Let us review problems area by area.

Polynesia

Principal students agree on two important points: the obviously close relationship of all Polynesian languages, and the special relationship of the group to a set of languages in Fiji and the central New Hebrides. This is only suggested in Dyen's list.

The view of Polynesian internal relationships which emerges from the writings of Elbert, Pawley and Green is as follows. There existed a language, Proto-Polynesian, located in western Polynesia, which 'formed the end-point of a long period of isolated development'. Because the Polynesian languages all share a great number of innovations separating them from the related languages in Melanesia, their period of isolation must indeed have been long, lasting from about 1000 BC to a few centuries before the Christian era (and so roughly agreeing with glottochronological dates cited by Grace). At that point the original Proto-Polynesian underwent a series of splits which obviously reflect the migrations of communities colonizing Polynesia generally. These are the steps [188].

Proto-Polynesian split into *Proto-Tongic* and *Proto-Nuclear*, the latter fathering all the present-day languages, at least the following, including those of the Outliers, excepting for Tongan and the language of Niue Island.

Proto-Nuclear, a few centuries later, divided into Proto-Samoic and Proto-Eastern. This would be early in the Christian era.

Proto-Samoic gave rise to Samoan and, among others, to the languages of the Ellice and Tokelau groups and of the Outliers, the Polynesian-speaking colonies westward in Melanesia:

1. Sikaiana, Luanguia (Ontong Java) and Takuu, and probably Nukumanu and Nukuria, all north of the Solomons.

2. Fila and Futuna-Aniwa, in the New Hebrides.

3. Nukuoro and Kapingamarangi, south of the Carolines.

Proto-Eastern Polynesian did not break up until about AD 500, when the language ancestral to Easter Island separated from that ancestral to the rest of Eastern Polynesia, i.e. a Proto-Central Eastern Polynesian; the final pattern is therefore:

Easter Island
Proto-Central
    Tahitic
        Tahitian, Cook Islands, Maori
    Marquesic
        Marquesan, Mangarevan, Hawaiian.

The final major divisions are estimated to have occurred 1,000 years ago or later, the major east–west split 2,000 to 2,500 years ago, and the separation of Proto-Polynesian from any other relative 3,000 years ago. Note at once how happily this fits the evidence of blood: an isolate, probably small to begin with, later expanding eastward into new territory, with its special gene proportions resulting from genetic drift and gene loss during this phase, and preserved from later mixture in the empty islands of eastern Polynesia. The present blood picture must have been established at the latest by the beginning of the Christian era, if that is the date for the split between Proto-Samoic and Proto-Eastern.

But this picture might carry back still further. An Eastern Oceanic subgroup of Oceanic has been proposed by Pawley and others [188].[1] The group, for which a parental language, Proto-Eastern Oceanic, can be reconstructed, shares traits of grammar and vocabulary of which many, Pawley thinks, are innovations unique to the group. Within it he includes Polynesian, Fijian, various languages of the central and northern New Hebrides, and languages of the Solomon Islands east of Ysabel, as well as some possible members further away to which we shall return. Not included are the more isolated, old-guard languages of Tanna, Eromanga or Aneityum of the southern New Hebrides, or of Malekula in the north of the group. The parent language, Pawley estimates, last existed in about 2000 BC. The meaning of all this for Polynesia lies in his detailed analysis of Fiji.

Pawley [188] finds that the Fijian dialects are extremely varied and can most conveniently be regarded as falling into two distinct

[1] First named by Bruce Biggs, it would correspond, though disagreeing in some respects, with Dyen's Heonesian, and with a subgroup of Grace's Oceanic. Grace would place the center of dispersal of this subgroup (not given a name by him) in the central New Hebrides, and allot it to the same members in general as Eastern Oceanic, though adding more of the Micronesian languages.

languages, East and West Fijian, each with its own set of dialects. He reckons that the western group, sharing a number of special features of its own, underwent a period of isolation from the eastern, beginning not less than two thousand years ago, followed by diversification.

All Fijian dialects share many common retentions from the Eastern Oceanic parent, as reconstructed, as well as a variety of innovations special to Fiji. The eastern Fijian branch is more diverse than the western. This seems to indicate, by the genetic model, a still earlier single Proto-Fijian dialect from which the western branch split off; but Pawley does not so interpret it. He finds some words, or arrangements of syntax, or prefixes, which occur all through Fiji but are related *only* to one or another of the other non-Fijian Eastern Oceanic languages, not to the reconstructed Proto-Eastern Oceanic itself. Still other features are found only locally in Fiji and again can be related only to specific Eastern Oceanic languages elsewhere, not to all of them or to their ancestor.

So a single, uniform, Proto-Fijian language cannot be reconstructed. As far back as linguistics can trace, Fijian seems to have been composed of a number of distinct dialects or closely related languages. Some of these were probably already distinct before their arrival in Fiji, but all derived from Proto-Eastern Oceanic, and very likely were still similar enough to be mutually intelligible. From an early period, then, a complex dialect chain has existed in Fiji. Over the centuries many common innovations have spread over the entire archipelago, with the effect that all dialects have remained rather alike. At the same time, a few of the original differences persist, while other differences between dialects have developed locally.

How did this come about? In contrast to the case of Fijian, there was definitely a spoken Proto-Polynesian language. reconstructible as a parent for all the existing languages of Polynesia. While none of the various early Fijian dialects can at this point be shown to be a sole direct ancestor of present-day dialects, and no Proto-Fijian can be set up, Pawley concludes that the dominant contributor to the mix was an early form of the language that later became Proto-Polynesian – that is to say, a pre-Polynesian language. This is because innovations which are uniquely shared (within Eastern Oceanic) with Polynesian languages (and therefore present in Proto-Polynesian) occur in all present Fijian dialects. At a date in the range of 1500 BC to 1000 BC, this primal ancestor, Pre-Polynesian, split for the first time, one branch moving east into western Polynesia, the other remaining in Fiji. Other contributors to the Fijian complex were a language or languages whose closest relatives lie in the New Hebrides, specifically in the northern New Hebrides and Banks Islands on one hand, and the central New Hebrides, centering on Efate, on the other. (There are some other features shared exclusively by Fiji and languages of the eastern Solomons, which Pawley thinks may have different reasons for existence.)

At some point New Hebrideans arrived in Fiji. Either they came only after the original separation of a Pre-Polynesian and some kind of a 'Pre-Fijian' had already taken place, or else they did not make contact with the ancestral Polynesians before the latter left Fiji. This conclusion arises from the fact that the Proto-Polynesian language, as reconstructed, is devoid of the specific language innovations which came into Fiji from the New Hebrides, and in place of such terms it retains words from the reconstructed ancestor of all Eastern Oceanic.

We might boil this down to its evidence for movements of peoples, as suggested by Pawley's analysis. Colonists arrived in several parts of eastern Melanesia speaking an original Eastern Oceanic language, or closely related dialects of it, before 1500 BC. Pawley would put the break up of Eastern Oceanic, in fact, at about 2000 BC. Sooner or later dialectically differing communities settled on Fiji, the most important and probably the first being Pre-Polynesian. From this source, after some centuries, a further colonization took place to western Polynesia. We may get a little ahead of things here. While Pawley is commendably cautious about this, a later study by him and Kaye Green [189] points to Tonga as the Polynesian landfall, and further on we shall see how strongly archaeology supports this.

Other colonists, speaking now diverging Eastern Oceanic dialects, also came to Fiji. They did not affect the region from which Proto-Polynesian derived, doubtless in the east, but their contributions established the Fijian complex and speeded the differentiation of Fijian and Polynesian.

A physical anthropologist walks softly among linguists. But, as with blood, the correspondence with physical evidence is admirable. The living Fijians are somewhat variable, but under their dark skins and frizzy hair – and making allowance for broad noses – they are Polynesian in skull and skeleton, as in general body form. And yet skulls from Fijian caves and other repositories – unfortunately these precious objects are poorly documented as to age – are in some cases clearly Melanesian in character. All this fits the same picture. The first settlers of Fiji were physically Polynesian. Some of them left this first homeland, and were the first to occupy any part of Polynesia. The 'Polynesians' who stayed in Fiji were then Melanesianized by amalgamation, both physical and linguistic, with other settlers from eastern Melanesia. Such people were by this time beginning, like the Polynesians, to command wider water crossings. But the Polynesians were there first.[1] The meaning and the character of the other original speakers of Eastern Oceanic languages is something to return to later.

Melanesia

We must note once more the distribution of Papuan languages in Melanesia: much the greater area of New Guinea; parts of New Britain and New Ireland; in the Solomons, much of Bougainville, on Vella Lavella and Rendova in the New Georgia group, in the Russell Islands, and on Savo, off Guadalcanal. Finally, east of the Solomons Wurm [273] lists four such languages in the Santa Cruz group. Signs of Papuan languages are not specifically reported further to the southeast. Still, in the Solomons we see a slight overlap with the range of Eastern Oceanic as already defined.

As to Melanesian languages (i.e. Austronesian), the primary fact, we saw, is the great diversity; the secondary fact is the divergence of present-day views regarding them – altogether such a thicket that our own purposes will not be served by getting very far into it. To follow Dyen's view, we have seen, is to emphasize exclusion: his arrangement simply suggests the great variation, with some languages falling into the Heonesian subgroup of Malayo–Polynesian, but with many set down as separate and isolated units, lacking other connections within Austronesian. Grace [95] represents the other view, actually an older one: there is a major division of Austronesian, the Oceanic, which takes in

---

[1] This is by no means a new idea, having been put forward by Hocart as early as 1919, and restated by Green [97]. I have long felt [120] that only a Melanesian addition to a fundamentally Polynesian population, not the reverse, could satisfactorily account for the predominantly Polynesian nature of Fijian physique.

not only the Micronesian and the Eastern Oceanic (Polynesian, etc.) but all the Melanesian languages as well; a great cousinship, with some close relatives, others less close. In the background of the argument there is also disagreement as to special likenesses or connections with the Indonesian languages.

Ascribing Melanesian diversity to the passage of time, on the genetic model, Dyen places the center of origin of the whole Austronesian stock here, probably in the region of New Britain, and proposes that early offspring from the parental form moved both east and west. From an eastern descendant in the New Hebrides–Banks area, many or all subgroups of the Malayo-Polynesian family spread out. Murdock, as a greatly-informed ethnologist, agrees quite fully with Dyen's scheme, only pointing to a few previous suppositions as to culture history which would have to be abandoned. The essence of all this is the presumption of a considerable time depth since parental Austronesian hatched in western Melanesia, to be followed by a dynamic language dispersal from what was surely a simple culture base in the assumed center of New Britain and perhaps eastern New Guinea; not one, I should think, to be a likely source of vigorous migration and mobility. I must say that I do not believe all this myself: I cannot see why Austronesian languages, originating in the New Guinea–Bismarcks region, should have been able to prevail throughout Indonesia, an area by that time of more advanced culture, while they did not more strongly overrun the Papuan languages so close at hand.

The second view, that of Grace and others, also takes note of the great diversity in the New Britain region; but Grace views this as the hatching-place only of the Oceanic wing, not of the whole stock. Oceanic is none the less a major branch, which Grace has taken to be the result of the first differentiation within Austronesian. Then, he holds, Proto-Oceanic split into the various subgroups of Melanesia at a date he has estimated to be 2500 BC, though he feels this may be a little high. One of the fission products spread from a home in the New Hebrides to Fiji, Polynesia, Micronesia and elsewhere; this corresponds in general distribution, if not exactly, to Pawley's version of the Eastern Oceanic group.[1]

---

[1] A further explanation of the great Melanesian diversity, supported long ago by Ray and more recently by Capell, is 'pidginizing'. That is to say, Austronesian-speaking migrants from Indonesia, in more than one wave, affected

These interpretations are stimulating and suggestive, but it may be rather too soon to move on such a major scale, relying on primary factors and on linguistics alone. There are probably many secondary factors to consider. As leading toward diversification, Pawley suggests that different processes have all operated, especially constant borrowing among the Melanesian languages themselves. He thinks it likely, also, that the north coast of New Guinea has been subject to Indonesian influences at various times, as cultural evidence also shows. However, as Pawley notes, others have shown statistically that several major Indonesian migrations into Melanesia are unlikely, and he cites Capell's own observation that Oceanic (Eastern Austronesian) languages share a good deal of vocabulary not found in any Indonesian language. Cultural anthropologists [29] are also disinclined to credit more than one major movement of population into Melanesia, that is, more than one basic settlement. As to influences from outside, it is my own impression, based particularly on evidence of physique, that Melanesia, at least from the center westward through New Guinea, has been affected at least as much from Micronesia as from Indonesia. Whether diverse visitations from this quarter could have contributed significantly to Melanesian linguistic diversity is something I would leave to linguists.

So much for the main point: Melanesian language variety and its effect on ideas of population movements, extending far beyond the bounds of Melanesia proper. I doubt that we shall make much real headway with history until Dyen's kind of lexicostatistical framework has been amplified and checked by attempting reconstructions using as broad a range of evidence as possible, and preferably addressing themselves to restricted regions. Pawley's analysis of Fiji, with relation to Eastern Oceanic and Polynesian

existing Papuan languages in Melanesia. They imposed a 'Melanesian' grammatical structure, but underwent radical diversification as the result of mixing with the highly diverse Papuan languages which formed the substratum. The picture of great age would be fictitious, since the process would not require the greater time depth of gradual diversification on the genetic model. Though supported in various ways by various people this hypothesis is not in general favor. Grace and Dyen both flatly reject it (see Capell [31]) because, if it were true, two effects should be expected: (1) the Austronesian element would show broader similarities at least in parts of Melanesia, and (2) the supposed non-Austronesian elements could be matched here and there in existing Papuan languages, and this has not been found. All the same, most linguists agree that pidgin and creole languages in some sense have mixed origins, and Wurm (see Grace [93]) find possible cases of mixed Papuan–Austronesian languages in New Guinea.

linguistic origins, is an example. Here are a few more points which seem to call for precise settling by devoted future attention.

One is the exceptional unrelatedness of some languages in easternmost Melanesia. In the southern New Hebrides, Tanna and Eromanga (definitely not Eastern Oceanic according to Pawley) are decidedly isolated. Eromanga, according to Dempwolff [31] has only twenty-nine per cent of words which can be identified as Austronesian at all, and Tanna is structurally even more divergent. Although Dyen groups the Loyalty Islands with New Caledonia,[1] Capell sets the Loyalties off as equally distant from the languages of New Caledonia (internally diverse) and the southern New Hebrides. The eventual relating of all these languages (so much work to be done) is most important from the historical point of view. At the moment they do seem to suggest ancient settlement of the whole southern area.

Quite a different matter relates to languages within, not outside, Eastern Oceanic in the same region. There is substantial agreement as to relationships in this group. We have noted above that the Oceanic languages have in common a good deal of vocabulary not found in the languages of Indonesia. At the same time Grace [95] cites Ray as remarking in 1926 that the exact languages which Pawley has now taken as the core of the Eastern Oceanic subgroup (Nguna of the central New Hebrides; Mota of the Banks; Nggela of Florida in the Solomons) 'show many more words of basic [Indonesian] origin than the islands adjacent to them'. These languages are not close neighbors of one another. What does this mean? Some special connection of Eastern Oceanic with Indonesia?

Finally, Pawley and others find possible members of Eastern Oceanic well away from the eastern Melanesian center: in the Motu area around Port Moresby in the Gulf of Papua; among the Nakanai of the central north shore of New Britain; and in the Gilbert Islands. I shall return to this when we come to Polynesia, but the involvement of Micronesian languages with this same eastern group is an important problem. Grace [95] has in fact joined the Micronesian languages with those of the Polynesian Outliers as a major subgroup of it.

[1] He finds a small sharing of cognates between Polynesian and the language of Lifu in the Loyalties.

Micronesia

I have shown the positions of Micronesian languages in Dyen's analysis (his elbow being joggled in this matter by Murdock). As a result of American administration of the Trust Territory since the war, a great deal of new work by trained students has been and is being done; this has been summarized by Bender [10].

The four isolated languages remain a matter of great interest. There has been a general belief in Indonesian connections or outright relationship for Chamorro (of the Marianas) and Palauan. Bender finds that structural features argue Philippine affiliations for Chamorro. In both cases Dyen found the largest number of shared cognates to be with the Bareic subfamily of Celebes; he also suspected that much borrowing from Spanish by Marianas Chamorro might have had the effect of reducing its word-sharing with other languages, though this would not apply to Palauan. The two are certainly not closely related mutually, but Bender is satisfied to separate them as being of 'Indonesian type', which the remaining Micronesian languages are not. Nevertheless Dyen [57], in a special consideration of all aspects of Palauan, remains positive that its position as suggested by lexicostatistics is correct: a position 'co-ordinate' with the Hesperonesian, Formosan and Heonesian groupings and as distinct as as all these are from one another. The implication is that the 'age' of Palauan, or time of its separation, is as remote as the ancestors of those groups. So the full significance of Palauan remains to be understood.

The two remaining languages, of Yap in the west and Nauru in the east, are extremely isolated and distinct in both vocabulary and structure. Nauruan, for example, has not two noun classes (like French and Italian), or three (like German), but thirty-nine. In Murdock's version of the Dyen tabulation Yapese and Nauruan appear as a 'family', but they are not so related and I should doubtless have separated them, as Dyen did originally.

Nevertheless, Bender thinks (as does Grace) that they might possibly be placed in a general Nuclear Micronesian family, since they show no other affiliation. Within the Micronesian group, Bender finds an increase in diversity from west to east. Everything from Truk to the western extremity (excepting of course the oddities) is so closely related that discrete languages are hard to specify. This is the group referred to below as 'Trukic'. Languages of Ponape and nearby atolls are related to the Truk-west group less closely. Next in diminishing relationship is Marshallese, followed by Kusaie and the Gilberts; relationship among these last three groups is rather low. Here are the shared cognate percentages supplied to Bender by Dyen:

	Trukic	Ponapean	Marshallese	Gilbertese
Ponapean	36·1			
Marshallese	29·0	32·5		
Gilbertese	23·2	25·9	21·3	
Kusaiean	22·2	25·7	23·8	15·3

The four isolated languages give no figures as high as any of the above, except Palauan, which shares 18·3 per cent with Trukic and 16·3 per cent each with Ponapean and Marshallese, all low figures in the absolute sense. (See Map 13, page 242.)

The very low value between Kusaiean and Gilbertese is remarkable. Dyen found Gilbertese equidistant between 'Carolinian' (everything else), with a figure of 23·9 per cent, and Polynesian with a figure of 23·2. Pawley rates it as a possible member of Eastern Oceanic, but he points out that Gilbertese has been strongly influenced by borrowing from Polynesian, which might have the effect, especially in lexicostatistical analysis, of pulling it away from other Micronesian languages and toward Polynesian. In any case, Bender does not doubt that it is a legitimate member of his (nuclear) Micronesian group.

Bender concludes from the greater diversity among languages there that the historical origin of Micronesian languages should be in this region, at the eastern edge of the Carolines.[1] This would be agreeable to Grace's suggestion of a movement of languages out of the New Hebrides into Micronesia, and to one of Dyen's movements of 'Malayo–Polynesian'. Things may not be so simple, however. Bender's review suggests that the Micronesian languages have an integrity of their own.[2] He makes his Micronesian group a distinct subgroup of Austronesian, which would seem to leave it outside the major Oceanic group of other writers. We should note

[1] Judging from Dyen's figures, the internal diversity of the Micronesian languages (of course omitting the four special languages) would match that of the Heonesian group, or of Eastern Oceanic.

[2] He cites Izui as saying that the language of Truk has few Oceanic (or Eastern Austronesian) word roots which cannot be traced back directly to the reconstructed Proto-Austronesian. This implies a direct, unpolluted descent from original Austronesian, which was surely not located in eastern Melanesia, or the central Pacific anywhere.

that Dyen did not place the Micronesian languages (Gilbertese excepted) in his Malayo-Polynesian – this was Murdock's doing – since his Carolinian group had a shared cognate percentage of only 19·4 with Polynesian, its nearest linguistic neighbor.

Another factor might betray simple deductions of movements based on languages. Micronesia may not be the best model for the working of the age–area principle, by which the region of greatest diversity is taken to be the primary point of dispersal, all else conforming. If atolls in the Carolines are relatively close linguistically, it is possible (and it has been suggested) that a small number of immigrants or castaways may have a greater impact culturally and linguistically. This would be especially true if destructive typhoons caused occasional flights of refugees from an atoll, or substantial replacement from outside.

Ignoring this, the following seems to be the important evidence from Micronesian linguistics. The languages form a unit whose greatest diversity is indeed in the east where Kusaie, the Marshalls and the Gilberts are particularly distinctive. Gilbertese is in fact ambiguous, with suggestions of connection to Eastern Oceanic. But a movement from east to west may be underlain by an earlier movement from west to east; signs for both are there. The languages of Palau and the Marianas are obviously really old establishments, and the even more isolated languages of Yap (in the west) and Nauru (in the east) cannot be got around; Kusaiean has some structural peculiarities in addition. These things all imply settlements of antiquity, with Nauru possibly connected to the general Micronesian group.

Indonesia

Here also there are some highly isolated languages in the extreme north and south: Formosa, to which we shall return, and Enggano, one of the small Barrier Islands off the south coast of Sumatra. (The other islands in this chain are said by Capell also to 'stand rather apart' from western Indonesian languages, and Dyen found supplementary evidence, not used in his classification, of the same thing.)

Elsewhere the languages are not as diverse. According to Capell [31] they can be grouped into these divisions: a northern (Philippines plus), an eastern (the Lesser Sunda Islands) and a western (the large islands plus a few on the Asiatic mainland).

Dyen's groupings are something like this but include, in Murdock's version, two subfamilies ranking equally with the subfamily (Heonesian) containing Polynesian and other eastern Austronesian languages. These subfamilies are Hesperonesian (northern and western) and Moluccan (eastern).

Grace [93] cites a glottochronological study by Thomas and Healey for the Philippines. This suggests a parent splitting about 1300 BC into three branches, a 'Philippines superstock', a 'southern Mindanao family' and a 'Malay stock'; later dates are computed for subsequent separations among their descendants. The first branch supposedly gave rise to most Philippine languages of the present; the last, though not traced out in full by the authors, was responsible for, among others, Malay and the Austronesian languages of South Vietnam. Dyen's West Indonesian branch (I-D-7 in the tabulation) would imply, since it includes Malay as well as Cru of Vietnam, that the 'Malay stock', coincided with this branch and was parental to the languages of Java, Sumatra and much of Borneo. Although the studies do not correspond fully enough, there is a suggestion here that Dyen's important Hesperonesian subfamily had a common ancestor at about 1300 BC – in the Philippines? – which Dyen's own figures might place at an even later date. The main point is that a large body of Indonesian languages represents a secondary dispersal within Indonesia, replacing an older, more diverse set of Austronesian languages. Grace proposes exactly this, at least for the Philippines. Certainly it would fit the picture of relics of an earlier stratum, marked by high diversity and surviving in the fringes: specifically the Barrier Islands on the south, Formosa on the north, and Palau and the Marianas to the east.

As to Formosa, Dyen [55] and Ferrell [60] have done special studies later than the former's statistical analysis. Dyen thinks it most likely that the Formosan languages make up a single, extremely diverse family; he suggests that a factor of word-taboo (dropping a word for some religious reason or because it was used in the name of an important dead person) may have hastened vocabulary change and thus the loss of cognates. But figures are figures. At any rate, he apparently continues to prefer the Melanesian homeland for Austronesian. Ferrell, in a more detailed study, thinks it will take more than 'superficial vocabulary resemblances', due in many cases to borrowing, to demonstrate a single family for Formosa. He distinguishes three: Atayalic, Tsouic and Paiwanic. The antiquity of their divergence seems plain. On present appearances Formosa could well be the Austronesian 'homeland' for the Pacific, as many think. We should, however, not forget the possibility – I would say the likelihood – that some other area, for example the Philippines, once contained a similar diversity, since blotted out by spreads of junior forms of Austronesian. In that case Formosa would simply represent a relic of a former state of affairs.

Austronesian Origins and Dates

There are a few Austronesian languages on the mainland, but these give signs of having come there from Indonesia and having been strongly influenced by non-Austronesian languages (for example by Chinese). Nobody appears to think them significant for origins.

Because, however, human beings in the Pacific came from Asia, relationships for Austronesian have been sought with Asiatic languages, and a number of writers agree that there is a distant relation to the Kadai group, including Siamese. One of these (Haudricourt, cited by Capell [31]) thinks the homeland should be looked for in southern China, between Formosa and Hainan Island. Others see no evidence either for such connections or for any point of mainland origin. Whichever the case, all the present signs are that the Austronesian dispersal was from some area in the Pacific itself, and no specific Asiatic homeland for speech or people is pointed to by what is known.

Grace thinks that the series of splits, like that giving rise to Polynesian, goes back through the differentiation of the eastern Austronesian languages (Heonesian of Dyen) to the division of eastern (Oceanic) from western Austronesian, and eventually the separation of Austronesian itself from whatever original stock it derives from. He supposes each step must have preceded the next by several centuries to a millennium, which should put the time of origin at 2500 to 3000 BC. Now Dyen believes that his Malayo–Polynesian family itself is older than Indo-European, for which much better records are available and which is generally given an age of at least 2500 BC. Therefore Dyen thinks that his proposed migrations of the 'Malayo–Polynesians' began before that date, 'and possibly well before it'. This does indeed seem likely. If a pre-Polynesian language existed on Fiji at about 1500 BC, as Pawley quite plausibly suggests, then Eastern Oceanic, Oceanic, and original Austronesian represent steps of separation which may make Grace's estimates modest. Ferrell thinks Atayalic of Formosa had separated from any other language by 3000 to 4000 BC, and unless Formosa is the exact site of Austronesian origin, this need by no means have been the earliest division.

Papuan (Non-Austronesian) Languages

Here the scale of differentiation becomes quite different. Half covered, as though with a blanket, by the Austronesian stock, much of Melanesia and all Australia use languages so numerous and diverse that the number of actual groups they might form was long unguessed at. As Wurm [266] says, before 1950 it was thought that the many Papuan languages were not a single group or anything like it, but only a conglomerate of highly diverse, exceedingly complex languages, mostly spoken by very small speech communities and mostly showing no recognizable trace of genetic relationship with one another. All this has changed, in an increasingly rapid pace of work by a number of able linguists exchanging ideas and collecting information from hitherto blank areas. In late years publication has not been able to keep up with fresh developments.

Cowan (see Wurm [266]), for example, found relationships between language families of the northwest end of New Guinea and of the Indonesian island of Halmahera (the two separated by Austronesian speakers on the coasts); and he joined these families in a stock. He then added other West New Guinea *stocks* and one covering Indonesian Timor and Alor to make up a West Papuan *phylum*.

This is typical of even larger events. Wurm discerned a large East New Guinea Highlands stock, spoken by three-quarters of a million people using about fifty languages (some spoken by over a hundred thousand people, some by perhaps a few dozen), and made up of five families of languages. Taking a couple of small and isolated families or single languages showing a more distant relation still, he created an East New Guinea Highlands phylum. After that, with the establishment of other phyla in eastern New Guinea, he has recognized 'more or less distant' relationships among some of them to form a Central New Guinea *macro-phylum*, made up of:

East New Guinea Highlands phylum
Huon Peninsula phylum
Southeast New Guinea phylum
Central and South New Guinea phylum
West New Guinea Highlands phylum

This leaves for the present (but probably only a short present) other recognized phyla (e.g. of the Sepik region) which might eventually be included in this macro-phylum, as well as a number of phyla, families or single languages for which no higher connections can now be shown, and of course those languages still quite unknown. The important West Papuan phylum already described is an example.

Such extremely remote connections among numerous languages obviously suggests time depths far beyond any which can be suggested for Austronesian as a whole. It looks as though some linguistic dispersals, of ages comparable to and greater than that of Austronesian, have given rise to the larger stocks and phyla of New Guinea. Lexicostatistics would put the original break up of the East New Guinea highlands phylum alone at about 6,400 years in the past (computed by Wurm, quoted by Pawley). Pawley suggests that any general common ancestor for more remotely related groups would go back 10,000 years. As he notes, the point is reached at which no further tracing can be done, since linguistic replacement and renewal will have obliterated still older situations.

There is particular diversity near the east central north coast, but there also would appear to be actual dispersals of great age in the highlands of the interior of New Guinea. This also corresponds with signs of marked genetic drift and differentiation on the biological side, everything bespeaking a great antiquity of occupation.

Australia and Tasmania

Three points can be made for the continent: all the languages are 'Australian'; they have no connection with those of New Guinea or anywhere else; and they are extremely diverse.[1] Capell began the organization of all this some time ago, and subsequent workers have substantiated his basic points repeatedly. Within the diversity he found fundamental common features. Occasionally reported

[1] Tryon [246] has brought Australian language problems up to date in a very good review.

'non-Australian' languages, such as a 'Tasmanoid' one at the base of Cape York (where 'Tasmanoid' tribes were also reported), turned out on closer examination to be Australian in form. The diversity has plagued attempts at organization because of the abruptness of differences. Languages compose what elsewhere would be dialect chains, in that B-speakers can understand A-speakers on the right and C-speakers on the left, while A and C are much more different than this would suggest; that is, they are not dialects of one language. Lexicostatistics has not yet been successful because, in spite of a fundamental similarity in structure, there are very few common words or cognates across languages. This has resulted in a sort of bastard term, phylic families, to recognize likeness in structure but not in vocabulary. Wurm's latest count of these is twenty-five, and linguists are apparently ready to put them all into a monstrous Australian macro-phylum.

Capell, with others supplementing, first discerned certain languages situated around the edges of the continent, which were more divergent from the rest, but which in some cases, though geographically distant, shared a degree of vocabulary. Capell suggested that these represent an Original Australian group, the remnants of a first radiation of Australian languages, pushed to the margins by the spread of a later Common Australian. This might be the burgeoning of one member of Original Australian, or might be an immigrant, though one basically like Original Australian. It does suggest a linguistic and historical event, a 'surge'. And the already great diversity of Common Australian, occupying most of the continent, would indicate, 'if any reliance can be placed on glottochronology' [246], a birth date for this group between 3000 and 8000 BC. We will look at this again.

The prompt extinction of their speakers over a century ago (see page 121) makes the study of Tasmanian languages a special one. But assiduous work with preserved words and names has given results. So has analysis of the punctilious journal of G.A. Robinson, who made several expeditions on foot among the natives all over the island, often making notes on dialect differences, and on which native could understand which other native [134]. The consensus is that five related languages were present, having as a group no connections with those of Australia.

Greenberg [95, 270] who is a leading general linguist, has proposed a whopping Indo-Pacific supergroup, to include Tasmanian and all the Papuan languages, as well as those of the Andaman Islands.[1] Australian languages are excluded although, according to Grace, Greenberg thinks they might be allied as a more distant branch.[2] In either case in this hypothesis the greatly varied Australian languages would remain rather remote from the relationships that can be seen among the others; and this would reinforce the views of those who think there is no connection between Tasmania and Australia linguistically. Otherwise the lack of a connection is somewhat strange, and we remember that various supposedly 'non-Australian' languages on the continent have all eventually been accepted into the Australian macrophylum.

As to the Indo-Pacific group otherwise, its establishment would have some interesting implications for an ancient but unified Melanesian realm, as we shall see.

Points and Problems

The linguists have gone a long way in following the tracks of prehistory and the problems, if not all solved, are at least at bay. The following seem to be the important points in what we have been reviewing:

1. The Australian languages on one hand and the Papuan (plus Tasmanian?) languages on the other do form natural supergroups, i.e. groups having a time depth which can only be called enormous. A distinction between them along these lines, implied by Greenberg's Indo-Pacific supergroup, would be significant. Papuan languages penetrated Island Melanesia – at a time unknown – at least as far as the Santa Cruz group beyond the Solomons. If they ever reached the New Hebrides and New Caledonia, as the physical nature of the people would suggest, no signs survive.

2. Proto-Austronesian appeared in about 4000 BC. The original community of its speakers must have been physically either non-Melanesian (some Indonesian-like people, the Proto-Mongoloids mentioned two chapters ago) or else Melanesian, not both. If, as Dyen has suggested, the locality was in the New Britain region

---

[1] Greenberg [270] says the connection of the language of Little Andaman to Indo-Pacific is 'highly provisional'. Wurm [280] considers that a relationship of Andamanese languages to Papuan is not demonstrated.

[2] Most recently Greenberg [270] appears more doubtful of connections between Australian languages and Indo-Pacific.

this first community was Melanesian racially, and the source of Austronesian was a Papuan language. The deduction can hardly be avoided, and needs to be supplemented by another hypothesis which would carry Austronesian in a very early stage to Formosa, where no signs of Melanesian missionaries or culture exist. If the original Austronesians were non-Melanesians in the west, no such difficulties arise, since Austronesian languages and non-Melanesian physiques are clearly the intruders in many parts of Melanesia.

3. This is not to say that Austronesian languages did not arrive and spread early in parts of Melanesia, doubtless before 2500 BC; their diversity in the region remains impressive no matter how they are classified. The New Hebrides strongly suggest two levels of Austronesian development. One has such isolated languages as those of Tanna and Eromanga, seemingly early. The other has the members of Eastern Oceanic, a group whose time of origin would be about 2000 BC but whose place of origin is problematical. Linguists would apparently prefer this place to be local: Dyen sees the New Hebrides as a point reached by one of the very earliest offshoots of original Austronesian; and others view Proto-Eastern Oceanic as a local descendant, in the New Hebrides, of Proto-Oceanic generally. But could it be an immigrant, bearing a special number of Indonesian word roots foreign to the region (see above)? There are other good reasons, we shall see later, for suspecting an actual immigration of Proto-Eastern Oceanic peoples into eastern Melanesia.

4. For Polynesia, the story is clear and satisfying. For Micronesia it is less so, though the future looks bright. Here both population and Austronesian languages must have a respectable antiquity, the languages certainly pre-dating by far any occupation of Polynesia. They forcibly argue an early settlement in the sizable western islands of Palau, Yap and the Marianas, while they also argue another dispersal, of lesser but still considerable antiquity, out of the east. These two things must be reconciled.

5. In Indonesia, the key area, a great deal remains to be learned. For large parts, especially the Philippines, there is an appearance of recent, doubtless secondary, linguistic spreads, leaving only Formosa (and perhaps the Barrier Islands south of Sumatra) to reflect a primary plantation of Austronesian. The surprising fact,

to me, is the thoroughness with which earlier languages, Austronesian or other, would have been replaced over major areas. And so, while we wait for the linguists to do more here, we may assume that in Indonesia the slate has been wiped virtually clean of a record which might have told us so much about Austronesian origins.

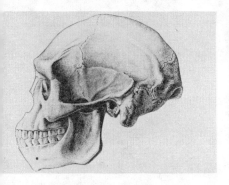

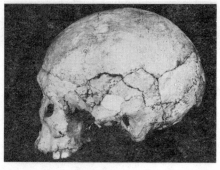

Above left: Skull of Solo Man, Java, reconstructed by F. Weidenreich.

Above: Skull from Keilor, Australia.

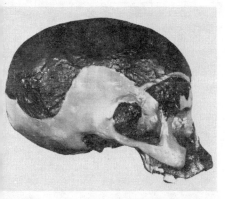

Left: Skull from Niah Cava, Sarawak, reconstructed by D. Brothwell.

Skull from Kow Swamp, Australia.

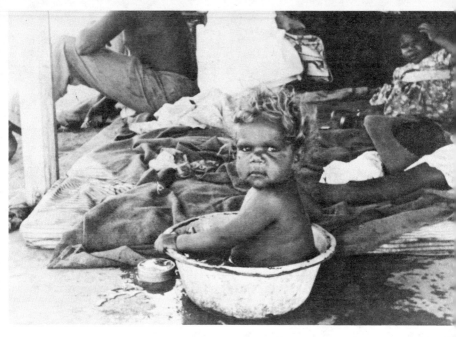

Aboriginal baby, Alice Springs. Central Australia.

Group of the last surviving Tasmanians.

Tiwi, Melville Island,
Northern Australia.

Groote Eiland, Northern
Australia.

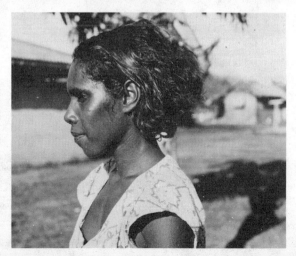

Arnhem Land, Northern
Australia.

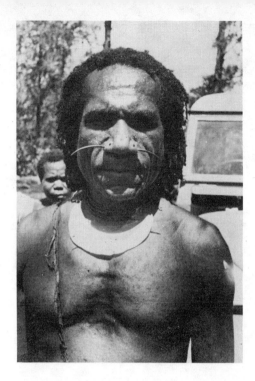

Far left: Girls from Mount Hagen, New Guinea.

Ufeto villager, near Goroka, Eastern Highlands District of New Guinea.

Tolai, near Rabaul, New Britain.

Baegu girl, Malaita,
Solomon Islands.

Man from Tanna Island,
New Hebrides.

Right: Girl from
Trobiand Islands, Papua.

Left: Men of Espiritu Santo, New Hebrides, with masks and figures produced for export.

Woman and child from New Caledonia.

Old warrior from Mare, Loyalty Islands.

Fijian from Suva.

Senoi aboriginal of
West Malaysia.

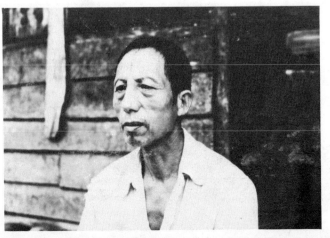

Atayal aboriginal o
Formosa.

Right: Dusun girl pla
a nose flute, Sabah, E
Malaysia.

Aeta men, Luzon,
Philippines, with Mr.
C. D. V. Knight who is
5 feet 10½ inches tall.

Tonga Islanders.

Right:
Maori girl, New Zealand.

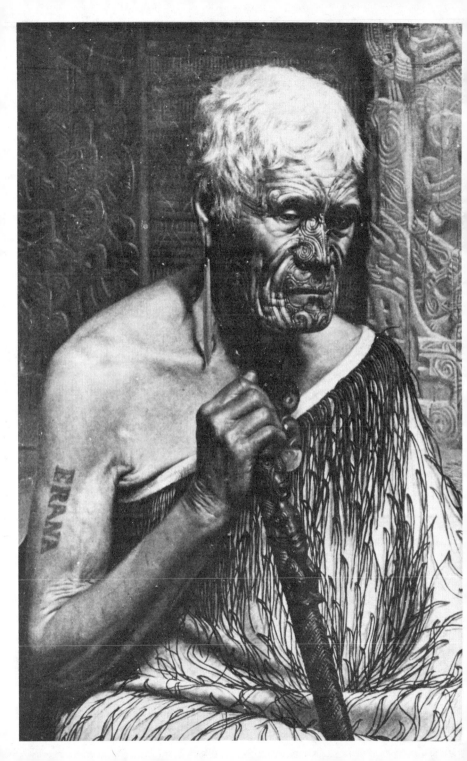

Far Left: Maori with face carving.

Tahiti girl photographed by Challenger Expedition, 1876.

Girls from the Gilbert Islands.

Majuro Atoll, Marshall Islands.

Truk, Doblon Island.

Below: Truk, Moen Island.

6

Australia
and Tasmania

Anthropology would have been much the poorer without the Australian aboriginal. Primitive man in our midst, he has dazzled us by his ability to survive in atrocious deserts, by his elaborate systems of kinship, and by his religious notions of himself. No other uncivilized people have had so many whole books addressed to them, and they will go on being studied as long as they exist. Here we will take account primarily of some things about them which seem important at the moment: theories of their origin; the nature of the vanished Tasmanians; the antiquity of their existence in Australia; the meaning of fossil skeletons.

The Stone Age nature of aboriginal culture was early remarked upon. A picture grew up, as seen in the 'ethnographic present', i.e. the moment of contact. The aboriginals were pure nomadic hunters and gatherers, innocent of any domesticated plants or animals, although they had the dingo as an aid in hunting. They were none the less enormously expert stalkers, birders and fishers along simple lines: watercraft were limited in distribution and primitive. No bow and arrow, though they had efficient weapons for hand throwing: spears, sped with greater force by a spear-thrower or woomera; and throwing-clubs and boomerangs (the familiar returning kind is a toy, the real one is a heavy whirling bent wooden blade, meant to fly straight and do great injury to prey or enemy). Working tools were of stone, roughly flaked. Stone axes with edges formed by grinding, and hafted to handles, which were found in some regions, were assumed to have been introduced recently from New Guinea; in other parts of the world such edge-grinding is associated with the beginnings of advancing culture. The natives of Tasmania were still more culturally deprived: no dogs, no ground axes, nor any hafted tools at all (and so no stone-tipped spears, but only pointed wooden javelins), no boomerang and no spear-thrower. In addition, while they collected shellfish in plenty, they did not catch and eat ordinary fish of the scaly variety, a surprising neglect of an important food source.

Archaeological work was frustrating. Sites stratified into occupation layers were virtually unknown, either in Australia or Tasmania, and some prehistorians felt that digging would be in vain. Only the veteran anthropologist Norman Tindale was able to show, forty years ago, that this was not so. He uncovered a succession suggesting great antiquity at Devon Downs; but with no direct evidence of age, he had to fall back on a supposed sequence of evolution for the types of tools found here and there.

Fossilized skulls for which antiquity was claimed all lay under deep suspicion, and understandably. Consider the case of Keilor.[1] In 1940 it was reported that a skull and five pieces of another had been found in a river bank northwest of Melbourne. First assessment of the skull's age, from the river terrace in which it lay, was 'Last Interglacial', or perhaps 80,000 years. So preposterous did this seem, especially in those days, that professional interest soured entirely on the find, which was written off as being a hundred years old. The second skull turned out to be the fiction of a gentleman disappointed in the rewards, coin or kudos, he had anticipated from his connection with the business. But the first Keilor cranium became a highly important document in prehistory through the efforts of Edmund Gill of the National Museum in Melbourne. Actually a most conservative geologist, in recent years he faced no little skepticism in establishing the skull's date, which he placed at about 13,000 BC.

All in all, most scholars doubted that man could have been in Australia more than a few thousand years at best. Such was the picture from long and avid study up to about 1960. Much of the picture persists, but important parts have changed astonishingly. As far as antiquity is concerned, the floor has not merely been lowered, it has virtually dropped off, and nobody now knows the limit. If ground stone axes were borrowed from New Guinea this happened over 20,000 years ago, because that is the age for such

[1] Pronounced 'Keelor'.

axes found in Arnhem Land living sites, the oldest ground-edged tools yet known anywhere on earth. Solid dates of equal magnitude, from long stratified deposits, have been determined in the south. A few others indicating human presence go back 30,000 years, and tools at Lake Mungo are associated with a sequence of dates reaching to nearly 31,000 BC. And in Tasmania good cave sites – full of fish bones! – go back 8,000 years.

The Living Australians

Let us turn first to the aboriginals themselves and some speculations on their origins. The things that mark them off from other world populations are fairly clear.[1] Skin is a warm chocolate brown running in places to very dark. Hair ranges from entirely straight to frizzly, though probably never to woolly – perhaps the scale nearly coincides with hair differences among Europeans. Hair distribution is also European-like: men are well bearded, and hairiness of body and limbs approaches that of Caucasoids, though Abbie believes that on the average it is very much less. Men go gray and white and are also liable sometimes to baldness – none of these piliary effects are characteristic of Africans, or of Mongoloids. In addition, children and young women of the center of the continent commonly have 'tawny' – actually quite blond – hair, which darkens in later life. This is positively not due to mixing with white Australians.

Apart from color, his appearance makes an aboriginal instantly recognizable. He tends to be longer-legged and longer-armed than a European. But his face and head are most characteristic. His mouth is large and his lips are full, without the characteristic eversion of those of Africans, and this gives a special chubby-cheeked look to young children. His nose is flat but more bulbous than an African's. Above all, his eyes are set deep, under a sloping forehead usually embellished in front with strongly developed – 'beetling' – brows.

The same look carries over to the skull with its marked brows, its generally sloping forehead and its flat sides. The cheekbone is prominent without being heavy, and the lateral edge of the eye socket is receding, curving back with respect both to cheekbone and brow, so that the eye is indeed deep set and the cheeks seem

---

[1] See Abbie [4] for a general recent description based on long acquaintance, and Macintosh [152] for an historical review of work.

that much fuller. In fact, though the root of his nose is set so well under his brow, his eyeballs are altogether so deep-set that the bridge of his nose is actually prominent with respect to them, as in Europeans.

This is 'the' aborigine. It is his passport photo, as seen by the first visitors and as classified by the early students of race. Considering the really vast size of the continent, most observers were impressed by the homogeneity of the natives and said so. Collection of measurements and other exact data was slow in coming. No really methodical examination of them was made until 1938, when J.B. Birdsell, now of the University of California, Los Angeles, joined forces with Norman B. Tindale of the South Australia Museum, Adelaide, a man with an enormous storehouse of information on the tribal and local distributions of the aboriginals. These two visited all major areas, with Birdsell making measurements and observations and taking blood samples (this was still in the early days of blood-typing).

In his results Birdsell saw what he felt to be overwhelming evidence to overturn the notion of unity of the aboriginals. He noted local differences among his population groups: taller, darker men in the north, stockier, lighter-colored men in the south, and Negrito-like tribes in Queensland. On this basis he proposed a tri-hybrid origin for the aboriginals [15, 16, 17].

As to the Negrito-like people, these had been photographed as long ago as 1890, though generally ignored. They focus on an area in the forested Atherton tableland, west of Cairns in northern Queensland. Here stature is low, according to Birdsell's measurements (in one small locality men average 155 cm, or 5 ft 2 in), faces are short, bodies relatively hairless and head hair very curly.[1] Birdsell termed this racial element the 'Barrinean', for Lake Barrine, on which the dwarfish tribes are centered.

Actual Negritos, Birdsell suggested, arrived as the first of his three components, the oldest stratum on the continent, but he thought that this stratum was relatively unimportant in the sur-

[1] Various kinds of Melanesians have been imported into Queensland for labor, in times past and times recent, from the Solomon Islands and the New Hebrides in particular. The latter, if of the dwarfish population found there, might have affected the local aborigines several generations ago, but they were apparently employed as cane cutters only in southern Queensland. In addition, Tindale satisfied himself that the individuals studied did not have any such foreign ancestry. So we should accept them at face value.

viving aboriginal population, having its effect only in the one small region. The other two elements, named 'Murrayian' and 'Carpentarian' by Birdsell, are best represented by the south–north scale of difference, being nearest their original forms at the extremes. The 'Murrayians' (called thus because the people of the Murray River drainage expressed their least mixed form) are fuller-bodied, more inclined to hairiness and baldness, and not very dark of skin. Their skulls are long and low, and Australian though their appearance is, they had for Birdsell a 'coarse and rough-hewn' Caucasoid cast of features and are not especially projecting of face. They are, in fact, kin to the Ainu of Japan, he believed, and to the White stock generally, and they came to Australia later than the Barrineans.

Variously mixed with this strain is the 'Carpentarian', so named because as a component in the aboriginals it is most evident in the extreme north, around the Gulf of Carpentaria. Its best examples are tall and lanky in build but small-skulled and broad-nosed; they are apt to be intensely dark-skinned and not particularly hairy. These, said Birdsell, are the real 'Australoids'; they are what other writers were seeing when they wrote of the Australians as a fourth major race of man in addition to the traditional Caucasoid, Negroid and Mongoloid, since the Murrayians are really 'White', and the Barrineans Negrito.

These three components, Birdsell said, represent three population waves. They arrived successively during the last glacial period, when lower sea levels (due to so much of the world's water being held in the continental ice sheets) bridged some of the sea passages to Australia and narrowed others remaining to be crossed. First were the 'Negritos', coming according to Birdsell from forested regions in Southeast Asia and northeast India, probably deriving ultimately from the same root stock as the African Pygmies. They reached the Philippines, the Andaman Islands and the former New Guinea–Australia–Tasmania continent. In original form these Negritos survive only in the Andamans, having been elsewhere modified to different degrees by later mixture with other peoples. They spread through Australia and beyond into Tasmania; the Tasmanian aboriginals and the Barrinean tribes near Cairns are their only visible remnants south of the dwarfish peoples of interior New Guinea.

Next, said Birdsell, came the Murrayians who, with the 'closely related' Ainus of Japan, stem from the Amur region of Asia at a time when ancestral Caucasoids extended, in a zone below the glaciated areas, from Russia right across to the Pacific shore. Toward the end of the Pleistocene, or after, came the Carpentarians who, one gathers, are mainly responsible for the primitive character of Australian skulls and faces. Birdsell traced them, like the Negritos, to India but to a quite different environment, that of the hot and sunny plains. Here, perhaps from a still more primitive Caucasoid ancestor than that of the Murrayians, the Carpentarians developed their very dark skins and their heat-dissipating lankiness by natural selection. In India itself they have left traces in some aboriginal peoples like the Davidians or Veddas. In Australia they found their most natural habitat in the sunny north. They mingled rather thoroughly but in varying proportions with the Murrayians and these two absorbed the Barrineans, leaving traces of them only in Queensland and Tasmania. But this mixing happened in Australia. The Murrayians and the Carpentarians both arrived there without having extinguished Negritos along the way (Malaya, New Guinea), because these last lived in the rain forests, as they do today, and not on the more likely paths of the other two elements. Thus time and environment kept the three lines separate.

I might agree with Birdsell at some points and not at others. That is neither here nor there. His hypothesis was formulated thirty years ago, long before the recent mushrooming of information, and was based on study of living aboriginals only. It is necessary to start afresh, rather than to look for holes in older attempts at reconstruction. I present Birdsell's view because it has constituted one main interpretation of the Australians, and he put it vigorously and coherently; one must still consider his suggestions on remaining regional distinctions, Ainu connections, or Tasmanian origins. In addition, it has been highly influential in anthropology. It was taken up by Hooton [117], and used also by Coon, Garn and Birdsell in a general book on race published in 1950 [45]. Since then it has been followed by perhaps the majority of those writing in English who have discussed racial origins and classification. Small wonder, because it has such wide implications in the Old World, and in various ways gives some appealing explanations of human distributions in Asia and Melanesia.

But it has not swept all before it. Professor Andrew Abbie of the University of Adelaide, the only man who has worked with living aborigines on the scale of Birdsell, takes exactly the opposite view, believing the natives show an exceptional homogeneity [1, 2, 3]. He thinks certain local distinctions have been overdone, such as the actual depth of skin color before tanning, or the pronounced hairiness of the southern Murrayians. N.W.G. Macintosh of the University of Sydney, another exceptionally well-informed and critical-minded student, concludes [152] on the basis of full reconsideration of the evidence that 'the Australian Aborigines constitute one basic pattern and the Papua–Melanesians another'.

Skulls as well as living people have entered this discussion a number of times and comparative cranial studies within Australia continue (e.g. E. Giles, in process). Earlier writers tended to see local distinctions in different degrees; later students have not found them. Macintosh and Larnach [143, 144] have published two monographs on crania from all of Queensland and the coast of New South Wales. Their method is the tabulation of many highly specific features of cranial anatomy (e.g. foramen of Huschke, or position of anterior ethmoid foramen) and of shape; they use measurements only to a slight degree. They fail completely to find distinctions such as would agree with a mingling of different founding strains, and specifically not in the area of the 'Barrineans', in the Cairns rain forest, where Birdsell spotted the submerged Negritos.

In other work Macintosh and Abbie have both noted a good deal of variation within any one tribe of living aboriginals, which is a different matter from variation between tribes. As for other comments on the hypothesis of multiple origins, Coon [43, 44] has abandoned the Birdsell view: he believes all the dark-skinned people of the Pacific are the gradually differentiated descendants of the earlier Solo Man of Java (see page 152). Local adaptation over a long span of time would, for Coon, explain the variation in Australia. Birdsell, who explicitly thinks some local adaptation would have had effect, has called Coon's view that of 'easy evolution', ignoring the complexities of other evolutionary processes. Simmons [215], dealing with the blood evidence, points out that 'for the tri-hybrid origin to be genetically tenable each of the three postulated components must lack at least the blood factors B, S of MN, rh [cde], rh" [cdE], Kell (K) and Fy^b of the Duffy blood group system'. This is quite an order of course, but Birdsell, rightly I think, says [17] that blood gene frequencies will prove 'very unreliable measures of relationship between populations separated in time by millennia, in space by thousands of miles, and adapted to quite different environments'. He believes as do I that more complex traits (of form, etc.) are less changeable over time.

For myself, I think Birdsell has considerably over-emphasized local differences among aboriginal groups, both in general and in his statistical usages. He supposes that for a population to be 'homogeneous', i.e. presumptively of single origin, it should display few or no average differences which a statistician could find, by mathematical tests, to exceed the limits imposed by chance in taking samples from an ideal 'homogeneous' population. This is more than anthropologists can expect; such statistical homogeneity is demonstrably absent, for example, among villages of one small language group on New Britain [237] or Bougainville [184]. In my general survey of Pacific peoples by measurements in Chapter 3, the Australians were not found to fall into different divisions – specifically not according to the divisions set up by Birdsell – although there were some signs that the 'Barrineans' approach small New Guinea people. Whether these last represent a Negrito strain is the question. I do not now think so, though I once did. We will look this in the face when we come to Melanesia.

Australians and Ainus

Birdsell in his statistical treatment [17] indicates that Murrayians diverge toward the Ainu of Japan, and Barrineans toward small tribes of New Guinea. His method is to compare measurements and indices (ratios among measurements), and to inspect the agreement, in the direction of divergence from Australian mean figures, in each case: i.e. to see whether Ainus and Murrayians differ in stature, etc., in the same way. Let us look into the general questions of Ainus and Tasmanians.

For the Ainus, there is a considerable agreement with Murrayians in the above direction of divergence. The problem remains: would the Murrayians resemble any *other* people, and do the *Ainus* resemble any *Australians*? Yamaguchi [261] did an analysis of Australian skulls (grouped by him as north, central, south and Murray River regions), grading each specimen, according to details of appearance, along a scale of 'most aboriginal' in type to the opposite, or least Australian-looking. He found that skulls placed at the latter end (least Australian) not only resembled Ainu skulls in appearance, but also were commonest in the Murray River area. This highlights the importance of that area, home of the best 'Murrayians', for our discussion here. However, as a result of his study of a variety of measurements and other traits, he felt that the evidence was generally unfavorable to any relationship between Ainus and Australians, though positive indications were not entirely lacking. On the other hand, when Yamaguchi calculated summary 'distance' figures, Australians clustered tightly with two Melanesian populations, while Ainus clustered with Maoris of New Zealand and were somewhat closer to Japanese and to Dyaks of Borneo than to Australians. Yamaguchi's comparison of bones of the rest of the skeleton made Australians equally distant from Japanese and Ainus, who were closer together. In these comparisons the aboriginal skulls were divided into two lots, the Murray River area on one hand and all other regions on the other; and no closer approach to non-Australian peoples was made consistently by one of the two Australian groups.

Another, highly sophisticated analysis [50] was made by my colleague Arthur Dempster, Professor of Statistics at Harvard, on early data of my own. This showed Ainu and Japanese skulls to be closer to one another, and equidistant from Australians (New South Wales) of both sexes.

One of the multivariate studies of skull measurements already described in Chapter 3 may constitute more positive and weighty evidence. The measurements of skull shape are numerous, and the study includes, in addition to Ainus and Murray River Australians, fifteen other populations, mostly intervening geographically between these two. In a summary and simple distance analysis (Figure 3, page 46) Ainus are seen to array themselves with medieval Norwegians, and then with Polynesians (Hawaii), American Indians and Eskimos. These in turn are related to a cluster of seven Asiatic peoples. Murray River Australians, Tasmanians and New Britain Tolais make a cluster widely removed from the rest. In the individual population distances (which the clusters summarize) those for the Australian males run as follows: Tasmanians 3·31, Tolais 3·92, Norwegians 6·52, Ainus 7·00, Peru 7·64, Guam 7·82, Eskimos 7·83, Arikara 7·98, Philippines 8·02, Atayals 8·32, Hawaiians 8·77, north Japan 9·02, Chinese 9·29, south Japan 9·36, An Yang tombs 9·67, Buriats 11·60.

Ainus are closer than most. But, to turn the tables, distances measured away from Ainus are these: Norwegians 3·22, Guam 4·12, Atayals 4·23, north Japan 4·32, Philippines 4·35, south Japan 4·51, An Yang 4·80, Chinese 4·83, Hawaiians 5·17, Peru 5·22, Eskimos 5·32, Arikara 5·53, Tolais 6·11, Tasmanians 6·64, Murray River Australians 7·00, Buriats 7·37.

Notice that, in the first list, giving distances away from Australians, there is a marked jump in size after the Melanesian Tolais, and that in the second, giving distances away from Ainus, these are smaller and increase gradually, with the distances to Australians, Tasmanians and Tolais virtually at the end of the list. So, forced into this framework, Murrayian skulls appear somewhat like Ainus, but the opposite does not hold. There is nothing exact about such distance figures – certainly not to two decimal places – and a different handling would produce different values, perhaps with small shifts in the results. But the main arrangement should be stable, and these figures are actually well loaded with information.

To go all the way to individual skulls in the study (the reader may take a short break here, or move on), the method used allows the computer to 'classify' specimens among the seventeen populations, and to estimate the absolute probability that a given skull could belong, on the basis of its seventy measurements, to a given group. Not a single Murrayian skull, out of fifty-two males and forty-nine females used, has an imaginable possibility (e.g. one chance in a thousand) of being mistaken for an Ainu, or even approaches such odds. For forty-eight male and thirty-eight female Ainu skulls the compliment is returned in kind. This of course applies to most other populations also, but occasional Ainus fall well within the possible confines of the Norwegian, Japanese, Chinese or Hawaiian populations. That is to say, in their total shape variety Ainu skulls overlap at points with the variety of these other peoples, but not with that of Australians.

This seems to be the nature of Ainu affiliation, although of course ultimate and ancient origins such as Birdsell is suggesting could be something else. In such a case, however, Murrayians could equally claim affiliation with Europeans and American Indians, not only with Ainus. With Birdsell I will ignore blood evidence. But archaeological and other indications are that Ainus are simply one tribe of pre-Japanese peoples of Japan, with some

Caucasoid affiliation to be sure, who, however, never extended beyond the confines of Hokkaido, except slightly into Sakhalin and northernmost Honshu.[1] Such remnant peoples have vital things to tell us, but we have an inclination, I believe, to recreate their past as something more mysterious and important than it was.

The Extinct Tasmanians

The same may be true in part of the Tasmanians, as supposedly remnant Negritos. As before, Birdsell inspects Barrinean relations to small New Guinea people by looking at their deviations in measured features from Australian average figures. The result is not very satisfactory: they agree in small size, and disagree in that Barrineans have narrow heads and broad noses – regular Australian features (see Chapter 3). Never mind: Birdsell thinks the 'Negrito' component in the 'Barrinean' populations has been well submerged by the Murrayian. But this brings us to the other suggested reflection of Negrito ancestry, the Tasmanians.

Tasmania lies as far to the south of the equator as New England does to the north; it has a temperate climate, beloved by flowers, with inviting landscapes and shores. But its aboriginals, as living people, are beyond our reach. In 1803 when the first British colonists settled at Hobart there existed about three to five thousand natives [134], wandering to hunt and gather shellfish in about nine major tribal territories. In 1876 the last of them was dead. Indeed by 1842 almost every one had been taken off the land and interned on the bleak islands in the Bass Strait or otherwise isolated and most of them soon died out. Early brutal treatment by colonists, new diseases and destruction of their hunting grounds brought the first quick declines. There followed a period of outright war, in which the aboriginals did so well in attacking farms that they nearly drove the settlers back into the cities. This was ended by two unusual people, a good-hearted Englishman, G.A. Robinson, and an able and lively young aboriginal woman,

[1] A fossil which frequently enters these discussions is the so-called Old Man of the Upper Cave at Choukoutien, north China, dated as probably late Pleistocene. When it (or rather a cast of it) is tested for possible affiliation by the method just described, it proves to be well removed from the populations used in the framework. It has almost exactly one chance in a thousand of falling into the Norwegian population; with estimated probability receding at the speed of light, the next populations are Buriats of Siberia (though these and north Europeans do make a plausible vicinity for the skull) and Tasmanians, Arikara and Ainu (these all well removed). Australians are quite out of the picture.

Truganini. Robinson got the governor's permission in 1830 to do what shooting had not done: persuade the natives to come in voluntarily. His voluminous journal, published only recently [196], is a long, dismaying record of wanton murder and brutality, seen and heard. Robinson was known among the aboriginals; he had their trust, and he had the diplomatic and courageous Truganini as a companion. In four years he brought in all but one family of the natives – by then a mere two hundred – to perish in hardly disguised captivity. Truganini herself was the last, dying a forlorn old woman in Hobart in 1876.

The earliest explorers do not seem to have noted that the Tasmanians were different from the Australians; but the first anthropologists recognized, when it was already too late, that they were not just an extension of the Australian population. They were quite dark-skinned – it is impossible to be more precise – and hair was uniformly woolly in appearance, that is to say a tightly curled up mop. It was probably very tight curls rather than the intertwined mat which constitutes African hair.

This is what some photographs seem to show, while in other drawings or photos natives are seen with hair drawn out in ringlets by the application of grease and mud. And two early visitors, Bass and Flinders, said that the hair was not woolly. Finally, still from photographs and drawings, some individuals, including Truganini, with short faces and broad noses call to mind some Negrito-like people of other places. So opinions on the Tasmanians have run from that of Hrdlicka [125] (working with skulls) that they were 'merely a subtype of the Australians' to the general (but not universal, as Gates said in 1960 [75]) classification as Negritos. This last view is accepted in a recent popular book on the aboriginals [244].

What were they really like? Only a few men had the curiosity actually to remark on the aboriginal physique. Very early observers from exploring ships sound as though they had exaggerated the stature, talking about huge men six foot high or more. But these navigators should be good observers. A later visitor, the French zoologist Péron,[1] measured fourteen men from one tribe and found them to range from 168 cm (5 ft 6 in) to 173 cm (5 ft 8 in), except for one at 179 cm (5 ft 10 in). Perhaps the

---

[1] Péron was actually designated 'anthropologist' for his expedition, perhaps the first use of this designation for professional work [109].

impression of small size was fostered by groups measured by Robinson in their Flinders Island captivity. These were men and women over twenty years of age, thirty-seven of each, and the figures give averages of 5 ft 4½ in for men and 5 ft ½ in for women, low but not dwarfish; some of these were published in anthropological literature by Bernard Davis.

Truganini was certainly tiny, not over five foot. Robinson measured another woman of only 4 ft 3 in. A skeleton in Canberra, discovered in 1926 and obviously aboriginal, is that of a female who must have stood just about 4 ft 10 in in life; but the delicacy of the skull compared to others shows that she was an individual small and delicate for the population at large. Other surviving skeletons, or parts thereof (very few), give equivocal answers as to being over or under medium height [157]. But the fact is that the settlers from England did not remark on small size in the aboriginals they saw. On the contrary, Robinson in his journal noted only the reverse, referring at several points to large individuals of either sex. For instance, at Bruny Island (near Hobart) a 'female deceased was a fine stout woman, rather taller than the general standard (being about five foot ten inches) . . .'; and of natives of the Oyster Bay tribe: 'Very tall and straight some 6 ft but scabby'.

Again, Robinson writes of Port Davey natives in the southwest:

They were fine looking men, about five feet nine inches in height and several of them six feet, well proportioned, broad shouldered, their features resembling that of the European, intelligent countenances, and the beard like that of the Poland Jew, growing long and to a point, and at the extremity of the chin leaving the upper part of the underlip bare. The beard on the upper lip was in the form of moustaches which gave them a truly majestic appearance.

Further north on west coast: 'We were met by two tall aborigines. Each of these men were at least six feet in height and well-proportioned . . . were the stoutest men in the tribe . . . these two men being the finest belonging to their tribe'. Noland Bay, north coast (six men): 'They were all fine young men, stout made'.

Clearly, Robinson was using 'stout', as he did repeatedly, in the now old-fashioned sense of 'strongly built' rather than 'fat'.[1]

[1] Nor was Keats, in the lines at the heading of Chapter 1, implying that Cortez was overweight.

Robinson was no anthropologist, but he had been in the building trades and he was given to estimating heights, since he recorded such estimates for seventeen sealers on islands in the Bass Strait, apparently mostly English but including an American 'mulatto' and a Tahitian. He rated them from five feet five inches to six feet. Could Robinson have been a small man, often overestimating men towering above him? I think not; I do not know that his height was ever recorded, but his weight was eleven and a half stone (161 lb) and thirteen stone (182 lb), on two occasions four years apart during travels when, a friend wrote, he became emaciated by privation and overwork. So if Robinson had been a short man he would, even in an emaciated state, have been much too fat to carry out his exceedingly rigorous journeys.

One other piece of information has come down from Péron. He does in fact seem to have been an anthropologist (in 1802!), because he used a dynamometer, to test the strength of hand grip, on fourteen Tasmanian men from eighteen to forty years of age. He found them weaker in this respect than his own sailors. Does this signify a people small in size, and stout rather than strong? It does not, and here I can speak with authority. I have used the same device on natives of Malaita in the Solomons, and was astonished to find men distinctly larger than myself (I am five feet seven inches and shrinking), as well as more strongly built and younger, unable to come up to my modest marks, in spite of appropriate grimaces indicating all-out effort. Such men have endurance, and strength in paddling, but may not do work which tends to develop a strong hand grip.

I am not trying to demonstrate that the aboriginals were actually large men, but only that the descriptions cited are odd ones for Negritos. We must conclude the same from the only real evidence, that of the skulls and a few life-masks. They are certainly not those of a pygmy people or of descendants of pygmies. The crania are thick and strong-browed; they are rounder than Australians', but the average of the main dimensions – length, breadth and height – is slightly *above* that for Murray River skulls, in both sexes [124]. Foreheads are not particularly sloping, nasal roots are narrow and slightly elevated. While skulls are broader than in Australians, faces are somewhat smaller, though the eyes are deep-set, and the root of the nose is tucked even further under the heavy brows. Such skulls suggest not Negritos like the Andamanese but, instead, particularly rugged and primitivized Europeans.[1] This of course is simply an impression. In a set of distance figures like those cited above, but on a different set of populations, distances of male groups of skulls are, from the Tasmanians:

Tolai 2·88, Murray River Australians 3·74, Europeans (three groups) 5·22 to 5·91, Andaman Islanders 5·48.

The female skulls give the same pattern. Once again, the Australians seek a friend who has better friends: closest to the Australians are the Tasmanians, but closest to the latter are the Melanesian Tolais. Negritos of the Andamans are not in the picture.

The notion of a Negrito element in the Tasmanians should be laid to rest, along with much of the mystery as to their nature. They are one with the general Melanesian population, something I shall deal with later. Melanesian peoples can and do vary in body size, some being definitely small. This is an adequate explanation for the Barrinean component in Australia as well. I think the contrast in views has been overdone. Birdsell may be right as to the Australians having more than one ancestral strain. We should be careful about *a priori* viewpoints: we should not build models peopling a continent from a single boatload; at the same time we should not expect 'ancestral strains' to be like strains of laboratory mice, restricted as to their genetic variation and incapable of considerable response by adaptation to the environment. In any case evidence from prehistory should carry us further than speculations from the living, since all the new information has overtaken the old controversies.

Prehistory

In fact, archaeology suggests the outlines of a pattern, as well as some new problems.[2] The pattern is this: men came to Australia,

---

[1] Robinson remarked, as to seven natives being held in gaol in Richmond, that they had thin lips and were not unlike Europeans, and that they were 'stout' and well-proportioned. This is a little surprising, in view of life masks and photographs, but it does serve to counter notions of strongly Negroid or Negritoid features.

[2] Particularly useful are D. J. Mulvaney's general book, *The Prehistory of Australia* [172], an article by Rhys Jones [132], and a symposium volume by many writers, *Aboriginal Man and Environment in Australia* [176]. There is an excellent review of older views and speculations about Australian and Tasmanian origins in *The Osteology of Aboriginal Man in Tasmania* by Macintosh and Barker [157], which alone serves to show that it would be almost impossible now

certainly well before twenty thousand years ago, settling down with a set of stone tools, simple but not crude, which persisted everywhere without real change for most of prehistoric time. The men themselves were not Negritos, being if anything larger and more robust of skull than the living aboriginals. Also, from the still slender evidence, groups diverged slightly more than now in cranial form in two directions. This is a first problem. One direction was toward typical Melanesians, or the known Tasmanians, and it was groups of this kind who eventually extended human occupation to the cold Tasmanian peninsula.

At the end of the Pleistocene, the melting ice of the world's glaciers raised sea levels and Tasmania became an island, preserving its inhabitants in isolation. Only after this did some distinctly new ideas in stone-working appear and spread on the continent of Australia, and only then did the dingo make his entrance. These things are a second problem. Finally, the Australians became more uniform in physique, presumably by amalgamation of the apparently differing strains present before.

Now to archaeological details. The last few years have clearly established man in Australia since before 20,000 BC, and Mulvaney has recently said that stone tools must be granted an age of at least 30,000 years. Some scholars are evidently preparing their minds for dates like 50,000 BC, and Dr Alexander Gallus of Melbourne argues human presence in Australia before the beginning of the last major glacial period (the Würm of Europe), perhaps over 80,000 years ago.

But these last two suggestions are still beyond the edges of solid knowledge. Before we taste the temptations of such adventurous possibilities, let us eat the meat and potatoes of the safe record of the last 200 to 250 centuries. (Remember, the 'safe record' of today was considered a pipe-dream a very few years ago.) The record comes from cave shelters near Oenpelli in Arnhem Land, in the far north; from Keniff Cave in Queensland; from Koonalda Cave on the Nullabor Plain, in the southwest corner of South

to suggest something not already put forward. For an example, Mulvaney [172] (p. 133) notes that the present view of the Tasmanians, accepted generally only recently – that they walked across Bass Strait when it was dry land, but before the dingo could come the same way – was propounded by Sir Thomas Mitchell in 1839! Many ideas, of course, have been proposed for wildly mistaken reasons, or on little or no evidence. All that a present-day writer can do is to try to synthesize solutions from the vastly better evidence now in hand.

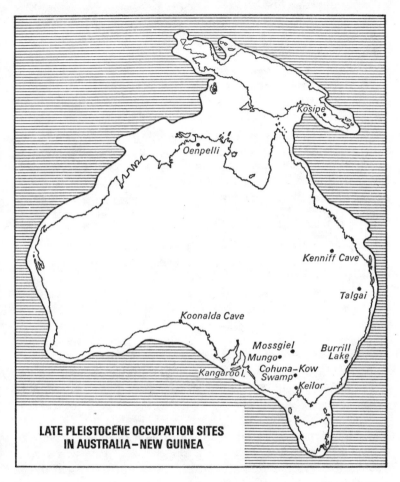

4 Late Pleistocene occupation sites in Australia – New Guinea. Some sites of finds of skeletal or cultural remains from the period 10,000 to 30,000 BC are shown. The outer line shows the coastline existing during much of this period.

Australia; and from Burrill Lake Cave near Sydney.

The first phase of prehistory was marked by an immense conservatism and a surprising uniformity in the manufacture of stone implements. These were flake and core tools: simple struck flakes, trimmed on one face into side-scrapers, and larger trimmed cores (a 'core' in general being a primary stone either fashioned directly into a tool or used to strike flakes from). Some of the latter are termed 'horsehoof cores'; other such were simple unifacially trimmed pebble tools.

In the Oenpelli sites no change in this modest assemblage is seen over 16,000 years. To paraphrase Mulvaney, a resident of northern Australia in 20,000 BC would have seen familiar things in the Kenniff Cave layers of 15,000 BC and later, and even in those of the Tasmania of 6000 BC. These tools were for hand-held use; the idea of hafting them to a wood or bone handle did not exist. The one anomaly, and an important one, was the presence, beginning in at least 20,000 BC, of edge-ground axes, some of which show a grooving or waisting, presumably for binding to a handle. (Such objects, though not definitely known from elsewhere in Australia, appear to have early relatives in New Guinea.) But spear points or hafted cutting tools apparently existed nowhere; and it is unlikely that the spear-thrower or the boomerang were present.

Next, about 5000 BC, there came a major event, the opening of Phase II, which Mulvaney calls the Inventive Phase. Older tool types survived, but new ideas appeared with apparent abruptness and stone-working techniques advanced markedly, with fine pressure-flaking producing excellent unifacial and bifacial points (earliest, apparently, in the north). Microliths are another innovation: very small blades, often 'geometric' (crescentic or trapezoidal) and generally blunted along one side. They became prevalent in the southeast though occurring sporadically in other parts. (They were not made in the fashion of microliths of the European Stone Age, in which a longer stone blade was broken into shorter fragments, but were small trimmed flakes in themselves.) These show that natural gum was being used to put points on spears and to haft knives, saws and chisels with wooden handles – aboriginal manufacture of very strong and durable gum adhesive is still carried on. Thus a series of new ideas, certainly including a new introduction of hafting, and possibly including spear-throwers and boomerangs, had become continent-wide, though without reaching Tasmania. However, all too little is known now of the actual direction and course of the spread of these things.

Nor can it be said whether they were frank introductions, an actual immigration and dispersal of the 'small-tool makers'. The microliths, so well developed in southeast Australia, have not been found in New Guinea, or Timor. Mulvaney worked in Celebes in 1969 and has confirmed that a small-tool complex occurs archaeologically there, as it does in Java. These are clearly not recent, though actual dates remain to be fixed.[1] They are the only known parallels for the Australian microliths until we go as far west as India, where microliths were present by at least 6000 BC. But, while we are on it, we do not know for certain that the small tools did not go from Australia to Celebes and Java, instead of the other way.

And there is the dingo. No signs of him appear in Australia in all the long early occupation, but his bones are now reported at 5000 BC or before. Like the small tools, he is unknown in Timor or New Guinea at any time, or anywhere else; dogs in Indonesia and New Guinea are much later, derived from east Asia. The dingo's closest relative is the Indian wolf, not found east of Bengal, although there is a social wild dog, distinct from the dingo in form and genetically, in Burma [86]. Now it is most unlikely that the dingo could have made the water crossings to get to Australia except as man's companion. So the prehistorians (especially Golson) are feeling obliged to connect him with the new ideas in stone-working and hafting, as an introduction about 5000 BC. This in turn acts to put capital letters on the Small-Tool Makers, as an actual body of people, and not merely as a body of good new technical ideas traveling across the landscape.

Phase II dissolved in fairly recent centuries, giving way to what Mulvaney calls the Adaptive Phase. What dissolved was the elegance of stone-working and the degree of geographical unity which still persisted. Recent stone points for spears were usually simple struck blades (but do not imagine that 'simple' means you or I could make them). Microliths have been used by the living aboriginals in blood-letting ceremonies, but they are surface finds of ancient ones, not made afresh. What was adaptive was apparently the result of long and close acquaintance with the special resources of different areas, leading to greater use of bone, wood, shell and other materials for the implements and artefacts needed. Whatever the further reasons, this late phase acts to hide from us better understanding of the precise uses and handling of the small tools

[1] Mulvaney and Soejono [272] give dates for such a culture, from the Leang Burung cave, of 850 BC and 1430 BC, certainly no great age.

of the Inventive Phase of the millennia following 5000 BC, since such knowledge is lost both to the aboriginals and ourselves.

Signs of the Earliest Aboriginals

What I have related is the organized, blackboard part of pre-history, something like the post-Columbian history of America. It goes back to a baseline when Phase I is known to have extended from the north to present-day Sydney. Evidence of settlement goes back further, and importantly, but more spottily. These are three key cases before the court.

The Koonalda Cave lies fifteen miles from the shore of the Great Australian Bight in South Australia. The dated sequence, down to almost 20,000 BC, has been excavated and reported by Gallus [72] and R.V.S. Wright [258], and the bottom has never been reached. Now such a date does not mark the first time that an early aboriginal, hurrying down from the hot north, popped into a handy cave for shelter from a storm. The cave then stood over a wide plain stretching about a hundred miles southward to the sea. It is a big cavern and the signs of its use are five hundred feet from the entrance, in the dark: the charcoal used for radiocarbon dating must have come from torches, for there are no cooking hearths nor meat bones. The place was a mine for a very good kind of flint-like stone for tools, a rare and valuable deposit for the aboriginals; and the debris in the excavation comes from taking out blocks to carry away for working elsewhere; very few tools occur in the floor itself. Still further back is a long gallery, another three hundred feet of decorated walls, some showing macaroni-like finger tracings in the soft surface, others being checkerboard-like markings produced with a stick. At one spot in this area Dr Gallus dug up a piece of limestone carrying such markings, from just under a hearth (sic) which gave a C_{14} date of 29,050 BC. The reliability of this date is now being questioned, but other radiocarbon dates in plenty cluster around 20,000 BC, and Dr Gallus [72] believes that both the deposits and the increasingly cruder tools point to a continuous human occupation going back much further. In any event the cave, with its desirable raw stone material, was most probably discovered only after man had made himself at home for some time in what is now South Australia.

Lake Mungo is a new scene of great significance. The 'lake' is now a dry pan, one of a string of late Pleistocene lakes in New

South Wales north of the Murray River and east of the Darling. In the changing Ice Age climate the lakes were sometimes full (Lake Mungo measured about fifteen miles by perhaps four or five), and sometimes dry or muddy pans. When they were full, westerly winds blew beach sand to form dunes on the eastern side; when they were low or dry, the wind blew salty clays and silts on to the dunes, or else nothing, allowing soils to form on them. Downward leaching of salts later hardened lower layers, but in recent times much of the upper part has blown away, leaving exposures and sections through older parts of these fossil dunes. Three cycles of wet and dry (roughly speaking) can be seen, and have been dated from charcoal and shell in them. These zones are named Zanci, with C_{14} dates from about 14,600 BC to about 21,400 BC; Mungo, with known dates running back to about 30,800 BC, and Golgol, which is older but beyond the range of radiocarbon dating.

In July 1968 J.M. Bowler [21] was collecting stone tools and shells here when he marked down, on a wind-blown surface, a partly cemented block of burned bones; it turned out to be a human cremation. Because of the blowing away of so much of the former dune, the actual position of finds within it must be worked out by checking back and forth with surviving columns showing its composition. But Bowler and his archaeological colleagues, Jones and Allen, believe that they can establish a human occupation marked by stone tools, hearths, burnt animal and fish bones, food shells, and a burial, fifteen or twenty yards from the edge of the former lake, and they date the occupation to between 30,000 and 23,000 BC. The tools are horsehoof cores and steep-edged and flat scrapers, all good members of Phase I of Australian prehistory. The animals, interestingly, contain no extinct species except the Tasmanian wolf (*Thylacinus*), which, however, is known to have survived until late times on the continent. The burial itself awaits further attempts at precise dating; it is believed [21] to be close to 28,000 BC.[1]

Perhaps the most likely place for antiquity-probing is still Keilor, which is both the name of a place and of a terrace in the

---

[1] More dates have now been published [265,266]. Two of them, one from collagen of the skeleton itself and one from a hearth nearby and just above, date the burial as close to 23,500 BC. Nine others, from hearths or from shell associated with tools, run from 24,020 to 32,750 years ago. Thus while the skeleton is somewhat younger than first estimated, the whole occupation containing it does indeed reach back beyond 30,000 BC.

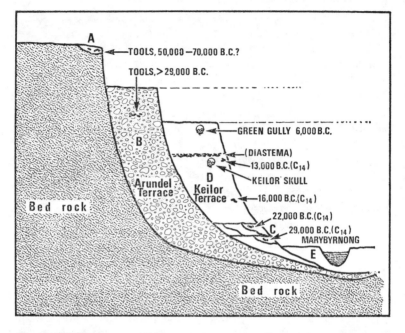

Figure 5. Marybyrnong River terrace system. (Drawn from diagrams and demonstrations by Dr A. Gallus, also information from E. Gill). An idealized cross-section of the valley, showing structure, C_{14} dates, human remains and finds of tools. The sequence of events is as follows:

A. Bain's Quarry River Bed. Deposits in a filled stream bed cut into the old land surface before the late Pleistocene downcutting of the Maribyrnong valley. Dr Gallus reports crude stone tools from these deposits with a possible age (which is beyond the range of radiocarbon dating) of perhaps 70,000 years.

B. Following the deep cutting of the valley into bedrock, a depositional phase of the river filled most of it again with the Arundel formation, until the valley flood plain reached the top level shown. Stone tools were found in the upper part of this formation by Dr Gallus, with an age presumed to be well over 30,000 years.

C. Another erosion cycle cut through most of the Arundel formation, leaving only the present terrace. At a low level the river spread much of the removed Arundel material on the valley floor, in a succession of complicated stream beds in shallow channels. From these Dr Gallus recovered stone and bone tools, and material giving dates of 22,000 and 29,000 BC.

D. A subsequent depositional phase built up the Keilor formation, which has a 'diastema' or marker bed at one point. C_{14} dates are 16,000 BC from well down, and 13,000 BC from material just under the diastema, where the Keilor skull lay. The Green Gully bones came from a higher level.

E. A final erosional phase cut down through the Keilor formation, again leaving a terrace (in which were found the above materials). The lowest terrace is the flood plain of the river at its present level.

valley of the Marybyrnong River northeast of Melbourne. The valley has for years been under the scrutiny of Edmund Gill,[1] the careful and experienced geologist of Melbourne's National Museum, to whose labors have been added those of Dr Gallus and Dr Bowler. Gill some time ago showed that there were at least three terraces at different heights in the valley. The lowest, the Marybyrnong, is the present highwater flood plain of the river, which flattens out at water level as the river reaches the sea. The Keilor, next above it, and the Arundel higher still, both pass underneath the Marybyrnong here and continue, disappearing below sea level. Thus they are of Pleistocene date, having been formed when the sea was lower. Gill produced radiocarbon dates from the Keilor terrace going back to about 17,000 BC at its base.

The valley as a whole is the story of the entire last glacial phase (the Würm of Europe, the Wisconsin of America), which comprised at least two major cold periods, separated by an amelioration generally timed at about 40,000 to 28,000 BC. In this valley geologists have not agreed as to which combinations of colder, warmer, wetter or drier conditions were responsible for the formations they find. Be that as it may, here are the events as Dr Gallus sees them (e.g. [71]), with remarks on glacial phases which do not necessarily agree with his own views.

In the warm, pre-Würm interglacial the sea, as Gill has found, stood as much as twenty-five feet higher than now and the river flowed gently over the landscape, cutting a shallow bed in the

---

[1] To whom I am indebted for showing me the site, letting me study the skull, and giving me such information.

rock. The bed is recognized, and named the 'Bain's Quarry River Bed'; it cannot be dated radiometrically but must be over 70,000 years old.

With the Würm's onset (and the formation of continental glaciers elsewhere in the world), the sea fell, and the increased flow and drop of the river cut a deep valley through the rock. Then, with a change in runoff (cold but dry weather?) the valley silted to a high level, forming the Arundel clay, while the sea still stood at a low ebb.

A new erosion cycle (the second cold period? or the warmer interstadial?) cut the valley deeply again, leaving along its sides remnant terraces of the Arundel formation and spreading material eroded from it across the lower valley floor. In these redeposited clays the river, in a sort of resting phase, cut several different channels at different times. Two dates from the channels are approximately 29,600 BC and 22,000 BC.

Then this floor and its channels were buried again under the basal gravels of the Keilor formation, which continued, from about 17,000 BC, to build up the silts of the Keilor terrace. During and after the end of the Pleistocene, the river cut down through them once more, to establish the Marybyrnong with its present terrace and level.

Dr Gallus has found a few stone tools in the pre-Keilor channels, going back to about 30,000 BC: small squarish flakes and some larger cores. He found more bone tools, crude in appearance (to my own eye), which he recognizes as javelin heads (some looking like primitive harpoons), as well as spatulae showing polish from use, and such things as borers. He considers all this the technical equivalent of the Upper Paleolithic of Europe.

But he finds further flake tools *within* the Arundel terrace itself, that is, from the time it was forming, not after its cutting down. There are no C_{14} dates for these (and we are getting past the limit of such dates), but they must be substantially older than the previous lot; the tools are more primitive as well.

This is not all: Gallus recovered river-rolled chopping tools from the pre-Würm stream bed at the highest level! Logically these would be of the order of 70,000 years old and perhaps a good deal more. He finds them appropriate in shape for such an age, resembling the Patjitanian 'hand-axes' of Java. He further infers that the makers must have been an earlier form of man than the present aboriginals (or ourselves): pre-sapiens *Homo erectus*.

Dr Gallus is an able and experienced archaeologist, with a background in European prehistory as well. But even in the progressive midst of modern Australian delvers in the past (who are probably out of breath from recent finds anyhow), he is likely to have an argument on his hands persuading others of the bona fides of his earlier tools. The implications of such evidence just now are rather indigestible. Gallus serves us well in any case, showing that these river terraces, with their clear geological succession, are the places to look for earlier and earlier witness to the aboriginal presence. As he has remarked himself, the Marybyrnong cannot be the only river whose terraces would contain such material. It has simply been lucky in catching the eye of Gill. Other river valleys are beginning to get such attention, not for stone tools alone but for all they tell about climate and ecology for ancient man.

Land, Water and Elephants

This brings us to another aspect of the immigration of the aboriginals: the real Pleistocene map on which they lived and moved. For the sea did, as we have seen, fall in the late Pleistocene: great glaciers in the northern hemisphere made levels drop the world around, exposing large areas of the continental shelves. Deciding where the shore stood at any time is a difficult business, based partly on a myriad of local finds: for example, an old shore line off northwest Australia, now over four hundred feet below the surface, is dated at 15,000 BC by shells which grew on it [131]. There are many complicating factors besides water levels. Shores rise and fall themselves – the north shore of New Guinea has been warped drastically up; and the area of Sydney has been depressed as much as a hundred feet [78, 79], so that present water depth there does not tell the truth about how far the sea would have had to fall to surface the bottom. The continental shelves in turn have been pushed down by the weight of water now on them, so that again their present depths can exaggerate the amount of sea fall needed to expose them. People disagree as to the levels to which the sea receded in the coldest phases, but agree that it rose substantially between them, in the warmer interstadial.

It is too complicated to pursue here. Fortunately Gill [78, 79] and Jennings [131] agree that the edge of the continental shelf, at about the hundred-fathom (six hundred-feet) line, can now be taken as a fair mark for shorelines during the cold peaks about 20,000 years ago, again between 50,000 and 60,000 years ago, and possibly earlier still. For Australia this meant a broad connection with New Guinea because of the emptying of the Gulf of Carpentaria and the Arafura Sea to the north. After 18,000 BC these were gradually flooded again: a core from a representative bottom depth in the Gulf, about two hundred feet, shows an alternation of dry land and shallow sea [131]; and only in about 5000 BC or later

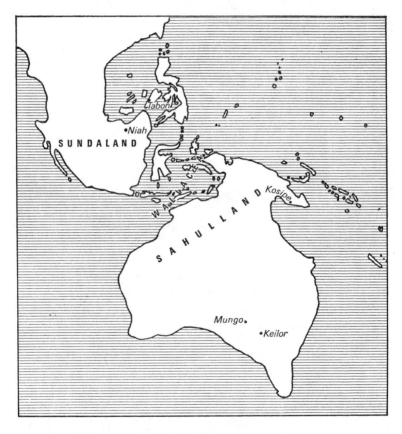

5 (a) Late Pleistocene land areas. This shows in general form the expansion of Southeast Asia (Sundaland, including much of present Indonesia) and of Australia (Sahulland, including New Guinea and Tasmania), due to lowered sea levels. Sites shown are those giving evidence of human occupation in the range of 25,000 to 40,000 BC.

(*b*) Present land areas for comparison.

do tide-water shells appear suddenly for the first time in the occupation layers of two cave shelters near Oenpelli in north Australia [252].

But what is the grand map? Map 5 shows it, following the probable shorelines. The Sunda shelf, under the shallow part of the South China Sea and south of it, stood exposed 20,000 years ago, joining all the large islands of Indonesia, except Celebes, to southeast Asia in the great peninsula of Sundaland. In the east, the Sahul shelf, north and northwest of Australia, made New Guinea part of the continent; and to this Sahulland were added not only Tasmania but also substantial plains along the south and east as well, over what is now the Great Barrier Reef. Such was the land mass open to any men who set foot upon its western edge.

Between Sundaland and Sahulland lay Wallacea, cut off from both and sliced through by deep channels which no Pleistocene sea fall could have bridged. To recognize this, Wallace's Line, named for Darwin's fellow naturalist, has been drawn along the deeps east of Bali, since few land mammals except small ones ever got across it into Wallacea. On the other side, the pouched mammals of Australia and New Guinea, isolated for a hundred million years or more, were also excluded from Wallacea. But there are exceptions. Somehow, species of the marsupial cuscus, or phalanger, did reach both Timor on the south and Celebes on the north. More important for us, at least two species of stegodonts, a primitive group of elephants, got from the western region all the way to both Flores and Timor [116], evolving into pygmy size, and by a different route, down from the Philippines into southern Celebes. This must have been well back in the Pleistocene, before the Würm glaciation. It is surprising; but land levels in Wallacea are unstable relative to the other land masses, and islands not now distant would have been still less so from time to time.

What elephants, even pygmy elephants, could do, man could do better. And he did: with *Stegodon* fossils in Timor have been found large, retouched flake and core tools. They are not dated, but they have many characters [81] of the Patjitanian stonework of Java, which is probably late middle Pleistocene. And, of course, Java was the home of primitive man, early and late: Java man, a million years and less ago, and Solo Man, probably within the Würm glaciation. So human beings from the earliest times obviously spread through Sundaland whenever it rose above water; and they must surely have penetrated Wallacea at different times and places, often standing at the various portals of Australia–New Guinea.

Arrivals and Dispersals

Here we can almost make up a narrative of the actual settlers.[1] They arrived before 20,000 BC and the previous maximum low sea stands would have been that of about 50,000 years ago (the date is not absolutely certain). Their arrival need not have been confined

---

[1] Helped by Rhys Jones's 1968 article [132] summarizing much of the background, by the 1971 symposium volume, *Aboriginal Man and Environment in Australia* [176] and by charts of ocean soundings.

to this event, but it would have been the most advantageous time, with many water crossings narrowed and land more likely to be visible in the distance. When we look at a modern map (Map 5b) the island of Timor seems to be the logical jump-off. But this is the map we must ignore. In those days Sahulland stretched far toward Timor (which did not reciprocate). But anthropologists do not favor an entry here, while not ruling it out. At the best of times the deep water would have been eighty-five to a hundred miles across, and at such distances the low exposed Sahul shelf would hardly have been visible to invite intentional crossings. And while we do not know its nature at the time, if it was bordered with mangrove swamps and guarded by crocodiles and deadly jellyfish, like much of the Arafura Sea today, it would have had its forbidding aspects. True, even with higher sea levels various islets would have been exposed, beginning only forty-five miles from Timor and making shorter steps to strips of mainland in the southeast. But if, in imagination, you will improvise your own 50,000 BC ferry, and bear those crocodiles in mind, you will read further.

To the north, from Celebes eastward, the maximum crossings were shorter (sixty or seventy miles and mostly less), usually with high land to be seen ahead. One might have gone over Buru and Ceram (which then stuck out a long tongue to the southeast) and then directly to New Guinea or via smaller islands to an arrival in Sahulland where the Aru Islands now rise. Or, north of this, small islands south of Halmahera would have made the easiest stepping-stones, though increasing the number of ventures over water, to the then western end of New Guinea. This last might have turned immigrants to the north side of the New Guinea mountain ranges, for an eventual arrival in Australia over what is now Cape York. Otherwise they would have moved south into and then down from the plains of Sahulland. Whatever happened, of course, we know that the first landfall, Australia's Plymouth Rock, is under water now.

Golson [85] feels that the real adventure would have been the move further south. The tropical forests, swamps and plains of North Australia and New Guinea have much in common with the Sundaland home of the migrants, which central Australia has not. So old food habits and practices would have served in the north, but elsewhere accommodation to new foods would be required, especially to seeds of grass species, much used by the living aboriginals of the interior.

Move south they did. They found an Ice Age Australia some-what greener then today's because of more rainfall. It was stocked with some surprising game. Today's marsupials were there along with some giant forms: nine-foot kangaroos; a colossal quadruped, the wombat-like *Diprotodon*, as large as a rhinoceros; and a marsupial 'lion', actually leopard-size, *Thylacoleo*, whose diet is not clear: was he carnivore, or carrion-eater, or even herbivore? But carnivores were relatively few and not especially dangerous: *Thylacinus*, the Tasmanian wolf, and *Sarcophilus*, the Tasmanian Devil. The latter, though not large, is well-named, a vile-looking beast, fleshy and fanged, with a thoroughly bad disposition.

By the end of the Pleistocene this hunter's Eden was no more. Not, however, says Jones, for the reasons generally given. It has often been assumed that Pleistocene rains transformed the con-tinent into lush forest and swamp and that when these disappeared at the end of the Ice Age in about 8000 BC the older, more varied fauna was decimated. But later studies show that, while the continent was indeed wetter and colder, and in parts greener, the arid core of central and western Australia remained. And there is evidence that the great marsupials could stand a drought as well as the small: fossil stomach contents of *Diprotodon* had vegetable matter of the present-day saltbush type, not swamp or forest greenery. In fact, the modern desert flora 'argues for an arid habitat of long duration'; furthermore a successful evolution of the marsupials, large as well as smaller, requiring millions of years, argues for adaptation to such a flora, not to dependence on the vagaries of Pleistocene rain cycles.

If the aborigine of historic times was an impoverished descen-dant of his ancestors, Jones holds, it was his own doing. He it was who killed off the giant marsupials, the largest and easiest to hunt. They vanished, not at the end of the Pleistocene, victims of a desiccating landscape, but well before this time, in the range of 25,000 to 30,000 years. Their bones are not found in the sites of 20,000 BC, nor at earlier Lake Mungo.[1] But *Thylacoleo*, the 'lion',

[1] As of now, there is a single disturbing exception. At Lake Menindee, New South Wales, plenty of giant marsupials occur, in apparent association with two stone tools, and with two C_{14} dates of 24,350 and 16,850 BC. The dates are not in agreement, and even the older is in discordance with the Mungo evidence.

and *Diprotodon*, the 'wombat', do occur in the sub-Keilor buried channels, whence Gallus has tools and a date of about 29,600 BC. Jones is favoring a school of archaeologists who point to the fact that, as in the Americas and a few smaller regions such as New Zealand and Madagascar where man had heretofore been absent only to appear suddenly from elsewhere, the disappearance of large animals (part of whose defence was size, and who may have therefore been especially docile) followed on one specific new factor: not climate but man. This is a plausible and possibly quite correct idea, but it has a degree of fragility[1] and not all subscribe to it. Direct assault, by a thin population of aboriginals not well equipped with weapons of the chase, might have been less of a cause than the incessant burning of the bush which was carried on by Australians and Tasmanians historically [133]. The effects are not clear: some species might have been endangered, while conditions for others might have been improved by the practice. Never mind: man came, and oblivion took the big marsupials. If man was an important agent, it is another sign that he had spread all through the continent by 30,000 BC.

The low sea level of 20,000 years ago and earlier might have tended to make a common province of tropical northern Australia, New Guinea, and the large plains and swamps that joined them, a province ecologically somewhat different from the rest. So might we explain the common presence of early edge-ground, hafted axes in these regions alone, as a tool not useful in the rest of Australia. So might we also explain those various blood distinctions of North Australia (see Chapter 4), likewise shared to a degree by New Guineans; but this is a long time range for any such assumption.

Pioneers to the south found the climate downright chilly, with a small glacier in the Snowy Mountains of New South Wales. The men making their ancient fires along the Marybyrnong River were not close to the sea, as Melbourne is now; instead, a broad plain

---

[1]For the Americas it has rested on the extinction of mammoths, camels, horses and other large animals after about 11,000 BC, presumably at the hands of the first American Indians, the Big Game Hunters, with their finely made projectile points for javelins thrown by a spear-thrower [160]. The fragile note is the recent evidence [167] that man had reached South America by at least 18,000 BC, long before the Big Game Hunters; but the latter may none the less have developed a specialized hunting culture which indeed destroyed these animals.

extended in front of them to the great headland of Tasmania. But only the frosty-minded would have traversed it. At the height of the last Pleistocene cold phase glaciers were widely distributed in Tasmania's highlands, with most of the interior therefore covered with ice and snow, or at the least treeless. Things would have been comparable climatically to Cro Magnon man's Europe at its worst, and no more than a narrow fringe of forest existed around the Tasmanian coast. Only in about 6500 BC did ice at last leave the western mountains.

So the now-smiling island was uninviting to naked nomads and for a long time could not have been occupied at all, except along the shore. Cave remains at several places show settlement going back to between 4000 and 6000 BC, seal and fish being overwhelmingly important in the diet. Below these levels the cave deposits are devoid of signs of man.

Now here is a momentary paradox in dates. No signs of man before 6000 BC at the earliest. But the sea is known to have been rising in late glacial times, and at some time now estimated to have been between 11,000 and 10,500 BC it made a critical advance from the thirty-five-fathom to the thirty-fathom line: instead of a land bridge fifty miles wide there was now open water forty miles across. Did man, after thousands of years when he could have walked, have to ferry himself to Tasmania after all?

No, says Jones. He walked, and as he did somewhat later, he depended at the beginning heavily on sea food and was therefore forced to stay near the shore. So his living sites in the time before 6000 BC are still there, under anything up to two hundred feet or more of seawater. One of the known later sites, Sister's Creek cave on the north shore, has its earliest human date at just about 4000 BC; the cave was not occupied until the sea had risen to within twenty feet of its present level.

The Tasmanians therefore became cut off from the mainland as the Pleistocene was coming to a close. (Macintosh [150] has shown from winds and currents that attempted crossings by crude boats from Australia to Tasmania would today be extremely hazardous.) In later times they could settle the rest of the island, though they never, early or late, occupied the rain forest of the western interior. For some reason they eventually lost interest in scalefish: in postcontact times none was seen fishing, although they were observed to gather ten or more different kinds of shellfish. They had no

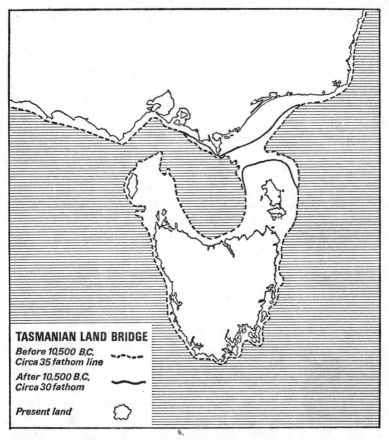

TASMANIAN LAND BRIDGE

Before 10,500 B.C.
Circa 35 fathom line

After 10,500 B.C.
Circa 30 fathom

Present land

6 Drowning of the land bridge to Tasmania. (After R. Jones.) In much of the late Pleistocene, Tasmania was broadly connected with Australia. Near the end of the Pleistocene, as the sea rose to the present 35-fathom depth, the connection had become a narrower bridge in the east, which in a relatively short time was cut by a sea channel at the 30-fathom depth. Drowning continued until present levels were reached at the end of the Pleistocene, leaving only the islands in Bass Strait as survivors of the bridge.

dogs, but not through lack of interest: they took eagerly to dogs when the English brought them in. But their culture, as known archaeologically, has some astonishing continuities with Australia. Stone tools, though they went through some refinements in

Tasmania, were part of the ancient Phase I core and scraper tradition of Australia. None was hafted; and the 'small tools' and fine workmanship of the Inventive Phase of the Australian mainland did not appear. Mulvaney [173] is willing to suggest that Tasmanian art motifs, engraved on rock prehistorically and painted on bark as late as the nineteenth century, had a specific kinship to similar motifs in the Koonalda cave which are 20,000 years old or more. (This is almost too good to be true.)

Quite late in prehistory, we have seen, there appeared on the continent the Inventive Phase, with the small-tool complex, as well as man's mammalian associate, the dingo.[1] These things came after the Pleistocene's end. One more thing happened, still later: the disappearance from the mainland of *Thylacinus*, the Tasmanian 'wolf',[2] and *Sarcophilus*, the Tasmanian Devil. Old inhabitants of Australia, they continued to flourish after the giant marsupials had become extinct some 20,000 years earlier. Both however became relatively scarce about three to five thousand years ago, judging by their archaeological remains; and then they vanished.

In December 1969 J. M. Bowler [22] in company with N. W. G. Macintosh [156, 158][3] found an extraordinary burial, that of a man aged about thirty-five to forty and at least six foot two inches tall, found crammed into a too small grave cut into 'brick-hard' calcareous clay. The latter was part of a fossil dune associated with Lake Nitchie, a generally dry pan today like Lake Mungo and about seventy-five miles west of it on the other side of the Darling River. In removing the skeleton, Macintosh found the remains of a necklace of canine teeth from *Sarcophilus*, the Devil. Not a single tooth hand-bored for such a purpose had ever been reported, early or late, in Australia. Here (after Mrs Macintosh and friends had spent many hours picking over fragments to put together) were

[1] Tools and dog alike failed to reach either Tasmania or Kangaroo Island, the latter lying off the south coast near Adelaide. This island was uninhabited at the time of European discovery, but Tindale long ago dug up artefacts archaeologically appropriate to Phase I, indicating that they date from the time when the island was part of the mainland. Lampert [271] reports a radiocarbon date of about 8970 BC at one site.

[2] This animal may now be extinct in Tasmania as well, not having been sighted in many years; *Sarcophilus* has also recently become very rare.

[3] Constant reference to his writings will show how much I and others owe to Professor Macintosh's many-sided work. Here I wish particularly to acknowledge his personal generosity to me with information, advice and help over a number of years.

over 285, all in a single necklace. This, says Macintosh, can only be not a personal ornament but an object of great ritual value, comparable to the churingas of modern aboriginals or even, for the context, like the sacred crown of a European empire – at any rate, something spelling much labor in boring the teeth, and perhaps generations of collecting. Differences in freshness suggest that the putting together was gradual, with some replacement of teeth over the years from wear and breakage. For *Sarcophilus* it spells grim slaughter: one animal could have supplied at the most four canine teeth with no allowance for breakage while boring; and Macintosh concludes that the whole thing may represent about one victim for every tooth. At the time, then, the Devil had by no means become a rarity. Accordingly, Macintosh had already surmised that the burial must go back to 4000 BC and perhaps much further (remarking also that the small-tool complex was not represented in soils around the grave), when a radiocarbon date from bone of the skeleton came the through giving a satisfactory date of 4850 BC. The burial, of course, could have been some centuries after the necklace had taken its final shape.

Three thousand years later both of these marsupial carnivores were dying out. Why? Because of the newly present dingo, evidently. Man may be blamed for extinction of the giant herbivores but, in spite of harvesting their canine teeth, he seems to have posed no threat to the survival of the Wolf and the Devil. In dogs, however, there appeared a different threat: direct competition for the same way of life from a very similar form of mammal, but from a placental mammal, not a marsupial. Placental mammals had replaced other amammalian forms elsewhere in the world many millions of years before, except for a few marsupials in the Americas such as the opossum. Placentals are evidently more advantageously organized and more intelligent (a kangaroo, though a speedy and alert leaper, strikes mammal-lovers as a little stupid). And the dingo is a perfectly good variety of modern dog, a very bright kind of mammal indeed.

So *Thylacinus* and *Sarcophilus* in the end lost the safety of their Australian refuge. But the dingo did not come before the drowning of Bass Strait about 10,500 BC (since he did not cross into Tasmania), and if he had reached southeast Australia by 5000 BC he did not do so in force, because *Sarcophilus* still abounded there. Nor did he banish the Devil and the Wolf overnight; but apparently there was a real replacement in a few millennia. The timing makes the connection of the dingo and the small tools look ever more reasonable and Calaby [30] calls the dingo, in so many words, the product of 'a new colonisation'. Was there a new population of men as well?

Prehistoric Men

I have mentioned the sour view of Pleistocene Australians prevailing not long ago. There was the Keilor find. Still earlier discoveries, the Talgai and Cohuna skulls, bore mineral encrustations and 'looked old'; but records of their discovery were so poor as to make them seem bad witnesses, and they ended by only increasing the suspicion attaching to man's antiquity on the continent.

All these have been rehabilitated and a new chapter has just opened. In this, the number of skeletons or skulls which can justifiably be put into the late Pleistocene and immediately after, or from 30,000 to 5000 BC, may come to exceed that for Europe and is already greater than for any other continent. Having said this much, I shall try to avoid the rhetoric of amazement, especially since new finds come faster every year.

These are general impressions of the moment: on the average, the prehistoric skulls are larger and more robust than those of their modern descendants (something holding good for Europe also); as Macintosh suggested [152, 153, 154], they tend toward two extreme forms. One expresses archaic traits like heavy brows and flat, narrow foreheads more strongly than in living Australians. The other seems more modern. These last are also more like skulls of Tasmanians, though robust and, like the Tasmanians, browfully endowed and having other primitive traits.

Both types, if they can be called that, none the less appear like exaggerations of distinctions existing among recent aboriginals and, although the contrast is greater, they do not suggest (at least to Macintosh, Thorne or myself) representatives of anything falling outside one general Australo–Melanesian population.

The contrast seems the key question. To be concrete about it, we are on firmest ground if we review the better-known specimens; the crowding new finds are still being put together in the laboratory and have been only fleetingly described. Let us look at the fine Keilor skull, which has been in part responsible for Gill's interest in the site and in the Marybyrnong terraces. A workman digging for commercial molding sand struck the skull with his pick. It lay in sand of the Keilor terrace, ten feet down from the present surface and just below a clearly defined layer, or diastema, of redeposited loess-like material, occurring only in this vicinity. Gill, beginning his re-examination, found the same material on and in the skull itself, together with an encrustation of secondary calcium carbonate. He has seen no reason to doubt its proper position in the deposit. He thought the skull showed signs of having been rolled somewhat by the river, but Macintosh has now cleaned off the carbonate and doubts the presence of such signs on the bone. In addition, there were associated with the cranium four pieces of bone which after being cleaned were found to form the upper two thirds of a left thigh bone. Though no other bones were recovered, it is possible that there had originally been a burial here.

The site is a wedge of land between the river and a tributary local gully, Dry Creek. Some time after the skull was found a new channel was dug across this wedge to divert the creek waters directly into the river. In the face of the cut, both above and below the skull level, have been found hearths, with charcoal, bone and organic material from food remains. And the charcoal has given dates running from about 7000 to about 17,000 BC, thus dating the formation of the Keilor terrace itself. From its position, Gill some time ago estimated the date of the skull to be about 13,000 BC, but Macintosh has used the thigh bone to give its own radiocarbon date (using surviving collagen or fibrous tissue), which he tells me will probably settle down to something 2,000 years younger, about 11,000 BC, though this is still within the Pleistocene. One piece of poor luck: Mulvaney believed he saw two stone tools embedded in the face of the cut below the skull level but, in 1965, while he was preparing a party to excavate these and the hearths, a flash flood washed the whole skull site away for good.

As to the skull's nature, it is of good size, with a large brain case and not especially heavy brows, a low nose and a broad palate. The cheekbones may be more robust than is usual in Australians or Tasmanians. Racially it does not strike me as strongly stamped, though it projects somewhat, in the mouth region. This is my impression; however, Weidenreich [250], who knew his crania, said it was practically an identical twin to the better of the two Wadjak skulls of Java, found long ago by Dubois when he was looking for Java Man. While the Wadjak remains are later in date, probably post-Pleistocene, this skull is recognizable as generally Australian in its features (and certainly in no way like Indonesians).

Macintosh classes Keilor in the modern-looking group of those I defined; he has been doing a thorough study of the skull such as it has long deserved, and we will know it better when this has been published. Adam [6] early remarked that palate and teeth were more Tasmanian than Australian in character; on the other hand Birdsell has suggested that the skull is a good representative of his 'Murrayians', and Wunderly [259] said that the form of its contours closely resembles that in South Australian males (same as Murrayian). Now let us refer again to Chapter 3. In this, the discriminant functions separated Tasmanian and Murray River skulls very well, and we have seen that other specimens can be tested on the same functions. Such a test is of course not absolute, but it is certainly useful evidence and it is objective, not a personal judgement. The Keilor skull is classed as 'Tasmanian', in spite of its size, with a stated probability that one male Tasmanian skull in four would be a less typical member of the Tasmanian population than is Keilor. As a matter of classification the skull has better than one chance in twenty of belonging to the New Britain Tolais. But its chances of occurring as a normal member of the Murray River population are less than one in a thousand and, strangely, poorer than its chances of being a Norwegian or an Arikara Indian! That is to say, by cold statistics based on a great deal of information from measurements, it is readily acceptable as a 'Tasmanian' but definitely not as a South Australian of recent date.

In 1965 a bulldozer working in the Keilor terrace little more than a mile away, in Green Gully, sliced the face off a skull with which was a collection of bones forming parts of the skeletons of a man and a woman, that is, a delayed burial of partial dried remains. This was higher up in the terrace, in levels which suggested a date of about 6000 to 9000 BC, but a more recent dating on the bones themselves gives a reliable date of about 4500 BC. After a lot of work in restoration, Macintosh finds the skull (allowing for sex – it is female) to be strikingly like the Keilor cranium.

The Nitchie man, with his somewhat earlier date of about 4850 BC, is also considered by Macintosh [156] to resemble Keilor in form, i.e. to have modern aspects of contour, but to be more rugged, and to exhibit a number of archaic or primitive traits (those recalling early man in Java). I would agree as to its place-ment with Keilor and I would ascribe the ruggedness and other features at least in part to its large size and to the large body size of its owner.

Quite the opposite, for antiquity and ruggedness, is the Lake Mungo skull of about 24,000 BC. The find gave every sign of a body cremated but not fully consumed, after which the bones were buried in a very shallow depression in the Mungo sand. (Burnt skull and skeleton parts of at least two other individuals were found nearby, too incomplete to be of much use.) This disposal of the dead was used to some degree among recent Australians, but was the typical method among the Tasmanians of the last century [110].

When disencrusted and laid out, the skeletal fragments came to about a quarter of the whole, all in small pieces, a four-inch bit of leg bone being the largest. Thorne [21] diagnosed the owner as a 'young adult female of gracile build and small stature'. The brain-case, which he was kind enough to let me see when he had reached this stage of restoration, is thin-walled, with small brow ridges and no special narrowing of the fore part. In my view this much of her could pass for a female European, and she certainly must be assigned to the more modern-looking group of skulls. (Thorne is at present of the same opinion, though in first mention of the frag-ments he had thought archaic traits might be present.)

All the above form a Keilor-like, or what I would call Tasmanian group. Other fossils contrast, as I said. Anecdotally most interest-ing is the Talgai youth [154, 155]. His crushed cranium was found, southwest of Brisbane, by William Naish, a contractor setting posts for a stock fence. This was probably in 1886. Naish gave it away; a later owner tried to sell it to the Australian Museum in Sydney for a good price in 1896 by threatening to send it to England, and finally did sell it to the University of Sydney in 1914, the first time it really came to notice. The skull is not adult, but it is nevertheless heavily constructed and flattish; primitive-looking compared to modern skulls, with rather large front teeth and a particularly long and protruding palate.

It was well mineralized, and encrusted with carbonate of a characteristic color. It gave every impression of antiquity, but by the 1960s the trail leading to its finding place was very cold. Nevertheless the indomitable Macintosh, getting a fortunate lead from descendants of Mr Naish, began an excruciatingly pains-taking search for the exact site of the fence. This included studies of old surveys, interviews with over fifty people who could give clues, and even the running down of such points as whether the car seen in the area on Saturday, 29 August 1914, was a Cadillac or a Buick. Taking Gill along to help, he finally bore down on what he felt was the proper site and stratum, the latter having an ap-propriate nature to match skull and crust in color, and being rich in carbonate nodules similar in composition to the crust. This began to suggest dates of about 8800 BC by radiocarbon.

To no avail. On a further, complete cleaning of the skull it turned out to be a different color, and Macintosh renewed the search, locating still another, more likely site. The skull's age seems to go ever upward, to at least 10,000 BC, and perhaps a good deal more since it was deposited after being rolled in a stream, and not buried in a grave. Its story is not yet over, but the early part suggests why ancient crania got a bad name in the old days.

Two adult skulls, Cohuna and Mossgiel, are excessively flat in the forehead and in general ruggedness are unusual to extreme, especially Mossgiel. This one is accompanied by a massive lower jaw and a generally massive skeleton. The Cohuna skull was ploughed up in 1925 some miles south of the town of that name, south of the Murray River in the state of Victoria. It had a par-ticularly heavy encrustation (Professor Macintosh tells me nine millimeters), but for a long time its age was purely presumptive. Now in looking at a single fossil one may readily forget how widely a whole population can vary in form, and may be carried away by the sight of an exceptionally rugged or primitive-looking fringe individual. This is the charge which, a few years ago, could be levelled against Cohuna and Mossgiel: that they were actually being honored for their low foreheads, not for any demonstrated antiquity.

They have now been brought out of the wilderness by a whole series of new finds near Cohuna [276]. Beginning in 1968 a team working with Alan Thorne had recovered, by the end of 1971, remains of at least forty burials. Most have been found in lake-laid or wind-blown silts around the borders of Kow Swamp, another former lake. This is where the Cohuna cranium was discovered. Other burials have come from sites a few miles away along Gunbower Creek, but these remain to be explored fully. The bones mostly owe preservation to mineralization by carbonates from ground water, often giving thick crusts like that on the Cohuna skull. The nature of sites and burials suggests a limited time range during which they were buried, and radiocarbon dates determined so far fall between about 8000 and 6000 BC (mostly before 7000 BC).

The skulls have a uniform and special nature (see plates), which is also that of Cohuna. They are thick and very long. The back has strong markings for muscle attachments but is also like that of recent Australians in form. It is the forehead and face which are most unusual and primitive. The forehead is flat and narrow; the brow ridges are strongly developed and wide; and, above all, the jaws are massive. According to Thorne all of them are too large to be fitted to the famous Broken Hill skull of Rhodesia, a large-faced early man. They are also virtually chinless; modern aboriginal jaws are similarly weak-chinned but far smaller. The Kow Swamp people were powerful chewers: teeth were heavily worn down.

Thorne views the population as an archaic form of modern man, especially with respect to the face, which preserves aspects of the earlier and really primitive men of Java (see below). At the same time it points toward modern aborigines. It is significant in being a whole, homogeneous population – isolated and remnant, Thorne suggests – which is clearly different in structure from skulls like Keilor or Mungo.[1]

The Problem

So the fossil men, as Macintosh has stressed, give the appearance of two extensions out of the head form of recent Australians, one toward a sort of enlarged Tasmanian, and one toward emphasis of archaic, not to say primitive, aspects of the Australians.[2] I do not

[1] Mr Thorne very kindly showed me the specimens in January 1971, in the state of restoration he had reached by then, and I am obliged to him for this and for later information.

[2] Macintosh [153, 143] is less impressed with the idea of 'extension', considering all the fossils to fall within the range of the total modern population. He bases this on a scaling analysis using a cumulation of specific skull traits which range from primitive to modern. I have had no chance to measure the fossils, other than Keilor, for purposes of the multivariate analysis of Chapter 3; but Keilor in such terms does fall clearly outside the modern Southern Australian population at least. And I must agree with Thorne that the center of gravity, so to speak, of the Kow Swamp skulls is displaced from the modern average form to a marked degree and is thus a natural parent group for Cohuna. We are, of course still making impressionistic if informed judgements about such skulls, and only further years of analysis will allow more objective statements.

like to sound paradoxical in talking about two distinct populations which (like my Australian colleagues) I nevertheless view as members of the same major stock, but that is the situation. I think the two groups, as discerned, are too distinct simply to be expressing the variation of a single local population, that of southeast Australia in the late Pleistocene, at least until such a sample as the Kow Swamp lot is shown to exhibit both forms, which it gives no promise of doing. The difference, I believe, has substance and is an important key to the Australian past. How may we interpret it?

In the first place, what might have caused it? What are the possibilities? Not two separate migrations from different parts of Asia, like Japan and India. Certainly not a migration of Negritos.[1] What did we learn earlier? Blood results are dubious: the homogeneity suggests long isolation more than anything else.

Recent crania? Much new work must be done, but that begun by Larnach and Macintosh [143, 144] has brought out no discernible differences between skulls of Queensland and New South Wales. Opinions on Tasmanians make a small library, but I find their skulls, by measurements and multivariate statistics, definably different from South Australians and slightly more like Melanesians.[2] The same holds for the living: in pictures and records, Tasmanian features, above all hair, are somewhat more Melanesian; the hair of Australians, usually wavy or nearly straight, is anomalous in the Southwest Pacific.

If one of the prehistoric skull shapes is a sort of Pleistocene Tasmano–Melanesian (as I believe), what made the other different? Here the conversation is apt to turn to Solo Man, a really primitive human being, known only from eleven braincases found in Java in the 1930s. These skulls are truly massive, with great brows in a straight line across the forehead, and a very thick skull having a bony crest across the back attesting to the muscle power in the neck needed to balance the heavy head. Unfortunately no faces or teeth were found. With so rankly primitive a character, and a brain distinctly smaller than any living population, he is generally classed

---

[1] Roundly rejected by Larnach and Macintosh [144] on somewhat different grounds: a comparison of recent skulls.

[2] Thorne [243], studying prehistoric fragments recovered by Jones, which cannot be used for measurement, failed to find the specific local features of the skull by which Tasmanians were traditionally separated from Australians. This is a different method from mine.

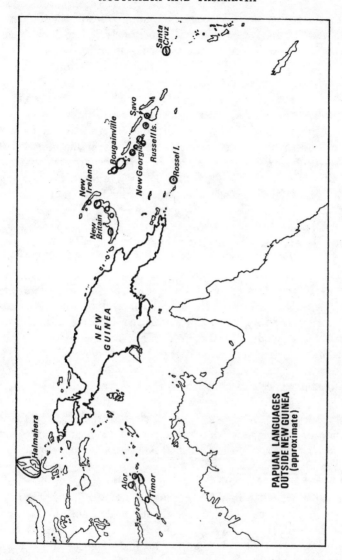

7 Papuan languages outside New Guinea. The general locations of these, in Indonesia and Island Melanesia, are given. New Guinea itself is mostly Papuan-speaking, with Austronesian found in spots along the coast. While rapid progress is being made in classifying Papuan languages in New Guinea, no attempt is made to show the still complicated situation there.

in that lower species, *Homo erectus*, along with the much older and still more primitive Java Man, who is believed to have been in Solo's own line of ascent. But Solo Man lived in the later Pleistocene, possibly during the Würm glaciation and, from accompanying evidence, perhaps quite late.

Weidenreich [251] and Coon [43] have viewed Solo Man as a direct ancestor of the Australian population, though Weidenreich (according to Birdsell [17]) modified this view to one in which Solo Man made a genetic contribution – that is, he mixed with a population of *Homo sapiens* – without being essentially parental. Macintosh finds the Cohuna-like people 'reminiscent' of Solo; and some details of skull form characteristic of Solo turn up in such specimens. None of this suggests that Solo Man ever reached Australia. But he might have contributed by mixture to one lot of migrants, which had started out by being a population of modern man of the same general kind as the other, Tasmanian-like, group.

Such a mixture, with a really primitive man, may seem bizarre, but perhaps it is no more bizarre than the presence, late in the Pleistocene, of Solo Man in Java – in fact, it becomes a question how a population of modern men could have avoided such survivors. Consider the situation. While we are imagining, let us call them the S (for Solo-descended) people and the T (for Tasmanian-like) people. It is the T people who have acceptable Sundaland ancestors or relatives of early date, in the Indonesian sources of migration: the Niah and Wadjak skulls, of whom more later. On Sundaland also, their miscegenation with Solo in one or more places, let us suppose, produced the S people. At least one group of each reached Australia, perhaps by different routes.

Here it is the duty of prehistoric crania to clarify things, a duty they have not performed. We could have a solution if only (1) the S and T people could be absolutely segregated and (2) they could be ordered in time. We might innocently conclude that of course the primitive-looking S people came first, followed by the more modern T people, who were perhaps connected with the small tools and the dingo. The 'perhaps' is just what can be excluded: it is the T people who reached Tasmania without tools or dog; the Nitchie man wears the absolute badge of pre-dingo age around his neck in the *Sarcophilus*-tooth necklace; and Keilor is also clearly of an age well before the dingo, while the earliest known skull

(Mungo), though small and female, is pretty certainly not of the S type.[1]

Then was it the other way around: the S people coming after Tasmania was sundered from the continent (as the later populations suggest), bringing small tools and dingo? An appealing solution, which might be supported if all dates for the S skulls were late, or post-Pleistocene. It does not seem likely that this will be the case. Instead it appears more probable that S and T people co-existed much further back, without actual signs (in southeast Australia, whence all the prehistoric skulls except Talgai have so far come) of separate migrations.

Possibly, with all these S and T people, we have been choosing up sides for a game of self-deception, but I think the distinctions remain real. It is a bad time to be guessing, with so many new things coming to light. Graeme Pretty, of the South Australian Museum in Adelaide, has found a unique cemetery at Roonka, on the Murray River; it contains a substantial number of skeletons apparently buried over a long period of time going back perhaps to 17,000 BC, perhaps further. That is one reason I said Australia might overtake Europe in the ancient skeleton department.

A Summary for the Present

We may leave it this way. Man entered Australia before 30,000 BC. The earliest remains now known are unquestionably those of modern man (*Homo sapiens* in the narrowest sense). We cannot pretend to have a clear idea of the variety of the early people, but a respectable number of skulls suggests a main difference between the 'S people', men with flat foreheads and often very robust features, and the 'T people', a kind more typical of Melanesia or Tasmania. None were Negritos.

Local isolation within the sparse population allowed such group differences, possibly present from the beginning, to persist over millennia; this, I assume, permitted the peopling of Tasmania by a population essentially of the 'T' kind. At the end of the Pleistocene not only were Tasmania and New Guinea cut off, but considerable living space on the east and the west was drowned, however

[1] Thorne, in an article [277] published after this was written, has a similar discussion. He gives some preliminary measurements of Kow Swamp skulls, and concludes that the S people probably came first.

gradually, by rising seas, which as Tindale has observed [175] must have caused substantial disruption and new adjustments to many groups. This alone might have led to a kind of homogenizing of the continent's whole population in recent millennia, reducing the distinction between our supposed S and T communities.

So might the appearance of the new culture elements, apparently coming in about the same time, perhaps together with the dingo. Were these from outside Australia? The distribution of the 'Common Australian' languages might reflect augmented internal movement like the one I suggested above; on the other hand, Greenberg's great group of Indo-Pacific languages stretching from the Andaman Islands through New Guinea to Tasmania would make the Australian languages, not thought to be part of the group, look like an intrusion into a once more uniform linguistic realm. Would 7,000 years fit such a history comfortably? I doubt if it can be said.

Just now, joining anything we know about anatomical Australia to the facts of prehistory is a baffling task. And the archaeologists have their own problems. They must bring in the dingo from no nearby source yet discovered. Golson believes we should be willing to think about a transmission direct from India, a most venturesome suggestion, but one which would at least combine dogs and microliths (a component of the small-tool complex), since India was producing microliths at just about the right point in time. There are other ideas for the Phase II introductions: J. P. White [253] has this one. Horticulture, we shall see in the next chapter, grew up from heterogeneous beginnings very early in Southeast Asia and was already spreading at the end of the Pleistocene. A patchwork front wave, incorporating a complex of tools and domesticated plants and animals, moved into Indonesia and New Guinea, where it became established. But the well-adjusted hunters and gatherers of Australia, as they are known to have done in historic times, simply rejected things that seem to us to be irresistible benefits: domestication, boats and so on. So a kind of bifurcation of culture elements took place in the advancing wave, with Australia accepting dogs and microlithic blades, which lacked appeal for gardeners with their polished adzes and domestic pigs (a situation which might explain the absence of dogs and small tools round about Australia).

But this is not the 'new colonisation' suggested by Calaby; the new wave gives us no new faces. If there was any addition to the human population of Australia – such as would be so helpful to explain Australian hair form – we cannot now show it from aboriginal heads, past or present.

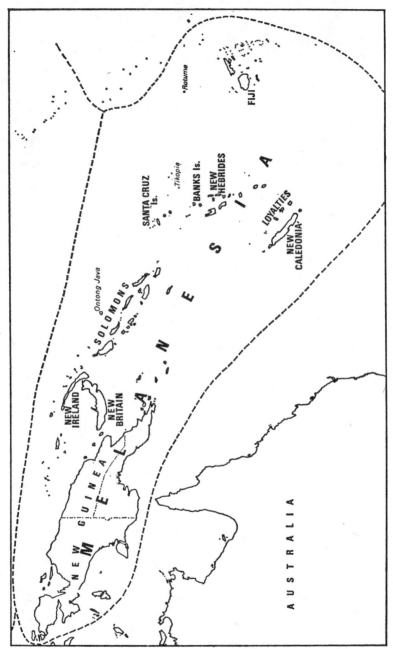

8 Melanesia.

7

Melanesia
and Indonesia

Melanesia by general agreement is easy to define geographically. It begins in the west with New Guinea and includes the islands off its eastern end (Milne Bay District) and the Bismarck Archipelago to the north; it continues on southeastward through the Solomons, Santa Cruz, and Banks and Torres, to the New Hebrides; a few hundred miles to the southwest and east respectively lie New Caledonia and Fiji. In the main, the islands are of good size, certainly in contrast to Micronesia and the typical groups of Polynesia; and all are 'continental' in geological character, lying outside the 'Andesite Line' which surrounds the deeper Pacific Basin. That is to say, the islands have the complex structure of mixed rocks characteristic of continents. Melanesia just touches the equator on the north and the Tropic of Capricorn on the south, and Fiji barely crosses the 180° meridian, halfway around the world from the Greenwich Observatory.

This nice package is not quite so neat linguistically. It contains all the Melanesian (Austronesian) languages; however, a dozen or so Papuan languages turn up in eastern Indonesia: in Halmahera just off New Guinea's western end, and in Timor and neighboring Alor and Kisar (Map 7). And definite Polynesian languages are found in various small islands, especially north, south and east of the Solomons (for example Ontong Java, Rennell and Bellona, Tikopia), and in Fila, Futuna and Aniwa of the New Hebrides. These are the so-called Outliers. More significant for historical reconstruction, as we have seen, is the particular likeness of Fijian and of some New Hebridean languages to those of Polynesia generally – that is, not direct membership, as with the Outliers, but an older, close relationship. Thus on both east and west there are vestiges of important contact, development and movement.

Physically also the edges are ragged. Over the western border in the Lesser Sunda Islands there are clear signs of a 'Melanesian' presence, expressed in frizzy, non-Mongoloid hair, dark skins and broad noses. These are to be seen in Sumba, and especially in eastern Flores and western Timor, and in the smaller islands Alor and Pantar just north of Timor [135, 142, 26]. Here there are occasional faces which could have come from New Guinea itself, as well as rarer faces which are strikingly Australian in appearance.

Considering the Papuan languages found in the same region, we might be emboldened to recall from the previous chapter that Timor's position, with the Timor Trough lying below it, is a little more likely to have made it, for people moving east without boats, a cul-de-sac rather than a best route to Sahulland. At the same time, Bijlmer [14] reports additional Melanesian-like people on the northerly route, in Amboina and Ceram, and there is some slight evidence of the same thing from crania [121].

At the eastern extreme the Fijians, though varying, are strongly like Polynesians in structure and skull form in spite of their dark skins and bushy hair; and their neighbors in western Polynesia return the compliment to a very slight degree, having some frizzy hair, rather large noses and dark skin. Across Melanesia's north an important note seems to be the whole rainbow of Micro-nesian–Melanesian intergrading, something very irregular, but running along the entire reach of the Melanesian arc. This has not heretofore been obvious from external appearances, which are poorly recorded anyhow, but it does emerge from the analysis of measurements already presented in Chapter 3. In the tree of likenesses presented there, it is manifested by the inclusion of Yap, Palau and the Marianas sample from Saipan in a general 'Melanesian' branch, as well as in the mingling of Melanesians and Micronesians in the more remotely connected D branch (see Figure 1). Linguistics do not reflect this degree of interconnection, but there are other signs of culture contact; and Shutler, an archaeologist who knows both areas, tells me there can be no doubt as to prehistoric contacts between the New Hebrides and the Gilberts. Finally, in western New Guinea there has in the past been undoubted Indonesian influence in addition to the Micro-nesian.

Meeting the Melanesians

Here we must undertake a pedestrian review of Melanesian physique, bearing two things in mind: the great variety in appearance of the Melanesians taken all together; and the fact that large areas have never been formally studied, with some important islands not known well at all. For distributions, and the precise description of populations and subspecies, certain species of Melanesian birds are far better known than Melanesian man. In trying to present the anthropology I must depend on the minority of peoples who have been measured and recorded for skin, hair, etc., and rely beyond that on photographs and some personal impressions relating to others, hoping that the blanks do not invalidate the effort.

In addition, too much of an attempt at simplification leads to the mistakes of the past, by making distinctions appear clearer than they are and thus creating 'types' in an uncareful mind. Types are only too apt to become 'waves of migration' in historical reconstruction. Nevertheless we must try a descriptive pattern, simply remembering that most areas about which we may be tempted to make broad statements turn out, like the surface of Mars, to be more complex and varied on close inspection.

To begin with, most Melanesians are short. A large proportion of male averages for height is grouped around 160 cm (5 ft 3 in), with most others running from this figure to 165 cm (5 ft 5 in). The Tasmanians, to hark back to them, would probably fall just here. For comparisons, Australian aboriginal populations mostly stand a little above such averages, and Polynesians are taller still, at about 170 cm. Melanesians, however, are not pygmies. Their skulls are those of full-sized men, and their bodies are well built. Body form ranges from a fleshiness which would strike us as normal for a man in good condition to one, seen in New Guinea and parts of the Bismarck Archipelago, of a muscular carcass with virtually no fat on it, quite outside the range of body composition in Europeans. I cannot be positive about either the distribution or the significance of this vanishing 'endomorphic' component, but it certainly occurs in the Admiralty Islands [107] and many parts of New Guinea.

Externally, Melanesians appear dark-skinned and woolly- to bushy-haired, with a protruding mouth region, a varying thickness of the lips, and a considerable breadth of the nasal tip. This is the complex of traits which led to their being called Oceanic Negroids, and to the assumption of some – by no means all – anthropologists of a connection with Africans. I was strongly persuaded of this at one time, but think the opposite now. The blood groups, Simmons [215] has pointed out, show no correspondence with Africa, though this is negative evidence only. The Melanesians also vary in beard and body hair, but many are far more luxuriantly bearded than all but occasional Africans. Skin color varies more than in African Negro tribes, while noses are on the whole more prominent in profile and more varying in width. Also, the brows are more prominent and there is a strong tendency for the root of the nose to be deeply depressed, something quite different from Africans but very similar to Australians. Again, it is important to emphasize that variation of this kind, especially skin color, is found within single communities as well as between them. It is significant that especially marked differences are seen within villages in the New Guinea highlands [151], because this region was opened up by Europeans only during the 1930s and so there can be no suspicions of mixture from that direction. The region is decidedly remote from general coastal and inter-island contacts as well. From all signs, the variation in skin color is an essential characteristic of the population gene pool itself and has nothing to do with non-Melanesian influences of any kind. (See also pp. 32–34.)

In addition, from the multivariate analysis of skull measurements described in Chapter 3 I find that Melanesian (and Australian) skull form is consistently and markedly different from African. One difference is indeed the projecting brows of the Pacific peoples; below this, however, and disguised by it, the nasal bridge root is more prominent and the nasal region narrower than in Africans; the nasal root in fact is virtually as prominent as that in Europeans, relative to the face as a whole. Below the nose the bony gum is definitely more protruding and prognathic than in Africans, whose facial protrusion in the living is due more to thick lips than to skeletal form.

In the interior mountains of New Guinea, body size falls in places to real pygmy levels. In western New Guinea (West Irian) the Tapiro and Goliath groups are now famous for recorded male averages of 145 and 149 cm respectively (4 ft 9 in, 4 ft 10½ in). Together with a few other short groups they are round-headed and not especially flat-nosed. The more lately explored Highlands of

Australian New Guinea have other very short peoples, especially in the Aiome region. There is no doubt of the prevalence here of short stature, only of its meaning. One savant recently made a quick visit to the Aiome to collect measurements. It transpired that the obliging District Officer, in expectation of the visit, told a native sergeant: 'The professor wants to see Pygmies. Go out and round up the twenty shortest men you can find.' Now this is not the sampling method approved of by statisticians. Whether the same favoritism was shown to very short men in the older reports I do not know, but I doubt it.

Among these same interior people face and skull traits vary over short distances. At Mount Hagen, picture magazines have already made familiar the natives of the immediate region, with their heavy beards, coarse features, with large noses and deep-set eyes, small ogres (157 cm or 5 ft 2 in) whose fierce-contoured faces are none the less suffused with charm. Other groups not far away lack these heavy features and have delicate, narrow skulls. This is one example of the checkerboard nature of New Guinea variation, corresponding in heterogeneity (though not necessarily in pattern) to blood variations and to languages.

In the plains and swamps of southern New Guinea, and around the west end, smallish narrow-headed people seem to predominate, often with narrow and prominent noses which have been dubbed 'Semitic' in surprise at their presence in a 'Negroid' people. There is, however, no earthly reason to ascribe this nose to any outside influence or connection, certainly not to a Semitic one, in spite of the historical spread of Islamic conversion right to the west end of New Guinea itself. Nor is such a nose seen among Indonesians. Nasal prominence, it is true, varies considerably in the Melanesians, but these noses are striking. They must be taken as indigenous and the reason for them is simply not known.

Southeastwards from the southern border between west and east New Guinea through Port Moresby, around Milne Bay and in the offshore islands, there is a marked tendency towards light skins and hair that is less woolly or even curly, especially in comparison with adjacent inland districts. Stature also varies, dropping from east to west. In this region the average lightness of skin, etc., does suggest (unlike what I said just above for highland New Guinea) an outright penetration, via migration, of non-Melanesian peoples, not only because of the physical appearance of the natives but also because of the important Motu language of the Port Moresby region. This (as we saw in Chapter 5) is a probable member of Eastern Oceanic; and in Murdock's compilation of Dyen's analysis, Motuan is placed in the Heonesian subfamily together with Polynesian, some eastern Melanesian languages, and Gilbertese and Carolinean of Micronesia.

Beginning with the north coast of the Territory of New Guinea including the Bismarck Archipelago, and going through the Solomons and on down to the New Hebrides, we have an area of continuing variety within which it is difficult to see any basic difference in origins. That is to say, no reason exists to conclude that there is more than one fundamental ancestral population, after we make allowances for the influences of obvious outsiders from Micronesia or Polynesia, for the effects of environment, and for long-time local change. In some places (as in Espiritu Santo of the New Hebrides) there is a great spread from small to large body size in various parts of the island; in others, a juxtaposition of differing peoples is evidently a matter of recent movement, as we shall shortly see. Islands thoroughly sampled (New Ireland [206], Bougainville [182, 65]) seem to have as great local heterogeneity as the whole continent of Australia, if not greater.

Let us look over this area in more detail. On the New Guinea north coast people are still short (with averages on either side of 160 cm), and seem like slightly larger versions of their inland neighbors. As far as I know – certainly around Madang – skin color continues to vary in one village from dark to quite light, and aquiline noses are common. In New Britain, the Baining of the mountains in the west of the Gazelle Peninsula (who speak a non-Austronesian language) are short, round-headed and dark, as are the Tumuip further south. Neighbors of the Baining but contrasting with them, the Tolai around Rabaul are taller and longer headed. The Tolai have come over in recent centuries from the shore of southern New Ireland opposite, where they resemble such people as those of the Lamassa district. In central New Ireland (Namatanai) are people again more like the Baining, while in northern New Ireland different writers (Parkinson, Friederici) have attested to a greater proportion of light skins. Schlaginhaufen also records skin colors in the south darker than the darkest shades to be found in the north, and Parkinson mentions hair of a Polynesian type in the north, whatever that means.[1] My own impressions and photographs of this region convey a wide range of color and appearance, running from a strongly prognathic Melanesian look to the opposite, a Polynesian-like form of high rectangular face.

Little is known of New Hanover and the Admiralties, though they seem to conform to the general type of the Tolai. Some smaller islands of the region, St Matthias or Pak, vary from this, in some cases with rather narrow noses, or with a resemblance in measurements to the New Guinea central north coast, so that both areas may suggest some Micronesian influence. This is particularly apparent in Tench. Of the barrier islands north of New Ireland, Tabar in the northwest is said to be relatively light skinned, but for those in the southeast, Tanga and Feni, I see no signs in Schlaginhaufen's photographs of anything other than a standard Melanesian face and physique. Thus we have, in this northernmost part of Melanesia facing Micronesia to the north, many populations which seem to be typical of the rest of Melanesia, and occasional ones which differ slightly and may suggest contact with Micronesia.

In the Solomons there continues to be the same kind of local variation on the main theme. Bougainville, the northernmost of the group, is one Pacific island which has been well studied. Oliver [182], working in 1938-9, found some consistent area differences, especially as read from measurements and such things as form of the nose or hairiness. In the central mountains the Rotokas and Keriaka are taller, with larger, and especially longer, faces and noses than the Siuai and Nagovisi peoples of the southern mountains; they are also hairier. All these are Papuan-speaking. From them other distinctions set off the Konua of the northwest mountains (Papuan-speakers) on one hand, and Torau (Austronesian-speakers) of the east coast. Friedlaender [66] in a recent, more intensive survey of much of the island also found that physical differences agreed with those of language. His grouping analysis tended to distinguish Papuan-speaking peoples of the north from those of the south, the latter aligning themselves more

[1] In the family tree of Chapter 3 north New Ireland is grouped, in the C branch generally, with some Micronesians and possibly Micronesian-like Melanesians but it falls in the sub-branch, C_1, with New Guinea peoples who do not suggest Micronesian connections at all.

with speakers of Melanesian (Austronesian) languages. The same result emerged from separate analyses of blood traits and of measurements.

In another study [67], a sophisticated analysis of blood groups testing aspects of genetic theory, Friedlaender has also shown that Bougainville (and New Guinea also) is quite extraordinary among other areas of the world which have been tested in the same way in its 'extreme population subdivision'. This is a social phenomenon which, however, leads to localized inbreeding and a low degree of interrelationship among communities in such an area, which in turn has tended to preserve or to induce marked local differences in physique and blood types.

I have alluded to such things in earlier chapters, and I emphasize it again for its general importance. In a region like the Pacific, isolation between different islands, because of supposed water barriers, may seem more important than it is. On the other hand isolation between small groups *within* well-populated areas – including especially New Guinea, where water barriers are not a factor at all – may arise from social factors of very long standing (not forgetting traditions of war and hostility) and may be very important. But the isolation, and its effects, may be more difficult to perceive until brought out by present-day methods of analysis and by well-planned village-by-village collecting of data. Even without such considerations, however, the well-marked language differences in the same areas point toward these very factors of long-enduring social isolation.

At the same time I do not see, nor do my colleagues Oliver and Friedlaender, indications that the physical differences are anything other than divergences within a strictly Melanesian frame of variation. One of Oliver's four groups of Nagovisi-speakers drops off to a male mean stature of 157 cm. Friedlaender got a figure nearly as low for one of his villages; others ran to 165 cm. Oliver reports some cultural and dietary differences (e.g. Bush people are almost completely vegetarian, while coast dwellers have plenty of fish); he nevertheless finds no cultural or environmental reasons for the physical differences. The small Nagovisi people are inland mountaineers, but so are the Rotokas of the central mountains, tallest of the island, and I [122] could find no consistent connections between altitude and body form.

Nothing so detailed is known of the rest of the Solomons. As usual, marked individual variation in skin color and facial form prevails, at least on the north side of Malaita and eastward in the small island of Ulawa, two places visited by Harvard expeditions. Santa Cruz islanders seem to be covered by anything which may be said about the Solomons. Banks Islanders are reported to have long narrow faces and noses. In the New Hebrides, the island of Espiritu Santo shows a particularly wide variation of body size in different parts (155 cm in the southwest to 167 cm in the northeast) which Speiser [228], who recorded this, ascribed to a less favorable environment for the smaller people, cut off from the sea. The short people of Malekula, just to the south, would fall into the same spread of variation.

However, from the central Solomons on eastward, account must be taken of probable effects from outside the range of Melanesian variation as I have been describing it. In the first place, I have, from my own experience, an increasingly strong impression that people in the eastern half of the Solomons tend to be less 'Melanesian' in their ranges of face form and skin color than they do either in the western half or in major parts of the New Hebrides or northern New Caledonia to the southeast. This is also the part of the Solomons where languages of the Eastern Oceanic group are spoken. I repeat that this is an impression, but it should be reported as something which may be more than a coincidence: something having to do with a possible very early component from Polynesian-like bearers of such languages. In any case, this slight shift in features in a Polynesian or Micronesian direction is supported by meager information in the family tree study [123] described in Chapter 3.

In the second place, and further to the southeast, such effects seem to be more specific and more local. In the Talamacco district, on Espiritu Santo, Speiser noted, as had Thilenius before him, an extension of body form to one of large size (and often fat, quite exceptional for New Hebridean Melanesians), and to a long face and broad head. This he puts down, reasonably, to an unrecorded Polynesian admixture. To the south, the smaller islands of Tanna and Eromanga have strongly Polynesian-like populations, [128, 227], especially Tanna, which has long faces and noses. The language of Tanna is not at all like Polynesian, but the nearby island of Futuna is linguistically Polynesian, and other New Hebridean languages have remoter relations thereto. Let us remark here that the linguistic evidence does not tell us whether intrusions of Polynesian-like peoples would have been late-coming Polynesians from the east, or others of such a physical nature coming much earlier.

New Caledonia and Fiji, at the margins of Melanesia, also depart from the main pattern. In spite of dark skin, frizzy hair and broad noses, Fiji is so much like Polynesia in measurable features and general cranial shape that the population should be viewed as Melanesianized Polynesian rather than the reverse. New Caledonia and the Loyalty Islands are more complicated. Face and skull form often appear strongly Australian in nature, with massive brows and particularly deeply recessed nasal roots, especially in the north. By contrast, Polynesian-like individuals, with long, rectangular faces are also not uncommon, apparently more so in the south. Both kinds of variation are to be seen in the Loyalty Islands, in what proportions I cannot say. However, the analysis of measurements in Chapter 3 places the north and the Loyalties with the Australians, and the south (Kanala) in a group containing Fijians and some Polynesians.

So, to review, we find in southeastern Melanesia physical indications of Polynesian relationships – Fiji, southern New Hebrides – and the same, more impressionistically, in New Caledonia. In the last, on the southern edge of the tropics, skulls and faces reminiscent of Australians are also evident. In many parts further west, there are varying suggestions of Micronesian influence, especially in places most logically exposed thereto, like the north shore of New Guinea and parts of the Bismarck Archipelago. Micronesia, we shall see later, returns the compliment by exhibiting copious signs of Melanesian admixture, in hair, skin or face. And the same zone reflects overlapping in measured features, as shown by the clustering of populations in Chapter 3. We may therefore assume that there has been, over recent millennia, a drifting and counter-drifting of genes between the two great areas. But a main problem is the component of variation in Melanesia which does not seem to hang on intrusions of other known kinds of population. I have tried to give an outline of geographic distinctions as far as they are known, which is poorly. But it is unsafe to do much commenting on this, not only because of the state of the knowledge but also because individuals in the same village may show striking differences in appearance and coloration.

I might suggest that in this genetic variety they recall the Europeans, who vary so greatly in individual appearance, face form, coloration and hair form – more widely than, say, typical African tribes (e.g. the Bantu-speakers), or Chinese, or American Indian populations. This is a broad statement and one difficult to demonstrate; I am trying to say that I think certain major areas may show this kind of genetic heterogeneity in appearance without its being the result of complex migrations and mixtures.

Beyond all this are a couple of special facts of coloration. One is juvenile blondness: the occurrence of light – actually blond – hair in children, darkening in adults, though some young women retain yellow hair, and others have hair which could be called dark strawberry blond.

Now some large parts of Melanesia have an aboriginal custom of bleaching hair with lime made from burnt coral; it was common enough in New Ireland so that Schlaginhaufen, who collected hair samples in his survey in 1907–9, felt obliged to discard a large number after he got home. Today, at least around Rabaul in New Britain, the people use peroxide from the Burns Philp store, and local opinion ascribes all apparent blondness to the practice. But it may be only a matter of touching up and so masking a real trait, since the natural tendency is actually widespread. It is very marked on the north shore of Malaita, where in the Lau Lagoon almost all children are yellow-haired, and sometimes straight-haired as well. The natives do not use bleaches – they are definite on the point – and think vaguely that constant swimming in salt water has something to do with it. However, people just inland from them, the Baegu, have the same lightness, though to a lesser degree, and the pattern of gradual darkening after childhood is not that of people who bleach.

In its lowest degree this lightness may possibly manifest itself in sun-bleaching of the ends of the hair, which grows out dark at the roots. The actual light hair, however, is so widespread that it seems to be a basic Melanesian trait. We must assume that it exists in the west, in New Britain and New Ireland, peroxide or not. I am told by Friedlaender that it is widespread in Bougainville, and by Shutler that it is common in the New Hebrides also, especially in the southern group. It is certainly not a present of genes from castaway Europeans, since it is far too prevalent, and is especially marked in Malaita where contacts have been very recent. It is also not a trait of Polynesians or Micronesians. Lessa [146] has reported frequent blond hair among children of Ulithi in the westernmost Carolines, ascribing it to sporadic mixture with Europeans. He is a good reporter, but I am inclined to consider it a possible importation from Melanesia. The atoll of Ontong Java, 200 miles north of Malaita, is physically essentially Micronesian. Bleached hair ends are fairly common here, and a very few children are actually blond. The people of the Lau Lagoon, where the blondness is so marked, have a tradition of coming originally from Ontong Java centuries ago and could well owe some ancestry to that source. But I can only suppose that the blondness comes from the Melanesian side of the family, and that any lightening in Ontong Java (or Ulithi) is also from Melanesian admixture, which has surely arrived in both places.

The phenomenon seems in every way the same as the juvenile blondness of central and western Australia, which we have seen already. It may well be a variation of a genetically simple kind which (like a few unusual blood genes) is a common property of the Australian and Melanesian populations, but I would not care to say more about common sources. Its distribution is actually poorly known – note the hearsay quality of much of the evidence I have been giving. It appears to be commoner in the Melanesian islands than in New Guinea. (In the New Guinea highlands reddish hair is seen in light-skinned individuals [151] and light hair is mentioned for other parts, but I do not know what the general occurrence may be.) Possibly it surfaces more readily in populations which are generally lighter-skinned, but evidence does not seem to favor the idea, and it is certainly a property of the darker-skinned populations as well.

Very dark skin is another phenomenon with a special distribution, and one which might be a sort of original Melanesian trait. The island of Bougainville has long been known for the extremely dark color of the inhabitants; in fact its native name, Buka (applied by Europeans only to the island at its north end), has become a widely used pidgin English word for 'black'. Oliver found the southern end to be darkest,[1] and this blackness carries on southward through New Georgia. Further on, in Malaita,

---

[1] Friedlaender was hard put to see any distinction in Bougainville, but says that, if he questioned natives' own views, they usually thought southerners were darkest.

skins on the southern side of the island appear darker to me than on the north, where the blond hair is.

Melanesians, Tasmanians and Negritos

Associated with this dark skin, I feel, there tends to be a face and skull form which is strongly like that of the Tasmanian aboriginals. Again, I have to say that this is a report based simply on my own experience, because skulls from these regions of Melanesia are rare or non-existent in collections; and for living Tasmanians one must turn to a few ancient photographs, poorly posed, of some sad survivors heavily clothed and capped in cast-off early Victorian attire. But the strong brows, the deep nasal root, the wide mouth – not as thick-lipped as in Africans, and often with a long and high external upper lip – all familiar from the nineteenth-century Tasmanian photographs, also appear frequently in faces running through the Solomon Islands: they occur occasionally in peoples of the area of the juvenile blonds in north Malaita but more usually in the other black spots already named. From published photographs it seems to me that such Tasmanian-looking populations or people occur both east and west of the Solomons as well. I am also inclined to think that these features are most associated with those same darkest-skinned groups already recognized, like the Baining.[1]

A general identity between the Tasmanians and a basic eastern Melanesian population certainly cannot be demonstrated now. But it cannot be disproven, and this is the foot the shoe is on, following the principle (Occam's razor) of not multiplying the number of major populations discerned. From this direction also then the Melanesians are 'Tasmanians' long present in the Pacific and differentiated locally by habitat and contact. The Tasmanian 'Tasmanians' were no more than one representative body of it, protected against exposure to genetic admixture from clearly different peoples like Micronesians and Polynesians.

The Tasmanians, we saw, have been classed by many writers as Negritos and used thereby as evidence of a Negrito stratum in the Pacific population, all in spite of the Tasmanians' rather rugged skulls and lack of dwarfishness. Smaller people, like the New

[1] I have been able to measure only two Baining skulls, for purposes of mathematical testing by the method described in Chapter 3. Of seventeen possible populations, both would be acceptable members of the Tasmanians and the Tolais of New Britain, one favoring the first, the other the second.

Britain Baining, or the very short villagers in Bougainville or Espiritu Santo, would be better evidence along the same lines. Impressionistically, a simple basal Melanesian nature for the Tasmanians seems compelling to me: from having viewed most of the surviving photographs of Tasmanian aboriginals, I have been struck by the feeling that I was seeing 'Tasmanians' in the flesh walking the roads of Auki on the south shore of Malaita, or at airports in New Georgia and Buka.

But this does not get us around the 'Negrito' problem. With Australia and Tasmania we faced it in the abstract; with the living Melanesians we face it in the concrete. Can there have been – distinct from a basic 'Tasmanian' Melanesian, normal in body and skull size, if sometimes shortish – a real pygmy stratum in the Pacific? That is, a now submerged strain, reducing the stature of peoples of another origin who moved in and mixed with it, and surviving in its most nearly primeval form only here and there, especially in interior New Guinea. Is there a break, a hiatus, between Melanesians generally and such 'Negritos'?

Here I must insist once more on the really great variation in appearance within many Melanesian communities. In North Malaita, of which I can speak with most confidence, one may see in the same village (forgetting the anomalous blondness) individuals who have almost a Polynesian aspect in facial features, through many combinations to others who do in fact suggest some of the 'Negritos', though they may not be relatively short in stature.

Now this kind of typing approach to an analysis of peoples is the old one which is properly condemned as 'typological', when it seeks by such recognition to divide a population into its ancestral 'types'. But the combinations of features do exist, and are rather compelling to the eye in certain populations. (The succumbing to such impressions is the root of all the gabble about 'Aryans', Nordics, Mediterraneans, etc., within European populations.) Such differences arise because of combinations of genes which are present in the population, however they got there. One possible cause is of course the introduction of genes from elsewhere, so that 'Polynesian' genes enter by admixture. Others arise by local mutation which may be favored by selection: perhaps blond hair on a dark-skinned body and head is an unusual mutation none the less useful in sunny tropics for reflections (see Coon [44] for general discussions of selection and racial features in man). But prevailing combinations really reflect the prevailing stock of genes of a population, and the commonest combinations are necessarily those of preceding generations.

I am assuming from evidence so far that the varying physiques of Melanesia reflect varying samplings or founding groups from a basic original population, perhaps best represented among others by the extinct Tasmanian aboriginals, by Bainings of New Britain, and by the darker-skinned areas of the Solomons described above, though this does not exclude as descendants such important populations as the Tolais or New Caledonians. We note that eastern Melanesian populations drop to especially small stature in two mountainous areas: west Espiritu Santo and the Nagovisi area in Bougainville. Bainings and Tumuip of New Britain are only moderately small, in a region (Bismarcks, north New Guinea) where stature is quite short in general. Now these New Guinea coastal people seem in turn to grade into their inland neighbors, maintaining specific similarities in form of head, face, and nose and differing only by a further diminution of stature. I am speaking of the Kai and Toricelli, who also resemble the Baining of New Britain in specific ways, but who are really short, at just over 150 cm (5 feet) on the average.

The core of the argument lies in the really small people, the Negritos or Pygmies of many authors: those of interior New Guinea, of the Philippines, of the mountains of the Malay Peninsula, and of the Andaman Islands. Let us look again at the grouping analysis given in Chapter 3. The very small New Guinea mountain people all fall into a single branch. A, which also includes the Kai and which, though separate because of size, is not radically isolated from the Melanesians as a whole. But the groups are indeed short (those here run in average male height from 145 cm (4 ft 9 in) to 153 cm (5 ft 0 in)), and in addition to being short, have smallish bodies and faces, with round heads but not broad noses. While highlanders are short in general, some are robust, and not all are dwarfish.

Modern students are suspicious of the idea that the New Guinea people are essential pygmies. In particular, Dr Carleton Gajdusek, wide-ranging biologist and nutritionist of the US Public Health service, has had a great deal of contact with them and others. He suggests that their small and wiry frames may in part result from a modest bit of selective evolution, since a small man (or, more probably, woman) carrying loads up and down steep mountain terrain is actually working at a more advantageous work/body weight ratio than a larger person. The really diminutive sizes, however, he ascribes to greatly retarded growth due to a low supply of protein and calories in certain mountain environments which are poor for crops and game. In some New Guinea communities, says Gajdusek [69], the height and appearance of a twelve-year-old boy is that of a six-year-old European child; and, by our standards, boys and girls from sixteen to twenty are easily mistaken for children of ten to twelve.

Fortunately, the acid test has been applied to this hypothesis of retardation. Schoolboys and young laborers going down to the coast, and there eating relatively enriched diets including rice, ample fish, and meat, increase in size so dramatically that on going home again they are hardly recognizable to their kinsmen. Parenthetically, Gajdusek also finds them now at a disadvantage in mountain hunting and farming in their own villages because of their altered work/body weight ratio in this difficult country and because their greater body size demands more water and protein than can be provided by the local resources and the culture.

So it would indeed appear that the little people are victims of the environment, when the disadvantage is critical, and that they actually have a genetic background similar to more favored inhabitants of New Guinea and Melanesia generally. I can only suppose the same reasoning must be applied to mountain people in Bougainville and the New Hebrides. Therefore I do not believe that the 'pygmies' demonstrate something outside the unitary, if not uniform, population stock of Melanesia.[1]

In the Philippines, the Spanish gave the Negritos their name ('little blacks') as soon as they saw them. If the explorers were mentally comparing them with full-sized Africans, the name is no surprise, for the Negritos are indeed small, as are some non-Negrito Philippine tribes. They survive in many pockets, from Palawan and Mindanao through other islands, up to the northeast coastal fringe of Luzon. Some Negrito groups have turned to, or

[1] A parallel case has been demonstrated among Quechua Indians of Peru by R. Brooke Thomas [241], in this case using laboratory methods for measurement of oxygen consumption, caloric intake, etc. People living at high altitudes have made the same adaptation of small body size, and without loss of ability to do strenuous work. Thomas interprets this, like Gajdusek, as a positive adaptation to maintain the population in the face of limited caloric availability.

been forced into cultivation, but others have continued as pure hunter-gatherers, nomadic within a limited territory. Those in northern Luzon, so isolated as to be almost out of touch with the world, tip their arrows with bamboo points, not iron; they fish from the shore and in rivers (they are essentially forest people), trap game and hunt wild pigs (partly for sport!) and dig ferns, wild yams and other such. Now this does not sound like a prescription for malnutrition, and Dr Robert Fox of the National Museum in Manila, who has had a good deal of contact with these groups and supplied the above information, says they have a great sense of security and freedom. As hunters, of course, they are different from all modern Melanesians, who are gardeners; they have some cultural similarities to the Andaman Islanders. Some have suggested that non-Austronesian languages might exist among them; Fox thinks not.[1]

Older reports and measurements of more accessible groups showed them to be decidedly small in stature; photographs of the period also indicated mixture with other Philippine peoples, with resemblances to those obviously mixed people of Timor and Flores. But recent anthropologists I have talked to, above all Fox, do not concede that there is a Negrito 'type' or a homogeneous population. While groups vary, the more short-statured having some particularly small individuals, in other groups Fox found men up to six foot in height. Skin is dark, of course, again with variety: Fox reports one group with exceedingly black skins; at the same time his pictures show a considerable frequency of reddish hair. Fox also pointed out to me a tendency in the Negritos to prominent noses, some even 'hooked', a trait which is neither Indonesian nor African Negroid but not inappropriate for Melanesians. The heaviness of Tasmanian, Australian or most Melanesian skulls does not appear, though bony brows are not absent. Altogether, nothing that I have heard or seen in pictures would exclude the Negritos, individually and collectively, from being smallish 'Melanesians'. Unfortunately, until very recent years these important people have been much neglected by anthropologists.

The Semang of the Malay Peninsula, also neglected, could be

[1] The recently discovered Tasadays of Mindanao, though not 'Negrito' physically, are obviously very small. They are reported to speak an Austronesian language.

covered by the same remarks, as far as I know, which is not far.

Provisionally, then, we may place all these pseudo-pygmies in a general Melanesian continuum, remembering that many Melanesian populations are of characteristically small size. But the Andaman Islanders in the Bay of Bengal give us pause – they seem to be different, though otherwise they would appear to be a natural extension of the 'Negrito' realm. They have their own language and enjoyed an isolation of unknown length before modern times; and their diet of wild pigs and dugongs, among other staples, should meet the caloric and protein needs of much larger people. But they are pygmies indeed, males averaging about four foot ten inches and being very dark, with woolly hair. If the other dwarfs and smallish people all the way to New Guinea look like little Melanesians, the Andamanese, with their infantile faces and bulging, browless foreheads, look like little Africans.

And statistically that is where their skulls belong. Turning again to the analysis in Chapter 3, Andamanese crania group themselves with three African Negro populations more closely even than the South African Bushmen. In individual 'distance' figures they are closest of all to Egyptians (not very odd, since the Egyptian crania also approach Africans', though grouped with Europeans'), and then to Africans. They are more distant from any Pacific peoples: among these they most nearly approach the New Britain Tolai, but are equally close to Europeans, so that they cannot really be thought of as close to Melanesians at all. By way of contrast, among seventeen possible populations from all over the world, the only individual Philippine Negrito skull I have tested in this way classes itself as 'Tasmanian'.

I cannot explain the Andamanese, and nothing is known about their past. At the moment I think they should be set aside, as another problem, while the Negritos of the Philippines can be connected with the protean Melanesian community of populations.

I have treated Melanesia to an especially comprehensive review because of its importance for human prehistory. Anything I have suggested so far – more implicitly than explicitly – has been based on the distribution of varying physiques, and we have seen in the case of Australia that such evidence has its limitations. What *might* have happened – this is the delight and the disaster of dozens of writers on the Pacific. What *did* happen can at least be checked and bounded by the remarkable and very recent work of the linguists and archaeologists.

Old Melanesia

The archaeology of Southeast Asia, Indonesia[1] and above all Melanesia is still in its infancy, though enormously illuminating compared to a few years back. For the present, in order to make the information hang together, we may indulge, as with Australia, in some hypotheses. We know that the Melanesians moved into the Pacific from Asia through Indonesia – that is the only possibility. They came into what is now Melanesia by expansion on their eastern front and by the encroachment of other peoples – the Indonesians – on their western front. This was gradual and piecemeal, and in the process important new items of culture and new languages came into their hands and mouths. They did not 'pass through' Indonesia in a migration; they owned it for millennia, although from time to time on the east one community occupied a vacant island and, on the west, mixture or dispossession was the fate of older Melanesian settlements.

This is the necessary outline of history. We are entitled to think of an Old Melanesia, not co-extensive with today's, and to begin hypothesizing about its boundaries and culture. I do not mean the settlement by really ancient men: Java Man of a million years ago, or the occupations of the Lower Paleolithic, known from an increasing number of places. I mean strictly modern man, the men in fact who are the essential ancestors of the Melanesians we know.

We can establish such a man in the Niah Cave in Sarawak on the northwest shore of Borneo. His skull lay at a depth where radiocarbon has given two dates of 39,500 BC and 37,600 BC [106]. It was not a burial: it was partly disassembled and lacked a lower jaw, though a few fragments of skeleton were present. This suggests a secondary deposition, like the Mungo find, and the date was taken from burned material including animal (and human?) bone just below it. This is one of the oldest finds of modern man anywhere in the world, and certainly more than 5,000 years older than any now claimed for Europe. Such apparently extreme antiquity (especially before the new finds in Australia) caused

[1] For anthropological purposes, Indonesia means not only the modern nation but also the Philippines and Formosa, since they all share a basic aboriginal culture.

queries as to the validity of the dates, but they are simply the oldest of an ordered series coming down from higher levels in the cave. Not far above the skull layer, pieces of large oyster shells, which were used as tools, begin to appear in the deposit. Their source was found to be a few fossil oyster beds in restricted parts of this and other caves close by, and a sample of shell gave a date [212] of 35,500 BC. The present coast here does not produce oysters, and in much of the late Pleistocene the shore would have been far away. So the supposition is that the oyster beds formed – and shell became available for the men of the cave – during the warmer interval between about 40,000 and 28,000 BC, when the sea came closest to the cave. So, perhaps tenuously, the evidence of sea levels and the position of shell in the deposit reinforces the radiocarbon age of the cranium.

The skull itself, though incomplete, has good parts of braincase and face, and three molar teeth. Dr Don Brothwell of the British Museum (Natural History) finds [25], from measurements and general aspect, that it most resembles skulls of Tasmanians. It is a teenager and a little smaller than either adult Tasmanians or Australians. In any event, it is not of rugged construction, having only slight bony brows as befits a youth, and it does not manifest the pinched forehead and keeled vault of the Cohuna–Kow Swamp skulls of Australia, or many modern New Guinea skulls. I see no reason to disagree with Brothwell, if we allow that classification as Melanesian or Australian would be almost as good.

This really impressive exhibit is the only physical evidence of man so early. The well-known Wadjak skull (the better of the two specimens found in Java by Eugene Dubois in 1889) is very close in form to Keilor and Green Gully of Australia, as I noted before. Its finding site was mined away long ago and its age is now thought to be post-glacial rather than early. So, instead of establishing great antiquity, it testifies to the Old Melanesian presence in Java at a rather late date.

Possibly in between are some sketchy remains found in 1962 by Fox in the Tabon Cave on the west shore of the long Philippine island of Palawan, which runs between the central Philippines and the northern end of Borneo. Not only are the bones fragmentary, but the part of the deposit containing them was later disturbed by megapode birds laying their eggs, thus destroying stratigraphy. However, one area, having strongly mineralized bones with some heavy encrustation is considered by Fox to belong most probably to a level dated about 20,000 BC, though in actuality he regards it as undated; another possibility is a later level which has given a date of 7300 BC. Dr Fox has generously allowed examination of the bones by Professor Macintosh and myself and some of our impressions – entirely preliminary and based on different parts – are as follows. An almost toothless lower jaw strikes Macintosh as definitely non-Mongoloid (in the sense of Japanese or Chinese, but not excluding Indonesian affiliation), but instead suggesting 'Negrito', with some Andamanese-like features. A well-preserved frontal bone, which I have attempted to analyse by the multi-variate methods already described, seems to want to be an Ainu, with Tasmanian affiliation the next possibility; other possible alignments are remote. Any Ainu–Tasmanian likenesses in the frontal bone are due largely to its being non-Mongoloid. The bone is rather gracile, without large brows, though I think it is likely to be male; thus in appearance it is not strongly Tasmanian, or Melanesian. But my analysis cancels an 'Andaman' likeness for this bone, and Macintosh's cancels an Ainu connection for the jaw. Whether jaw and forehead belonged to one person is not important. Finally, fragments of other skeletal parts suggest at least four individuals, and some of these are fairly robust, which is against 'Negrito' in the sense of pygmy stature. Important as the remains may eventually turn out to be, the above may occupy more lines of print than are justified by present evidence of either dating or racial affiliation. At best, it seems to me to constitute a slight plus for placing a Tasmanian or Melanesian population in the Philippines at an early date.[1]

All these human fossils are mere pinpoints of evidence. Archae-ological signs of ancient man in Indonesia have begun to spread rapidly since their first organization by Hallam Movius [170] and

[1] Here I should mention the Aitape skull fragment, found in 1929 on the north shore of New Guinea near Aitape and thought at the time to have come from a Pleistocene deposit. Consisting of the fore part of the braincase, it has been described as primitive, with very heavy brow ridges. The piece is actually rather thin and light, with only medium brows and a conformation entirely appropriate for a modern New Guinea native. After the radiocarbon method had been developed, the site was revisited by the same enterprising geologist who had found the piece in the first place, P. S. Hossfeld. Charcoal specimens brought back by Mr Hossfeld [118] date the skull at 3000 BC, so that its present value is to show that New Guinea natives of this modest antiquity cannot be distinguished from those of today, a satisfying but not startling piece of evidence.

others, but have only reached the stage of showing how rich this territory must be for prehistory. Work is in fact still very preliminary. To comprehend the time zone of Old Melanesia we should try to put it in the perspective of earlier periods and cultures, but this is difficult until a great deal more geology, paleontology and archaeology has been done. Today it is hard for one worker to make systematic comparisons of his finds with those made by others elsewhere, and the region's history is one which fosters all these difficulties.

In the first place, look at the evidence of fossil animals, mentioned briefly in the last chapter. Marked earth movements – rises and falls – evidently created land bridges from time to time across what are now deep channels, too deep to have been bridged in the later Pleistocene when the Australian ancestors were moving. With the Middle Pleistocene, perhaps a million years ago, a new group of mammals migrated into Java. This was the Sino-Malayan fauna, a sort of selection from among the *Stegodon-Ailuropoda* fauna of south China. *Ailuropoda* is our friend the panda, who did not make the trip; those who came included tapirs, tigers, orangs, gibbons and primitive elephants as well as *Stegodon*, who is an elephant uncle and not in the direct ancestry of modern elephants. These migrated not only by the 'mainland' but also over Formosa and the Philippines into Sundaland. One very early prong crossed from the Philippines into Celebes, which was *not* part of Sundaland and is on the wrong side of Wallace's Line [115] (see Map 5). The isolation of Celebes from then on allowed the fauna to become rather specialized compared to the rest of Indonesia, with both elephants and *Stegodon* diminishing considerably in size. This is the sort of thing that can frustrate attempts to date sites from the animals found in them, since relationships to faunas elsewhere cannot easily be established. Evidently another early land bridge formed from Java, running east all the way to Timor and Flores; and here as in Celebes the travel-minded *Stegodon* gradually evolved into pygmy size and specialized form.

A particular interest of this animal is the frequency with which his fossil bones have been found together with stone tools. *Stegodon* himself is no badge of antiquity, since he probably survived into late times in various places; his association with man, however, suggests the latter's early wide spread in the islands, and the possibility of his using the same migration routes. Whether land bridges to Timor, or between Formosa and the Philippines, might have existed for the use of man as late as the third glacial phase (Riss of Europe) is not known.

The earliest Java men belong to the early Middle Pleistocene. Tools of this time, found in Burma and China but so far not with the Javanese fossils, have been defined by Movius as choppers and chopping tools: these are crudely trimmed cores or pebbles, the latter worked on one face only. The oldest Javanese culture known is the Pajitanian, clearly later in time. It has been provisionally dated to the late Middle and early Upper Pleistocene. The assemblage consists of large and medium-sized choppers and hand-axes, and trimmed flakes running down to modest size. However, the relative age is not really well enough known to allow much that is useful to be said. Also it is not certain that the tools, showing a considerable difference among themselves in apparent technical development, all belong to the same time. The culture is reported to have been found in Sumatra and Borneo as well as Java.

From Tjabengé in southern Celebes comes another flake culture, apparently associated with the fauna I have just described for that island. The flakes are smaller than those of the Patjitanian (some of which are indeed large), and seem more sophisticated. On the face of it the culture should be later, but the date cannot be assessed at all closely from the fauna or other evidence. Finally, there is the little-known flake stone culture of Solo Man at Ngandong in Java (found in a few other sites also). *Stegodon* occurs here too in a highly specialized (late?) form; the fauna as a whole has a rather recent aspect, *Stegodon* being the only genus of animal actually extinct. Movius is willing to say that the Ngandong and Tjabengé tools are not dissimilar in appearance; he is emphatic that the Ngandong culture is entirely different from and later than the Patjitanian.

So two time levels are suggested. There are various finds made more recently, which are not yet clearly dated. I mentioned in the last chapter the large flake tools found with *Stegodon* bones on Timor. Unknown as to age, they occur in many cases on the surface; but when they have been found in context they were always lower down than any tools which could be dated by radio-carbon, or which were known on good grounds to be relatively recent. Mulvaney [174] thinks these flake tools should in fact be allied with the Javanese Patjitanian, a suggestion which would certainly imply a broad extension of really early men – pre-Solo – eastward through Indonesia. Fox has lately found a large number of Philippine sites, especially in northern Luzon, yielding *Stegodon* bones and a stone culture which has chopping tools and flakes; water-rolling of these is taken as indication of age. Fox thinks they have relations to the Tjabengé culture.

The useful connections still depend, as I said, on much more work. What we see now is simply evidence of man's long and continuous occupation of today's Indonesia, evidence which seems to predate his known use of the Niah and Tabon caves, excepting, possibly, the case of Solo man at Ngandong. The Solo culture, not yet properly studied, apparently lacked choppers and gave some writers an impression of recency, which may be quite false. Its date remains unknown.

To return to these caves, their diggers (Harrisson and Fox) have estimated in each case that culture-bearing deposits below the levels actually dated by radiocarbon would reach back to about 50,000 BC. (The caves do not contain remains of *Stegodon*, which may not be significant – in Borneo few remains of any kind of elephant have been found.) At both sites there is a very long succession of tools showing only limited basic change, though Jonathan Kress, who has been excavating in association with Fox [64] at the Tabon Cave and others near by, says there is a real evolutionary sequence. Kress and Fox note a likeness of the tools to those at Niah, and Mulvaney [172] has called the likeness 'striking'. Though chopping tools occur early at Niah, the bulk of implements are struck flakes showing signs of use but being only rarely retouched along the edge by the makers, actually less reworked than the apparently much earlier tools associated elsewhere with *Stegodon*. This use without retouch (a trait shared by the otherwise different mainland Hoabhinian culture, described further on) has suggested that wood was the real basis of implements and weapons, the stone flakes serving only to scrape and sharpen wooden javelins, or bamboo points to be hafted with thongs, or digging sticks, and so on. If we remember the simple but dangerous javelins of the Tasmanians; the copious use by Australian aboriginals of equally simple spears, as well as complexly barbed ones, made entirely of wood; similar things in recent Melanesia; and the bamboo-pointed arrows of some Negrito groups in the Philippines, then the idea is appealing.

There can be no doubt that the Niah and Tabon cave cultures belonged to men of modern type, in spite of the uncertainty as to whether the Tabon fragments have a substantial antiquity. The lack of abrupt change, and the apparently slow change in any case, argues strongly against either replacement or rapid evolution of the occupants themselves during possibly 50,000 years. In any case, the cave industries were contemporaneous for many millennia with the long Phase I of Australia, which showed little change in tradition (so different from what archaeologists find during the same time interval in the west), though it produced better tools. There is another common feature: edge-ground axes, already present in North Australia by 20,000 BC, are present at Niah, though preceded by simpler edge-ground pebbles which themselves go back only to about 13,000 BC.

So we have a first definition, a stage-setting, for Old Melanesia. Let us admit how slight our knowledge really is and go ahead. It began to be inhabited, conceivably as early as 50,000 BC, by Melanesians specifically of a 'Tasmanian' kind physically. Pockets of earlier men – Solo Man – may have continued to exist here and there. The territory we have been talking about was Sundaland, the whole dry land extension of southern Asia which then included Sumatra, Java and Borneo, and the shelf around them. True, at times the sea came in, approaching Niah Cave on Borneo's northwest shore. But at other times Niah had a possibly even more advantageous position: the sea was lower than at present, and a corner of what was then the South China Sea stood much further off, seventy-five miles due north. To the west and south the plains of Sundaland reached hundreds of miles away to the mountain ridges of Malaya and Sumatra (though not beyond them to the Andamans, separated by a deep ocean trough). Northward, Palawan was virtually a part of Sundaland, although it would actually have been connected to Borneo only when the sea fell about three hundred and fifty feet; at other times there would have been a water-crossing of four miles, and the typical late Pleistocene animals of Sundaland did not cross over from Borneo into Palawan. Obviously, however, there was no hindrance to man, who occupied the Tabon Cave about as early as he did Niah Cave. The seashore, today close to the Tabon Cave, was probably thirty miles away during all or most of the time it was occupied. This is indicated by the fact that Fox found no seashells whatever

9 The Sulu Sea in the late Pleistocene.

A detailed map attempting to show land areas and connections from the region of the Niah Cave, Borneo, to the Central Philippines in the late Pleistocene, as a background to human movement without boats. This is done by assuming a fall in sea level to 40 fathoms (240 ft) of present depth, as a good estimate for the last cold period following the warmer inter-stadial of about 40,000 BC to 28,000 BC and lasting to the end of the Pleistocene. (In the previous cold period the sea fall was apparently greater and more land would have been exposed.) The more general maps use the 100-fathom line, approximating to the continental shelf, in outlining Sundaland and Sahulland.

The shoreline was removed some distance from both Niah and Tabon Caves rather than being right at the base of their respective cliffs. The shore of the South China Sea ran almost directly west from Niah, and large and small islands were exposed. The island of Palawan was greatly extended, coming very close to the extension of Sundalar (Borneo), and may have been actually connected by a bridge. On the north, Palawan was much closer to the island of Mindoro and Panay, with many sma islets emerging to make crossings easier.

South of the Sulu Sea emergence would have extended the Zamboanga Peninsula of Mindanao halfway to Borneo, and consolidation of small islands into a few large ones would ha nearly completed a bridge along this route, although a few narrow but deep channels remained. Islands of the Cen Philippines (Negros, Panay, Masbate) were joined, but around them also dee channels persisted at many points. (Sources: US Naval Hydrographic Office charts HO/BC 5501, HO/BC 14,706, HO/BC 14,707 (old numbers).

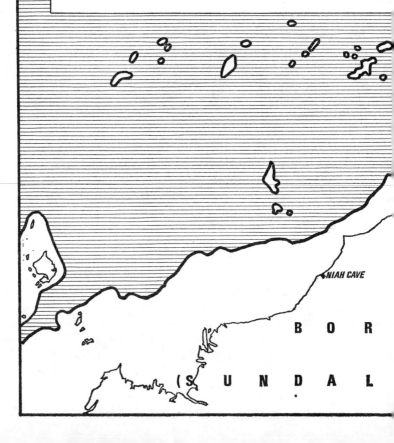

NIAH CAVE

B O R

(S U N D A L

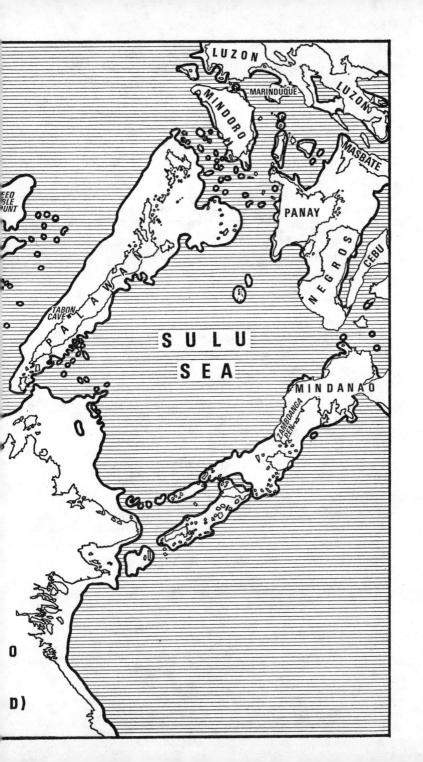

in deposits of any age earlier than the end of the Pleistocene.

At Palawan's north end there were deep-water channels cutting it off from the rest of the Philippines. But even a modest fall in sea level exposed a number of islets in Mindoro Strait; the most advantageous passage need not have covered distances of more than five or six miles across water, with easily visible land on either side. At times of somewhat lower sea levels land would also have extended some distance eastward, to within ten miles of Panay. I conclude that Old Melanesians from Sundaland – parental 'Negritos' – made their way throughout the Philippine archipelago. But the north end of Luzon was their limit and Formosa remained too far away; the day of *Stegodon*-bearing land bridges was long past.

So we may fix the northern limit of Old Melanesia at Luzon. How far it extended elsewhere in Southeast Asia we cannot say; that is something for the future. Eastward, however, we can see its first Oceanic extension: across Wallacea and into Sahulland, or Australia–New Guinea, which in human terms was annexed to Old Melanesia not later than 30,000 BC and probably earlier.

For Wallacea, the lack of information is downright exasperating: only in recent years have Indonesian and Australian diggers, sometimes working jointly, begun to get results. Those *Stegodon*-butchers are important but are not, I think, part of this story, being much earlier. Otherwise the oldest level known to have been reached in excavation, dated at 11,400 BC in the Uai Bobo 2 site on Timor, yielded flake tools associated with bones of a kind of giant rodent evidently used for food. There were also seed cases and one seed of Job's tears which was apparently pierced, as is often done today, for an ornament; however, the plant has also been used for food and may have been gathered here. The flake tools, although like Niah and Tabon in the apparent continuity of tradition, are more frequently retouched.

Since New Guinea was part of Australia for much of the Pleistocene, it was of course reached at the same moment. We cannot tell how it looked and felt to the pioneers. F. Keesing some time ago [136] suggested that the pattern of winds, with the rainier northwest monsoon, would have made the northern faces of the islands of Wallacea more habitable to primitive people, tending to pull early migrations along the more northern island routes to New Guinea rather than into drier grasslands, which he assumed existed toward the south. (We have seen that water-crossings would have been more favorable through northern Wallacea.) But this depends on what they were used to: very early man seems to have been hunting in the open plains of East Africa; and Solo Man lived in more open country than now surrounds his discovery site in Java, which contained skulls of a giant buffalo whose wide-spreading horns would have made existence in wood-land impossible.

In any case, an immigrant to New Guinea's western end would have looked straight at the nose of the great belt of mountain and highland running the length of the island, and would have had to turn north or south. New Guinea presents the archaeologists, who have barely started work there, with opportunities beyond their original hopes, but with problems also. The worst is that the first settlements, to a larger degree than in Australia, must have been coastal and their sites are now lost to us under water. Never mind; we need not presume that arrivals were early: we know it, because stone tools have been already dated to about 25,000 BC. (Here I must pause to gulp once again, remembering how im-possible such an age in Australia would have seemed early in the 1960s [254].)

Nor were these tools made by the first of the pioneers. They were found at Kosipe [279], which is at the eastern end, not the western, and the place is six thousand feet above sea level, not on the shore. Their users must have been making gradual adjustments to new foods and new country for some time to reach this altitude. (Unfortunately precious little is known about Pleistocene New Guinea animal life, and no bones were found at Kosipe.) Surely the people were hunters and gatherers, using pebble flake tools both retouched and not. But two other characteristic tools are puzzling: a so-called axe-adze, and a waisted blade, another axe-like tool with a narrowing or stemming near the butt end. They show worn surfaces but their use is unknown, since they are not likely to have been used for clearing the forest for simple culti-vation, or for hoeing a garden. (In spite of the fact that these were modern men apparently not obstructed by glaciers, we are not ready to think that the world's first horticulture was done in this corner of highland New Guinea.) Their shape does indeed suggest that the tools were hafted, even at this extremely early date of about 25,000 BC. Possibly their purpose was cutting or gathering new natural foods, like pandanus.

So the tradition diverges from that of Australia, though it is both neighboring and contemporary. It carried on for a long time and edge-ground axes, of the north Australian kind, made their appearance later and co-existed with the other axe-like forms. Were more islands added to Old Melanesia in early times? Here things get vague, though the question is important. On New Britain waisted blades and other tools like those at Kosipe have been found at several places, but only on the surface and they therefore cannot be dated. Naturally, they suggest an early and parallel occupation but they do not prove it because the types at Kosipe are not good time indicators, running from early to late and lasting to the Pleistocene's end.

Elsewhere no solid evidence of Old Melanesians has been found.[1] Papuan languages today reach as far as Santa Cruz, which is suggestive. And we may take a close look at Bougainville of the Solomons, the most broadly studied of any Melanesian island. Here an argument can be made for early occupation from indirect evidence, resting on a combination of differences between populations of the north and south which seem to be of long standing. Jonathan Friedlaender, who pointed out to me the force of this argument, has himself confirmed, in examining a long stretch of villages, the physical north–south distinctions (always within the general Melanesian variety) which were first noted by Oliver [182]. In a further study of Oliver's material I [122] was not able to ascribe the distinctions to such possible recent causes as altitude or regular genetic drift. Archaeological work by John Terrell of the Field Museum, Chicago, is also probably the most systematic yet devoted to any large Melanesian island. He feels, from his analysis up to the present, that the prehistory of the north and south has been quite independent as far back as the record now goes (only about two thousand years), and that altogether there may be three or four distinct archaeological provinces on the island, suggesting long-term cultural isolation.

Finally, the Papuan languages of north and south belong

[1] White [278] gives a preliminary report of his excavation of Balof Cave on New Ireland. This has pottery and also pre-pottery occupation levels. One piece of a ground stone axe was found, and White estimates, from a late radiocarbon date and the level of appearance of pottery, that first occupation of the cave was about 4000 BC.

respectively to two different *stocks* (by way of scale, remember that all the Austronesian languages form a single stock). These are related only extremely distantly [7]. All the above evidence might be taken simply to suggest two or more separate migrations, bearing the physical and cultural distinctions, which could have taken place in recent millennia. But the language may imply more. Professor Wurm in a major recent survey [280] of the Papuan languages (and work with these has been proceeding very rapidly) classed the two Bougainville stocks in a phylum by themselves. However, he tells me that he is now inclined, from further study, to place both in a larger phylum containing several other stocks of New Britain, New Ireland and the central Solomons (New Georgia to Savo Island); in this, the two Bougainville stocks do not seem closer to one another than either is to the central Solomons lot. If the pattern of relationship is a correct one, it would seem to extend the same indications of great time-depth – long divergence following early migration – which prevail for New Guinea itself. This may not rule out the idea of several small migrations into the Solomons, by groups already very distinct linguistically, at a rather recent time; but the relatedness implied by Wurm's finding does perhaps argue for one general movement followed by local isolation, at a time more remote. Further work in both linguistics and archaeology may make the answer clear.

In any case, Old Melanesians of 25,000 years ago and more, once having got to New Guinea–Australia, could hardly have been defeated by water-crossings to New Britain and New Ireland (which were and are minor), and could almost as easily have reached the Solomons. The real barrier was doubtless a lack of natural foods. Hunters and gatherers, probably with limited means of fishing, needed wild game and vegetables. In Old Melanesia generally these were plentiful: the Niah Cave, for example, contained food bones from fish, turtle, orang-utan, rhino, elephant, giant pig and wild buffalo [212, 106]; and the marsupials of Australia, whether giant or medium-sized, were a sufficient bounty for the aboriginals there and even in Tasmania, where hunting weapons and aids were the most primitive ever viewed in living human communities.

But the outer islands of Melanesia had no such animals and plant resources were poorer, though not lacking. The sago palm existed in most islands, and pandanus nut and perhaps the coconut should have been available. Combined with fishing, these should have made occupation of the shores possible. It seems likely to me, however, that settlement of Island Melanesia, whenever it took place, came only after an apprenticeship served in New Guinea in the command of food resources, whether the foods were wild or domestic.

New Guinea itself was apparently fully and successfully occupied by the end of the Pleistocene. Bands going along the north side would have discovered the main route up the Markham Valley to the hospitable and healthy highlands; and the acclimatizing and exploitation of new foods would have begun the process of more and more intensive settlement, of population expansion and of diversification of languages. The few early sites show some local diversification of tool forms, but also the spread of some common ideas, such as the appearance of edge-ground axes in the lowest levels of the Kafiavana rock shelter near Goroka, at 8800 BC. New Guinea flourished and went its own way, even if it was not yet physically separate from Australia.

Agriculture and the New Melanesia

The great fork in the road was the coming of domesticated foods. The Australians either did not receive them or else rejected them, but the New Guineans eventually became expert and specialized growers. They doubtless added further plants, and adjusted crops and gardening methods to local environments; today, as in parts of Island Melanesia, they often vent their virtuosity as nurserymen by adding flowering hedges and floral borders to their villages.

The food plants did not arrive in a single boatload, and it remains to be determined how far the New Guineans may have subdued particular natural foods themselves: that is, in addition to providing a staging and remodeling area for the whole art of horticulture from the west, how much they may have added by way of new plants. The botanists [105] are satisfied that they domesticated one species of banana native to the region.[1] In any case it is likely that New Guinea was far from being a passive recipient of food-growing.

Nevertheless the fundamentals came from Southeast Asia. New Guinea, we saw, had axe-like tools extremely early, though that

---

[1] When, in very late but pre-exploration times, they acquired the sweet potato, they remade their agriculture to accommodate it as their chief staple.

proves only something like cutting or digging. At 10,000 BC in the highlands there is evidence (from a change in pollen deposits studied) of forest clearing. It is only remotely conceivable that this was for deliberate cultivation. True, such an event took place on Formosa at the same time, but even here it is not known to have been a sign of horticulture. Later, however, things suggest the gradual mustering of a real gardening subsistence, by a population avid to take this road. Do not forget that proof of agriculture fossilizes poorly. But the bones of pigs have been recovered at least as early as 3000 BC in New Guinea. Pigs, like dogs, are introduced placental mammals needing human help to cross Wallace's Line, let alone to traverse the expanse of Wallacea as a whole. Now pigs in domestication must be fed cultivated food, even if they eventually run wild again at the end of their journey.[1] So the argument is that one such journey, with the dissemination of pigs and domesticated plants, had ended far up in the highlands of New Guinea (at the Kiowa rock shelter) perhaps as early as 3000 BC.

Another possible signal of agriculture is a totally new tool: the polished axe, no descendant of the old edge-ground kind, but smaller and symmetrically smoothed, with an oval cross-section, and of course hafted. It is unmistakably a wood-working implement and in the Kiowa rock shelter it appears full-blown, an intruder from elsewhere, above flaked tools at 4000 BC. Pottery, traditionally if mistakenly supposed to be the mark of the agriculturalist, appeared later still, about 3000 BC. In general, the antiquity of settled gardening in New Guinea is logically supported by its importance in making possible the complete occupation of the island, and by the fact that there are today no hunting groups at all to compare with the Negritos of the Philippines.

At any rate by these times Old Melanesia was a thing of the past. With the rise of the sea to present levels, important valves had closed, cutting New Guinea, Australia and Tasmania apart. Tasmanians had been locked up for good on their island; Australia went its way, changing by mysterious internal migrations or external introductions involving the dingo, new tools and possibly physical features not known elsewhere in Melanesia. But new valves opened with the appearance of horticulture and a new level

[1] The wild pigs of the Andaman Islands, where the people are not horticulturalists, could much more easily result from an accidental arrival.

of seafaring: to the west of New Guinea, Old Melanesia was eroded by the invasion of new peoples and culture elements, and to the east the New Melanesia took form as the eastern islands were occupied.

The pattern for this New Melanesia, or Island Melanesia as I have been calling it elsewhere, eludes us now. I mentioned earlier the difficulty but not the impossibility of settlement by non-horticultural communities. Still, apart from the great diversity of Austronesian languages, itself arguing respectable age, there is the spotty survival of Papuan languages well out through the archipelagos. And the physical variety of the peoples is considerable, from dwarfish folk in parts of the New Hebrides to large and rugged men in New Caledonia who have an Australian (perhaps this should read 'Tasmanian') look.

These things would support the possibility of a complex series of small-scale movements, some going back several thousand years. Withal, students of culture today (e.g. R. Bulmer [29]) do not think it likely that there was more than one major intrusion into the area. And, whatever the future, signs of man found so far anywhere beyond New Guinea (and perhaps New Britain) all fall into the range of 1000 to 1500 BC. Shutler [213], taking an overview of his own digging in the New Hebrides, concludes that settlement here might go back to about 2000 BC. It was achieved by people practising shifting agriculture (but also fishing), having pigs, dogs and chickens, and using shell tools as well as polished stone axes of the New Guinea variety. Now possibly there were pre-agricultural people, heavily dependent on fishing, who moved out from New Guinea and lived along the shores in places now covered by higher seas. But the sea rises were long ago; the people would have had to take refuge above present shores thousands of years before 2000 BC, and nothing belonging to such an interval has come to light. So for the present we must view the New Melanesia as taking shape only as the Old Melanesia had come to a state of advanced decay.

At the Indonesian extremity of Old Melanesia we must assume that there was a major population replacement and that it was likewise connected with food-growing, probably a more intensive kind of agriculture. This would have been an outright invasion of non-Melanesian peoples coming out of Southeast Asia, rather than a simple transmission of culture. But we should not think of on-the-spot annihilation of the Old Melanesians of Indonesia, or of whole communities being driven across Wallace's Line and down to New Guinea. This land was already occupied. Rather, when agricultural people, particularly with later crops like rice, settled solidly in country occupied by more nomadic hunter-gatherers, the latter found their game areas and their wild food restricted. The situation deteriorated until the hunters, perhaps over generations, merged with other surviving groups and eventually became reduced in numbers, taking refuge in interior forests away from major rivers. It is probable that many were actually absorbed into the new establishment. Others may have begun to live partially by trade with the agriculturalists. Such people, either Negrito or Indonesian physically, have carried on in this way into modern times: Negritos of the Philippines, Punans in Borneo, Toala in Celebes and Kubu in Sumatra; some were apparently still using the Tabon Cave as a dwelling when agriculturalists were present in the region [63].

In any case, this withering fate was not visited on New Guinea, where domestication simply fortified the existing inhabitants, leading to surprisingly heavy population densities in healthy fertile areas like the highlands of the eastern half of the island.

The direct skeletal evidence of replacement is unfortunately poor. We have considered the Wadjak skull of Java, which I take as a certified Old Melanesian of early post-Pleistocene date [180]. Elsewhere in Southeast Asia and Indonesia other skeletons, in indifferent states of preservation and excavated in the past by less than ideal methods, fail to help us much [129]. They have generally been labeled 'Mesolithic', a usage implying only that they are pre-agricultural and suggesting anything from the end of the Pleistocene to 4000 BC, or later.

Isolated teeth recovered in some numbers have tended to be of larger size than those in living Indonesians and thus more characteristic of Melanesians or Australians. There have been arguments about the worth of such evidence; I think it has merit and that the weakness lies in the dates, not the teeth. For Indonesia there are remains from Sampung, east Java, associated with animals some of which are extinct locally. The people were of medium stature, with large teeth. The remains include a large hip bone and one skull with strong brows and a brain case which could be Melanesian or Australian; the same could be said of a jaw. Burials from Liang Momer, west Flores, also have some Melanesian characters as to skull and face, though the indications are slight and un-satisfactory. A rock shelter, Liang Toge, also on Flores, yielded a fairly complete skeleton with a C^{14} date of 1600 BC and was associated with non-agricultural equipment (arrowheads, stone blades and scrapers, no pottery). It has been labelled 'Negrito' but, for a female, is not very small; it would be acceptable, I think, as a slight New Guinean individual, which is what the skull looks like from photographs. But since Flores today harbors people both Melanesian and Indonesian in physical character (and also lies in the sector of Indonesia where Papuan languages are found), these cases are telling us little about migrations or replacements.

On the present mainland in Malaya remains of skulls, jaws and teeth from the Gua Kepah kitchen middens have been viewed as mixed in type, but most of their characters seem to me to be quite non-Melanesian in their weakness of brows, breadth of nasal root, etc. Other fragmentary remains, taken in the last century from rock shelters and lacking clues as to age, were assessed by Duck-worth [52] some time ago. He considered them most like abo-riginals of the region, or the Nicobarese of the islands off Sumatra, and certainly not like Negritos; he also thought that they resembled Australians to a degree. They are in fact slender in the limb bones, and short to medium in stature. But in skull contour (as far as visible) there is nothing Melanesian or Australian; and in the lack of bony brows and the contour of the upper borders of the eye sockets (all there is to the face) they are, I think, quite unlike anything Melanesian, large or small.

Trevor and Brothwell [245], both highly competent anthro-pologists, examined skeletons of 'Mesolithic' and 'Neolithic' age from Gua Cha, Kelantan. They did not find differences between the archaeological periods; that is, I would say, no clear signs of replacement of peoples. However, they saw more Mongoloid traits in the later teeth, and less prognathism suggested by skull fragments. They ruled out 'Negrito' or definite Mongoloid assignments and, as far as they could judge, found the greatest probable likeness to be among Melanesians or Tasmanians. The photograph of the best skull does look to me somewhat like those of New Guinea in details of brow and nasal bones, but not in contour – certainly not a Tasmanian form of Melanesian. This may be the most reliable testimony available from the present mainland of Southeast Asia.

Northward, in Laos, of 'Mesolithic' or Hoabinhian age, we have the good Tam Pong skull [185] found some time ago but recently carefully reviewed by Olivier. It is certainly not Melanesian (in his and my opinion), being most like the primitive tribes of the region today, the Moi. 'Early Neolithic' skulls from a cemetery in Quynh Van, North Vietnam [179] though diagnosed as a mixture of 'Australo–Negroid' and Mongoloid, seem to me to be entirely Southeast Asiatic or Indonesian in nature, and specifically like Philippine skulls in all their characteristics.

The Sai-Yok skeleton from northern Thailand, found in 1960–1, is assigned a 'Mesolithic' or Hoabinhian date. Jacob [130] considers it too large to be a Negrito, but it is so fragmentary as to defy easy assessment. The teeth are rather large, but Jacob finds nothing incompatible with a Proto-Mongoloid affiliation.

Finally, to go back much earlier, one might argue that the Pleistocene skull from Liu-Kiang, south China, has a Tasmanoid or Negrito appearance. But Woo [257], who studied it, sees it as an early Mongoloid and its details, as far as they have been published, are not persuasive of a Melanesian likeness.

This is all a lot of detail, and I have ignored some older reports which seem ill-informed. Some writers have been deceived, I think, in distinguishing prehistoric 'Indonesian' skulls from 'Melanesian'. A projecting bony gum and an associated lack of sharpness of the lower border of the nasal opening are supposed to be 'Negroid' but are at least as accentuated in modern Southeast Asiatic crania. Better markers in the latter are a less flat forehead and less brow development, a face flat across the middle and flat, low nasal bones, together with a more pronounced occurrence of 'shovel incisors'. The inner surfaces, of the upper central incisor teeth especially, where you may feel them with your tongue, have raised edges like an old-fashioned coal shovel. It is a trait typical of Mongoloid peoples, though not exclusive to them (my own incisors are decidedly shovelled, and I am an authentic Caucasoid); such teeth are common in some Melanesian populations, rare in others. Indonesian heads are supposed to be rounder than Melanesian or Australian, but may actually be any shape. So, although such methods as multivariate analysis of whole skulls give good results, wrong diagnoses of broken remains are easy to make.

Such reading of skulls or fragments by eyeball is in any case a rather personal process, based on experience. From all this, I myself do see acceptable signs of Melanesian-like people (obviously so when we include the Wadjak material) among the meagre remains of late prehistoric date in present Indonesia. I do not see any clear evidence of them, nor of 'negroid' or 'Australoid' or 'Negrito' people on the mainland, possibly excepting parts of the Malay Peninsula. I would, in fact, have expected 'Old Melanesians' to be found here, but I do not really see them.

About the living inhabitants of Indonesia one may only generalize, since the detailed information, such as it is, has never been properly systematized. They are of a moderately Mongoloid appearance, with few of the very flat, round faces and lid-buried eyes of northern peoples like Koreans and north Siberians, or even the degree of these seen in Chinese and Japanese. The Indonesians are brown-skinned, short and slight of build (this is generalizing, of course). And the Mongoloid appearance is variable: some having it more, some less, some looking almost Caucasoid, or American Indian. Hair of Mongoloids is straight, and so is that of many or most Indonesians, but there is widespread waviness, and some very curly hair. I am inclined to think that there has been a very considerable absorption of Old Melanesians by the Indonesians. But I am also inclined to think that this is not the only cause of differences among Indonesian groups. Indonesians should represent migrants from already varied tribal populations of Southeast Asia and south China, who in pre-horticultural and early horticultural times were sufficiently isolated to undergo the same processes of drift and differentiation which are so manifest in Melanesia.

Asian beginnings: Hoabinhia, South China, Formosa

Granted that the Melanesians are central to many Pacific problems; granted that the New Guineans probably fostered their own command of cultivation through long intimacy with their plant resources (something like the Australian adaptation to the life of the continent), it remains a fact that pigs, yams and taro came from Asia. We still face questions of the Austronesian languages, of the origins of agriculture, of impulses from Asia toward the Pacific generally. Here the revolution in knowledge is as striking as anything I have yet recounted.

In order to sense the impact of what has lately become known about the paramount event, domestication of animals and plants, we might recall some traditional ideas from the western Old

196

World, especially Europe. Here, of course, the stage of cereal agriculture is known as the Neolithic. In arc̣ ̣eology's early days agriculture was supposed to have, as natural handmaidens, pottery for cooking oatmeal and other such stuff, and the polished or ground axe (Neolithic = New Stone Age), with its cleaner bite in wood-chopping, for clearing forests for gardens. This triad, planting, potting and polishing, rang like a comfortable chord down several older generations of university teaching, though lately it has sounded out of harmony. As corollaries it was assumed that, from the earliest center of domestication in the Near East, either grains themselves or the idea of food-growing traveled across Asia to China. From there, after the founding of Chinese civilization, knowledge of farming was bestowed on simpler folk in the south where, in the monsoon belt, rice, not wheat, became the staple.

All this has been stood on its head; the old triad is a discord. Ground stone tools in Australia at 20,000 BC – almost a cosmic joke. In Japan where rice arrived only with the ancestral Japanese themselves in about 300 BC (in the Yayoi culture phase) pottery began to be made not later than 10,500 BC in Kyushu, long before the western world had it, and before the end of the Pleistocene. Most disconcerting of all to high society, east or west: food-growing, the sine qua non of higher culture, also may have begun before the end of the Pleistocene in Southeast Asia, perhaps as early as 12,000 BC.

That very possibility had been suggested some time ago by geographers and botanists – at least as early as 1936 by Carl Sauer (see Sauer [204], also Chang [35, 36, 37]). Cultivation, they speculated, first took place in the Asian humid tropics with a rich flora, along the shore perhaps but especially along freshwater streams, with plenty of fish and particularly varied plants. Such waterside communities would have need of plant fibers for nets and lines and perhaps for bark cloth. In pounding out fibrous plants in streams they made the happy discovery that alkaloid poisons were released which stunned fish without spoiling them for food – at any rate this method of fishing diffused widely. Their education in usable plants led them to the idea of actual cultivation. But this was not by seeding, which means grasping the whole cycle of a plant's life; rather it was by setting out roots and shoots, an obvious and direct method of duplicating plants. Thus they came to the cultivation of taro, yams and bananas, among other things, which are Pacific staples today. Early inefficient cultivation called for the constant clearing of new ground, and the practice of slash-and-burn, or swidden, agriculture, in which trees and undergrowth are cut and burned and the crops set out with simple digging tools where tree stumps permit.

This canny hypothesis has now been given archaeological support. In trying to show how, I will be relying on recent work, writings and critical advice from Wilhelm G. Solheim II, Kwang-chih Chang and Chester Gorman. All have the gift of imaginative synthesis to a high degree and the agreement in the trend of their ideas is impressive.[1]

First we have the hunters of the late stone age. Chopping-tools, made by crudely flaking large pebbles on one face, were the typical implements, though in Indonesia the large trimmed flakes of possibly Patjitanian tradition, but undated, were widespread. About 50,000 BC, according to Solheim, the chopping tools developed into the earliest beginnings of the Hoabinhian[2] culture, found in south China, Vietnam, Thailand, Malaya and eastern Sumatra. (Sites are rare in southern Indo-China, but as Gorman suggests many may now be under water.) With a diminution in size of the pebble tools there also appeared flake tools, rarely retouched, of a broadly Upper Paleolithic nature. Occasional edge-ground artefacts on partially flaked or even unflaked pebbles occur from a date unknown but probably late in the Pleistocene [85, 88] and guessed by Solheim to be earlier than 12,000 BC.

Similar flake tools were being made at the Niah and Tabon Caves of Borneo and the Philippines, with the older chopping tools at Niah. But the mainland Hoabinhian forms of tool are not known from these places, nor from Java or Celebes.[3] (Hoabinhian tools

[1] Key articles are Solheim [224, 225]; Chang [35, 36, 37, 39, 40, 267]; Gorman [91, 92, 269]; Dunn [53]; Peacock [190]; Golson [85, 88].

[2] Originally named from Hoa Binh province of North Vietnam. Here Solheim is generalizing 'Hoabinhian' from its previously more restricted application to a 'Mesolithic', supposedly post-Pleistocene culture. Any such Mesolithic stage, as defined for forested post-glacial Europe originally, is now rejected for Southeast Asia by leading scholars as non-existent and merely confusing.

[3] This statement may not hold up. Jonathan Kress tells me there is a typical Hoabinhian site near Tabon, and he recognizes the later edge-ground tools at Niah as Hoabinhian in character. Altogether, the distinctions suggested here between Hoabinhian and Old Melanesian traditions and areas may turn out to be too sharp.

had more retouching, as well as more definite shapes such as points, scrapers or plain ellipses, though I find authors somewhat vague in describing them.) On the other hand, edge-ground pebble tools are found at Niah in a level bespeaking, from its depth [88], a date of about 13,000 BC, and these apparently evolved directly into fully developed oval axes by 6000 BC. Such axes are characteristic of New Guinea and the Solomons, so that it would be significant if they were native to the region containing Niah, but they are also known from parts of Asia as far as Japan and all their connections are by no means understood.

It is tempting to see some kind of a culture line here, perhaps lowland versus upland in some degree, but also perhaps Old Melanesian versus Hoabinhian, meaning between aboriginal peoples racially different. In both regions the stone traditions continued until very late times.

In Formosa, Professor W.H. Sung [236] has made a remarkable discovery of a stone culture. The first comparable in nature and age to those described above, it has a clear stratigraphic position. It lies underneath deposits made by agriculturalists in the floors of Caves of the Eight Immortals, on Formosa's east coast in territory of the Ami tribe of present aboriginals. Its exact date is not clear; radiocarbon readings as recent as 3000 BC seem too late and may have contamination errors. In any case, a wide gap in the stratigraphy exists between these layers and those of the farmers.

The Changpinian culture, as Sung has named it, occurs in several of the caves. Their mouths are at different heights up to a hundred meters above present water level; and since the caves have sea sand in them, they must have been in use when the beach stood at the levels of their various mouths. This is puzzling, because seas in the late Pleistocene were lower, not higher. However, Formosa itself has undergone complex land movements, especially uplifts. The culture is now most reasonably interpreted as belonging to late Pleistocene and post-Pleistocene fishing folk, using bone tools as well as stone, and surviving into times when more advanced cultures had arrived. Professor Sung thinks it most nearly resembles the Tabon Cave industry, but Chang [38] thinks its pebble flakes and pebble choppers ally it more with the mainland Hoabinhian of the south. For us here further study will be most informative to judge whether its connections are toward the mainland and Southeast Asia, or toward the Philippines and Old Melanesia.

Now comes a milestone. About 12,000 BC, possibly earlier, there must have been the first flickerings of some new ideas, especially as to plant use and perhaps including pottery for containers (in Japan at least). There were different flickers in different places, but especially in localities in Southeast Asia, in the Hoabinhian province. Here is the picture Gorman has constructed, from present information, particularly from his own digging in Spirit Cave, which overlooks a highland stream in northwest Thailand. The date is not later than 10,000 BC, and the cave's occasional inhabitants at that time were using, or eating, bamboo, bottle gourds, candle nuts, betel nut, almonds, butternuts, *Canarium* (a tasty, almond-like nut), water chestnuts, a bean, a pea and cucumbers. Many of these suggest mere gathering, but they also indicate broad exploitation and knowledge; and Gorman thinks that some imply a stage beyond gathering, i.e. early cultivation.

These uplanders were also hunters; they hunted pigs, deer, wild cattle and buffalo, goats, elephants, rhinos, monkeys, gibbons, and even rats, bears, porcupines and tigers. Oddly enough, the lowland plains are empty of signs of habitation, there being only a few known sites, all near the coast. Here the Hoabinhians were hunting many of the same animals found in Spirit Cave, but also sea cows (dugongs); and they were eaters of a large number of kinds of snails and shellfish, as well as scale fish and sharks. Gorman's conclusion is that many other such living sites along shores and river mouths have since then been covered by the rising level of the sea. They would have been most informative since Gorman (following Sauer's ideas) believes they were in just those areas where varied plants, different from those at Spirit Cave, would have been used (and perhaps deliberately cultivated) for food, for containers and for netting. We can be sure such natural materials were important from direct evidence: in Spirit Cave, the amounts of charred bamboo indicate that large bamboo sections were being used as containers in which to cook stews of cut-up meat and vegetables.

There can be no question that the drowning of Sundaland, ending about 8000 BC, blotted out such shore and river mouth sites. It also blotted out altogether great areas of lowland, sending people back onto higher levels in all directions and over several thousand years. Now if the earliest phase of horticulture produced

10 Old Melanesia and Hoabinhia. The apparent homeland of the Melanesians in Sundaland and the Philippines beginning about 50,000 BC with its first extension to Australia–New Guinea. A second contemporary province, Hoabinhia, probably having a different racial complexion, is suggested for the mainland just to the north. The boundary is meant to be indicative only, and was probably not sharp in any case.

the actual planting of yams and taro, to which the lowlands are well suited, these plants and techniques could have begun disseminating in what was left of Old Melanesia, moving toward New Guinea. But the new islands, to their cultural detriment, were now split off from one another and from the mainland.

In fact Hoabinhia (to give such a name to the mainland South-east Asian culture province) was probably influencing another major center, south China and, at one remove, north China, where agriculture became based on a cereal grain, wheat, as the foundation for eventual Chinese civilization. But south China and Hoabinhia, as far as they can really be distinguished in the story, began exchanging ideas or even complexes of ideas directly. Between the two they domesticated rice, which may first have existed as a common weed in taro patches (normally grown in wet ground) but was then cultivated for its own sake.

But let us not move too fast. Such waves of culture in eastern Asia cannot be well viewed through the tiny windows of a few sites. Nevertheless, back at Spirit Cave, another landmark was passed about 6800 BC. New things appeared abruptly, from somewhere else. One was cord-marked pottery. Such a pot is made patty-cake fashion, working a slab of clay between a paddle and an anvil. While the clay is still wet, before firing, the pot's surface is impressed with cord, generally wrapped around a paddle. A second artefact was a new kind of polished axe, quadrangular in section. A third was fragments of a small kind of stone knife, ground on both faces; though this is unique archaeologically, something similar has been used recently in parts of Indonesia to harvest rice by hand-cutting the heads. This does suggest rice, which might here have been dry rice which will grow on a hillside, but the crop might also have been millet or Job's tears.

This upland cave was by now probably a cultural backwater and it is likely that such things had been known earlier elsewhere. Chang notes the appearance of cord-marked pottery in north China and Japan, as well as in Hoabinhia, in about 8000 BC. Whatever this means by way of contacts, cord-marked pottery was present in Formosa, where Chang has been working, and events on this island, at the far end of the Hoabinhia–south China zone, are informative.

In central Formosa, Tsukada extracted a vertical core over forty feet long from the bottom of Sun-Moon Lake, the tourist spot. The core comprises sediments covering about 60,000 years, and has allowed a determination of the kinds of pollen which were settling in the lake and, by radiocarbon, the times at which they settled. At about 10,000 BC there is a shift in the pollens from those of forest trees to kinds of secondary growth, and charred fragments of wood and leaves occur. This forcibly suggests the appearance of slash-and-burn horticulture – the continuous clearing of fresh plots of forest for simple cultivation. Conceivably it could have been the work of hunters, like the people who must then have been present in the Caves of the Eight Immortals on the east coast, if we imagine that they were given to bush-burning like the Australians. But the pollen shift is a one-time affair. Chang suggests it was the doing of the next culture stratum in Formosa, the Corded-Ware people, even though the date is very early. These Corded-Ware people are known to have been present before 4000 BC at the latest, and remains of no other culture (except the fishers on the east coast) have been found during the preceding millennia, such as might explain the burning. However, even if they have not been detected, it remains possible that early pre-pottery horticulturalists, like those at Spirit Cave, could have come to Formosa, and dry-shod at that. For by present sea depths Formosa would have remained joined to the mainland until the sea had risen above the thirty fathom line, probably just about 10,000 BC.

But the Corded-Ware people, whatever their date, have their own interest. They lived, in fact, close to the sea, near the mouths of major rivers.[1] Their stonework includes chipped axes and polished adzes of various sizes and 'remarkable workmanship', which suggests special carpentry, not forest-clearing alone. There are also flat grooved stones, apparently 'bark beaters' to aid in making cord (and bark cloth like that of Oceania?), as well as other stones with notches so shaped as to suggest that they were fishing-net sinkers, and fairly large ones. However, there are no agricultural tools, unless some of the chipped axes are hoe-axes, as Chang in one place refers to them. The adzes and sinkers, if that is what they are, together with the coastal position of the villages, suggest to Chang that the Formosan Corded-Ware people were capable of offshore fishing in sizeable canoes.

In this case they might be legatees of the ancient Hoabinhian shore-using tradition, the assumed cradle of horticulture. In the south itself, however, Gorman finds the upland people of the early phase abandoning the high country sites and settling on the plains; in fact, perhaps obliterating some more ancient lowland sites in so

---

[1] Their living sites are now somewhat *above* water level, suggesting the higher sea rise just after the Pleistocene, which should date them some time after 8000 BC.

doing, thus partly accounting for the lack of such sites in the un-drowned regions.

We arrive at another marker date at almost 5000 BC. In north-east Thailand Solheim and others have been excavating at Non Nok Tha, where the lowest levels are now believed to go back that far or nearly so. Here there is no doubt of the presence of rice: rice chaff was used as a temper in making the earliest pottery at this site. Leg bones of cattle from these levels have been compared (by the very same method of discriminant functions described for skulls in Chapter 3) against several species of cattle and buffalo. They have been identified as belonging to *Bos indicus*, the zebu, arguing that cattle were in domestication [112]. And – a final blow for traditionalists – metal-working appeared here before 2500 BC, independently of developments in the Near East. This in itself has shaken the archaeologists, but for us it is another argument for the cultural primacy of Hoabinhia, which by now had lost its Hoa-binhian character.[1]

The rice-growing and otherwise progressive phase, however, had a cosmopolitan aspect, and Chang has called it the Lung-shanoid horizon. If I understand the writers, the end of the Hoabhinian saw south China in a role first as consolidator and then as missionary for what Hoabinhia had originated. Chang suggests that the naturally most productive crops of Hoabinhia, acre for acre, were taro and yams, and would have continued in use; and that adoption of rice was due to powerful influence from more northern cereal growers. The Lungshanoid, says Chang, touched on its southern fronts various Hoabinhian centers, producing pottery styles which were native growths within the Hoabinhian but bore the clear stamp of the Lungshanoid stimulus.

Whatever these fine points may mean – and much remains to be confirmed, especially as to relative dates – the Lungshanoid brought a new wave to Formosa. In the Sun-Moon Lake pollen profile there is a dramatic stepping-up of pollen from secondary growth shrubs and trees and of grass pollens at 2200 BC; about a third of the grass pollens are taken to be those of cereals. This marks the arrival of intensive farming with rice and millet, with a

[1] This primacy is supported by Benedict's finding that some basic agricultural terms, e.g. 'rice', 'cattle', in Chinese are actually of Thai origin and so were borrowed by China along with the things named. It is rejected by others such as Harlan ([105], p. 472), who says that the north China center of domestication was 'indigenous, endemic, and strictly Chinese'.

copious use of stone hoes, settling first about 2500 BC in other parts of Formosa. People of the Lungshanoid horizon [34] made tapa or bark cloth and put their houses on platforms, mounds or piles. This is a material culture of basic Indonesian type and, except for the cereals, has overtones of Polynesia.

The newcomers were the populations directly ancestral to the present aboriginal groups of Formosa, although how the links and lines run between present and past is not known. Chang distinguishes two archaeological divisions. A general Lungshanoid culture took up most of the west coast: it used varied pottery styles, and had stone adzes of rectangular section. The second, the Yuanshan culture, used simply-colored pottery with light surface markings, and had a 'stepped' adze and a shouldered axe. Pearson (see Ferrell, [60]) adds a third culture, the T'aiyuan of the east coast, which was generally like the Yuanshan but lacked the adze types, though having a lenticular unpolished axe which is also found in the nearby islands of the Ryukyus. A further note: this multiple migration implies a ready ability to cross water, i.e. a new level of seafaring.

What have we in outline? With labels borrowed from Solheim and Chang, and possibly used inappropriately:

1. *Early Hoabinhian* The Late Pleistocene Stone Age from about 50,000 BC on the mainland, with a parallel but apparently distinct culture of flakes, lacking Hoabinhian tools, in what is now Indonesia. A first approximation for a western border of Old Melanesia?

2. *Late Hoabinhian from* 12,000 BC Very early horticulture, presumably leading in different places to domestication of yams, taro, etc. These things, while taking place in Hoabinhia, a broad province, may have been shared with some western parts of Old Melanesia, and the effects may have been extended coastwise to Formosa.

3. *Corded-Ware Horizon from* 8000 BC The drowning of Sundaland, with isolation of Old Melanesia from the mainland, where intensification of agriculture and of internal exchange had begun. Pottery, quadrangular axes and some local offshore water craft were added to what had been the final Hoabinhian. Horticulture in New Guinea improved independently, but intrusions of new elements and population groups from the mainland took place into Indonesia generally, including Formosa.

4. *Lungshanoid Horizon from* 5000 BC   Establishment of full rice culture, with domestication of cattle in southeast Asia. Regional variety in pottery and stone axes and adzes. Marked improvement in seafaring capacities, renewing contacts with Melanesia, and leading to replacement of the Old Melanesian population in Indonesia through rather rapid introduction of advanced horticultural techniques.

There are other inferences to be made about Melanesia. One is that none of the cultural advances or intrusions within Hoabinhia itself, such as the appearance of pottery and quadrangular axes in the Hoabinhian of Spirit Cave at about 6800 BC, suggests profound population replacements. That is, there is no indication that the inhabitants were formerly Old Melanesians, rather than aboriginals of a generally Mongoloid nature like the Sakai or others. The one exception is Malaya, considering its present-day Negrito Semang population.

Another inference is that renewed contacts from the mainland, after the drowning of Sundaland, introduced such obvious benefits as domestic pigs: and that it was some degree of voyaging eastward to New Guinea which improved water craft to the level which allowed the peopling of eastern Melanesia before or after 2000 BC.

We really know very little about the connections of this general late stage in either Melanesia or Indonesia. Pottery was in Timor by 3500 BC and probably in New Guinea by 3000 BC, though it is not known from the Philippines until some indefinite date after 2700 BC.

The coming of deep-water travel opens up many new possibilities difficult to check. Solheim, largely on the basis of his statistical analyses of pottery traits, has made some bold suggestions. Tenuous contact, he thinks, may have existed with southern Japan along the Ryukyus – a natural route, and an area not inactive culturally at the time – and possibly taro was introduced as a crop to Japan in Middle Jomon times. (Certainly without some kind of vegetable food storage the long and strong Jomon pottery industry is difficult to comprehend.) But there are no archaeological signs of horticulture there.

Solheim also suggests that a return movement from Japan brought, or started the transmission of, a particular kind of axe and of *coiled* pottery. This is not shaped by paddle and anvil, but built up from the bottom, either spirally or by rings using a small roll of clay. The axe is the oval, or lenticular, polished axe of New Guinea, which turns up in the Kiowa rock shelter at 4000 BC. The suggested line of transmission went along the fringes of Formosa and the Philippines, mainly affecting Micronesia, eastern Indonesia (Celebes), and northern Melanesia and New Guinea. However, axes of oval section may have evolved in Borneo (in the Niah sequence), and so be an Old Melanesian development. All this needs a lot more archaeology to give it substance.

Austronesian Origins

Finally, in the balancing of dates and places, we have the Austronesian languages to put into the scale. Grace thinks (see Chapter 5) that they were distributed throughout Melanesia by 1500 BC. This may be a conservative estimate considering their notorious diversification, as well as known arrivals in Fiji and New Caledonia about this time, and taking into account Shutler's estimate that the New Hebrides were settled by a fully developed Melanesian economy perhaps as early as 2000 BC. Dyen, in contrast to Grace, has suggested that his Malayo-Polynesian grouping alone (necessarily younger than the whole set of Melanesian languages, since it does not include them all) may go back to, or beyond, 2500 BC, and that it dispersed from the general area of the New Hebrides.

Back to Formosa. Here Dyen [55] and Ferrell [60] both recognize three language groupings. Two of them are Atayalic and Tsouic, which are sharply distinct from each other and from all other Austronesian languages (including others in Formosa), matching a cultural distinctiveness of their respective speakers, the Atayals and Tsous. The third is a looser group which Ferrell calls Paiwanic, embracing a variety of Formosan aboriginals, having greater but not great internal likenesses and a greater possibility of relationship with Austronesian languages elsewhere. (Dyen assigns the group to his Malayo-Polynesian subfamily.) Atayalic and Tsouic, however, are each designated 'prime', that is one of a kind and obviously very long isolated.

Now Grace has suggested a date of 2500 to 3000 BC for the first appearance of an Austronesian language anywhere; and, following the strict arithmetic of glottochronology, he uses a date of 2640 BC for the separation of Atayalic, specifically, from any other language. But Dyen takes a date of 2500 BC for the origin of his Malayo-Polynesian subgroup alone, which should make the beginnings of the whole Austronesian stock considerably earlier. And Ferrell, specializing in Formosan languages, thinks that 3000 BC to 4000 BC is the antiquity necessary to account for the isolation of Atayalic, and perhaps of Tsouic also.

Such dates, of course, would set Formosan language separations back before the arrival on the island of the new cultivators at 2500 BC. Chang [40] says just this: that the two well-differentiated cultures must have brought two already different Austronesian languages. Ferrell admits the same possibility, though he accepts a third such archaeological culture and a third language group; the pattern is the same.

And the pattern is virtually irresistible. It points to some other conclusions as well: 1. The thesis of a Melanesian homeland for Austronesian languages is untenable. 2. The cultures arriving on Formosa at 2500 BC already had some earlier mutual relationship on the mainland, because of sharing Austronesian. 3. That relationship had to do with the Lungshanoid horizon generally, that is, with peoples using cereal agriculture, on the mainland.

Solheim [221] could find, in the existing state of knowledge, no specific culture-to-culture connections for Formosa in Southeast Asia, but only a general community of prehistoric artefact types and evidence of small amounts of movement and diffusion. He thinks the nature of the real connection would have been a common source of ideas in south China and northern Indo-China. This is just the zone which at least one linguist has been willing to guess is the homeland of the Austronesian languages. Now Formosa, old though Austronesian seems to be there, and important as it must have been for certain Pacific movements, cannot on several grounds have been the feeder point for Melanesia. Rather, the above pattern suggests to us other possible gateways to the Pacific, southward from Formosa.

Melanesia: an Embarrassment of Problems

I have said a good deal about known and hypothetical events in Southeast Asia, suggesting the force they exerted on, and the source they provided for, Melanesian history, economic, cultural and linguistic. They are at least as important for Polynesia and

Micronesia. For Melanesia itself, an outline of history appears to me something like this:

1. Old Melanesia takes shape at a possibly ambitious date of 50,000 BC, comprising Sundaland, the Philippine Islands, and perhaps part of Malaya. Sahulland (Australia–New Guinea) was added so soon (in terms of the passage of late Pleistocene time) as to be considered an integral part. I do not attempt to say what might have been the ultimate origin of the Old Melanesian population, which was completely modern anatomically at its first known appearance. But Old Melanesians spoke Papuan languages, or languages that were the source of Papuan languages. In fact, Greenberg's intrepid promulgation of the Indo-Pacific group would take in the Andaman Islands, and have the Old Melanesians carry such languages out to Santa Cruz and down to Tasmania. The continental Australians, and their languages, remain a problem here.

2. From 10,000 BC New Guinea must have had an accelerating differentiation from Australia culturally, with emphasis on the use of plants like the sago palm. This is a guess date; but it remains conceivable that not long after the beginning of the Late Hoabinhian in Asia some Old Melanesians received ideas of horticulture, if only because of their geographical position, and that the ideas or food plants were transmitted as far as New Guinea. However, signs of similar enhancement of horticulture are wanting in cave sites like Niah or Tabon.

3. From 4000 BC (perhaps earlier) to 1500 BC there was a period of drastic change in Melanesia, resting on different events in different theaters. The real nature of the events is highly speculative.

(a) In Indonesia of the post-Pleistocene, Old Melanesia was rapidly eroded by the entry of physical Indonesians with a developed horticulture (and eventually rice), and with pigs, goats and perhaps buffalo. They could only have spoken Austronesian languages, since there are no traces of other non-Papuan tongues, and their culture was of eventual Lungshanoid, or basic Indonesian derivation. They dispossessed and absorbed the Old Melanesians fully on the former Sundaland, leaving remnants only in the Philippines and, together with some Papuan languages, in the Moluccas and the Lesser Sundas in eastern Indonesia.

(*b*) In New Guinea food producing was intensified with the arrival of pigs. The useful arts were expanded by oval axes and coiled pottery, of unknown origin, but evidently not out of the Corded-Ware cultures.

(*c*) Austronesian languages spread from Indonesia to parts of the north New Guinea coast and into Island Melanesia. I have quoted the linguists enough already to show that they cannot agree on a plausible story for this. Logically, Austronesian might be connected with pigs and pottery, brought by seafaring Indonesians. But I think this would be reflected in a pattern of physical differences among Melanesians which does not exist; non-Melanesian traits of physique are much better explained in other ways. But this is not to deny some effects, in New Guinea particularly. If I had to guess (and guess I must), it would be to say that, in some part or parts of Old Melanesia (which would not include Formosa), older inhabitants of Melanesian physical type were adopting ideas from new settlers drawn from the spectrum of Lungshanoid cultures. They would in some cases have improved watercraft, and in some cases pottery, but not the growing of rice, perhaps merely because of cultural resistance. They also adopted Austronesian languages, from a not too diverse group. Many such Old Melanesians were absorbed or submerged, but some communities, under a sort of billiard-ball impact, migrated. If this area were the Philippines, for example, it is possible that the Austronesian languages of this phase have been replaced there by more recent spreads as we saw. And the departing groups, taking such languages, would have gone, not straight out to sea, but in the one direction still congenial to such people (with Indonesian settlers everywhere else): by Halmahera along the New Guinea coast and so eastward.

I am not greatly impressed with such a hypothesis but somebody bore the more varied Austronesian languages of Melanesia into the region, and I believe the bearers were physically Melanesian.

(*d*) I suggest that the settlement of Island Melanesia was not by one wave, nor by two, but by something more like an untidy series of leap-frog movements. The Kandrian stone culture of New Britain, proving nothing, nevertheless suggests a first step out of New Guinea by some of the pre-horticultural people. Next in line, the island of Bougainville has two full-fledged stocks of Papuan languages, which are related at a very low level to one another and to additional groups to the eastward. If that, and the physically distinguishable (but completely Melanesian) populations of their speakers, means differentiation on the island after the people settled, then that settlement was long ago and it may have reached further into the Solomons. Papuan languages extend to Santa Cruz, but beyond this point they give way today entirely to Austronesian, with nothing to indicate eastward movements, at this time, of non-Melanesian people. All conforms to Shutler's belief that a typical Melanesian economy was planted in the east perhaps as early as 2000 BC. Grace estimated in fact that Austronesian languages attained their distribution here by 1500 BC. It seems most reasonable to assume for the present that such a phase saw the coming of the highly diverse languages of the southern New Hebrides, of the Loyalty Islands and of New Caledonia. Only in Fiji, and special localities elsewhere, are there convincing signs, physical, archaeological and linguistic, of something outside this whole pattern of Melanesian occupation, something which belongs to the story of Polynesia.

11 Polynesia.

8

Polynesia
and Micronesia

In bidding for the attention of the sophisticated western world, Polynesia has had all the advantages. The scenic beauty of some of the islands – take Tahiti – is unparalleled, though Melanesia has much that is beautiful. Polynesia is healthy – in Melanesia, which offers malaria and parasites, one still goes cautiously, though the worst of its curses, bone-destroying yaws, is being suppressed in one of penicillin's easiest conquests. The Polynesians, especially the women with their long hair, light-skinned bodies and hearty outlook on sex, made an impression (to put it chastely) on European mariners which the Melanesians, no matter how friendly, could not match. And the elegance of Polynesian culture, visual, social and religious, has a similar compelling quality. So it was the Marquesas which drew Melville, not a place in Melanesia; Samoa which drew Stevenson, Tahiti which drew Gauguin.

Similarly there has been a special appeal for scholars: the unity of culture and language and the coherence of the rather explicit traditions and legends made it seem that the actual origins and history of the Polynesians were almost within grasp. These have been a main subject of writings on the Pacific, for a long time rather imaginative though now rapidly becoming scientific. But with all due respect I have to say that, for the history of man, the importance of knowing the origins of the Polynesians cannot hold a candle to knowing that of the Melanesians, and probably of the Micronesians also.

The older writings can by no means be ignored. They are the spectacles through which Polynesia has so long been viewed – and there is always money to be made out of the Mystery of Easter

213

Island. The writings rest on what I have just said: the feeling that Polynesian origins seem temptingly near understanding, that Polynesia is something that can be comprehended as a single entity, and that one only needs to read the clues of physical form, tradition and culture traits which point to their original home.

Here is more of the background. The Polynesians kept their genealogies, since chiefly rank and indeed the relative social placement of whole communities often rested on primacy of descent. These genealogies frequently seemed to lead back to a common ancestor, supposedly leader of the expedition which colonized a whole island group. Secondly, traditions of wars, long migrations, periodic sojourns and renewed voyages seem explicit in some of the sagas. Third, other things suggested a multiplicity of peoples and migrations. The Polynesians struck observers as being primarily Caucasoid, but with Negroid and Mongoloid elements as well. In various island groups, traditions spoke of the Manahune, the serfs, perhaps the first migrants, being subjugated by the Ari'i, a ruling caste. And there were differences in cultural emphasis, particularly in religion: the great importance of the god Tangaroa in Samoa and Tonga, much reduced elsewhere compared to the other important gods or to the interest in Maui, the culture hero who in some places originally fished up the islands from the sea. Sir Peter Buck, an anthropologist of Maori descent, held [28] that the major gods, Tane, Tu and Rongo, were actually deified ancestral navigators of a migration which came to eastern Polynesia direct from Micronesia, without passing through Samoa and Tonga where Tangaroa held sway. Linton [148], on the contrary, found in the Marquesas and New Zealand affinities with Melanesia in art forms, in canoe construction, in cannibalism and head hunting, and thus signs of Melanesian contact and influence in an assumed early stratum in some of the same eastern areas.

The many reconstructions are too numerous and detailed to review (see Williamson [255, 256], and Howard [119]), and I will only sample, to give the flavor. Fornander in 1878 traced the Polynesians all the way back to the shores of the Persian Gulf and pre-Aryan India, giving them the benefit of Cushite civilization. Such a tinge of biblical scholarship is hardly surprising for those days. Percy Smith (1910, and later) also brought the Polynesians from India, on the basis of legends. The homeland was named Atia-Te-Varinga-Nui, translated as Great-Atia-Covered-With-Rice. In epic wars the Polynesians were defeated and left India for Indo-nesia. Here from a long sojourn are further legends naming other more familiar places to be identified. Avaiki-Te-Varinga (compare Hawaii, and Savai'i in Samoa) was Java. Tawhiti-Nui, or Great Tawhiti (compare Tahiti, or Viti in Viti Levu, Fiji) was Borneo, and Long Tawhiti possibly Sumatra. The names were then carried in a new migration, or series of migrations, to Fiji and Polynesia.

Like these, virtually every writer assumed two, three or four migrations, over different routes. Handy [104] with particular attention to religion, and to Tahiti, settled for two. The first, which he called the Indo-Melanesian, survives mainly on the periphery. It came from Vedic India and was stamped with mystical ideas of mana (like Brahma) and tapu or untouchability (like caste). It carried the main gods of the pantheon and picked up some primitive ideas of social organization, as well as treatment of skulls, etc. The second wave, that of the Ari'i, brought the Tangaroa cult to the central and western area, where it was dominant or exclusive. These later people, though not themselves Chinese, came from the south China coast, where there actually are fish-eating Chinese seafarers in Kwantung, called Tan-Ka-Loh (Egg-Family-People). Now Tangaroa in myth existed first in a shell in the midst of nothingness, a void, before he emerged to create everything, by himself becoming everything. But the genius of these people was political and social, not mystical, though they converted their clan name into a god and introduced the idea of a divine chief. The kava ceremony, so important in Samoa, Tonga and Fiji, comes from the ritual Buddhist tea drinking, and the seated posture of a Samoan chief, with right foot on left thigh, is that of Buddha.

If this seems far-fetched – and it is – Handy was nevertheless writing within the modern age of anthropology, on the basis of a deep knowledge of Polynesian culture, as were such profoundly respected anthropologists as Buck and Linton. But all of these efforts and others, early and late, had a few things in common. They were untrammeled by the slightest archaeological evidence from Polynesia. They had only the facts of living culture to go on, and the above body of legend, which led to a concensus of opinion dating arrival at about the beginning of the Christian era. And everyone, much more so in the early days, unconsciously took a heroic view of Polynesian migrations. That is to say, they assumed that the voyages had come via Melanesia or Micronesia, certainly with contacts here or there, but preserving the real integrity of the culture and physique of their original homes (though perhaps losing the arts of pottery and the bow), as well as their traditions, to have them all flower again in the eastern Pacific. But the sought-for homelands remained elusive – no Asiatic Polynesia or Polynesians came to light.

Some of the others had evidence less slippery than culture traits. Linguists of the period also put their hands to tracing migration routes. So did physical anthropologists, using both living people and skulls; but I must save these for later. I am not bringing this story of theorizing into the present generation, because that is the stage of new evidence and different views.

But I must mention Thor Heyerdahl and the Kon-Tiki because, in spite of his originality in looking to the Americas for the start of migrations, his theory definitely belongs to the old school. That is to say, it rests on culture parallels (many of them decidedly strained) with Peru for Easter Island, and with the northwest coast of North America for Hawaii. It also must reject outright the real body of knowledge about the Polynesians and their relationships, even as this stood a generation ago.

Now there may well have been accidental voyages out of the Americas. The sweet potato of south America became an important food plant in Oceania, especially to the Maori, who faced difficulty in adapting the tropical plants of Asiatic origin to temperate New Zealand; and this was at a time after the original settlements of Melanesia and Polynesia, as we now know. Much has been made of the likeness between Polynesian *kumara* and Quechua *kumar* as names for the plant. Trans-oceanic contact has been a subject of lively study in recent years [201], and there are weighty reasons for accepting the case of the sweet potato, based on analysis of its varieties and so on. But there are perhaps weightier reasons against acceptance, including linguistic defects in the supposed *kumara-kumar* correspondence. The latest conclusions are that no hard and fast evidence now exists for the transfer of any known plant between the New and Old Worlds. Another recent opinion [273] is that the sweet potato did arrive from South America fairly early, and that *kumara* is a true Proto-Polynesian word, attesting antiquity, but that *kumar* in Quechua is not really Quechua, having been introduced by Spanish lexicographers who knew it. These are of course judgements on the evidence, not on the events, and arguments still go on.

Even if it is a fact, the coming from South America of the sweet potato is a thing quite different from the carriage of a whole tissue of American Indian culture and religion, to say nothing of American Indians in adequate numbers themselves. Heyerdahl has been discussed and answered at great length by others [234]. I apologize for neglecting this particular theory; it just does not interest me. I am interested instead in what the anthropologists have been bringing to light month after month, facts which are often quite as startling as the imagined voyages.

Incidentally, I do not consider the voyage of the Kon-Tiki to be relevant to all this. Historically it is at best an indication of just what the Peruvian immigrants might have constituted: one raftload of Indians, doubtless in poor shape, to be absorbed or killed by Polynesians already settled on Easter Island, and hardly an expedition likely to dominate such a population and impose an imported culture on the spot. I greatly doubt that Peruvians could have done to Polynesians what Pizzaro did to Peruvians.

Drift voyages or sailing-raft voyages are perfectly possible (and it is mean to remark that charts and radio communication make them much more possible). The Kon-Tiki somewhat inauspiciously landed on a reef in the Tuamotus east of Tahiti. In 1969 Eugene Savoy tried a repeat trip, without being towed well out from the coast like the Kon Tiki. This time the Peru current, two hundred and fifty miles wide, carried the raft to Panama. Another more prosperous venture was made in 1970 by four men under Vital Alsar, starting from Ecuador and bringing up over five months later north of Brisbane, Australia; they promptly sold the rights to their story for $60,000 Australian to the *Sydney Morning Herald*. They had landed briefly in Samoa, and it is interesting that their direction just afterwards was that in which the Outliers are found. They had previously passed well north of the Marquesas. This, like Kon Tiki, confirms the views of the Russian oceanographers, Voitov and Tumarkin [249], who find that, at best, the south equatorial current and the southeast trade winds would carry a raft from Peru not to Easter Island, but further north, perhaps to the Marquesas, perhaps to the Tuamotus.

I am decrying only Heyerdahl's ideas. His voyage was a fine conception, a heroic piece of seamanship in a time weak in heroes, and a compelling vision of what it is like to be right on the surface of the Pacific, for the rest of us who cross it encapsulated in a jet. Heyerdahl has in addition planned and led a professional archaeological expedition to Easter Island with important scientific results; and a specialist in Easter Island who thinks nothing of Heyerdahl's Peruvian theory [8] has nevertheless credited him with having provoked the upsurge in field archaeology in the Pacific.

There is one more peculiar fact about Heyerdahl's hypothesis, or any other such radical departure. The proponent, whether or not he wishes it, is apt to fall into the role of seeming to tilt against the Establishment, a fusty group of professional scholars who dogmatically defend existing interpretations. Such an attitude, I feel sure, has even supported some of the really mad writings of the past, such as those on the 'Lost Continent of Mu'. Now the fact is that, if a radical new interpretation can be made to stand up with the least degree of responsible argument, any anthropologist with an IQ in the normal range want to be the first proposer himself, because that is how the science is advanced (to say nothing of how the anthropologist is advanced). Certainly Dyen has been radical in proposing that the Austronesian languages originated in Melanesia. But in this case arguing pro and con calls for considerable and sophisticated acquaintance with the subject, not merely man-in-the-street images of glittering Incas and Easter Island statues. So a striking hypothesis like that of Dyen, supposing that it somehow reaches the morning paper, is simply not going to make anyone spill his breakfast coffee.

Prehistory in Polynesia: Language and Archaeology

Yet it is here, in the heart of professional work, that the real excitement lies. Again, the linguists and the archaeologists of the last few years have found out and analyzed much that is new. And it has led to agreement among some – perhaps not yet a consensus – that there were not two, three or four Polynesian migrations from Asia (or America, if you persist), but none at all. The new idea – and it is radical in the eyes of the past – is that the Polynesians, their language and their culture, took shape at Melanesia's back door, in Fiji and the New Hebrides, and then fanned out into the eastern ocean to produce the prodigy of Polynesia. Actually, as Green [98] points out, it was Kenneth Emory, the doyen of Polynesian studies, who first stated the belief that it was erroneous to imagine a migration to Polynesia of people identical with the known Polynesians in physical type and in distinctive features of culture and language. Though late on the scene, that is the more natural view, as against what I have just called the heroic one, so common in anthropological literature, in which a chosen group packs up its culture and pushes its way across a whole hemisphere, through and around other peoples and every kind of environment.

The students of language, who have lately been publishing energetically, are in considerable agreement. Polynesian languages are better known as a group than the generality of Oceanic languages. Even so, since linguistics is a field with built-in possibilities for argument, the extent of agreement is rather impressive. The linguists do agree, and firmly, on the close kinship of the languages, so that some at least refer to them as dialects only. The closeness was noticed by the first explorers to lend a serious ear, and was of course recognized by the Polynesians themselves. It is so marked that a local language in an unexpected place, such as an island in the New Hebrides or near the Solomons, can be readily recognized as strictly Polynesian. The inescapable conclusion is that all Polynesian languages are descended, in a family tree pattern, and in a spectacular blow-up compared to the rest of Oceanic languages,[1] from one original parent, which in those days would more properly have been classed as 'Melanesian'. There may be arguments about details of the pattern, but they concern us little (in any case I am entirely ignorant of the material itself). I have already cited one typical version of the whole pattern from Pawley (see Chapter 5), which we shall look at again here.

We may go quickly backwards through the generations of Polynesian languages. The living tongues of the marginal groups all come from one common parent which broke up about AD 500 giving off the original languages of Easter Island, of Tahiti (from which later came New Zealand Maori) and of the Marquesas (from which later came Hawaiian). The common parent, Proto-Eastern Polynesian, had a brother, Proto-Samoic, whose own brood was the present languages of Samoa, of the archipelagos northwest (Ellice, Tokelau), and of the Outliers in Melanesia. These brothers had a father, Proto-Nuclear Polynesian, who had a brother in turn, from which it separated shortly after the beginning of the

[1] A parallel in Africa is the enormous expansion of the Bantu languages from one local parental member of the much more diverse Niger–Congo group.

Christian era; the brother was Proto-Tongic, parent of Tongan, of the language of Niue and, in the minds of some of a few other languages in southern Melanesia. These two brothers came from the grandfather of all, Proto-Polynesian. And this had its origin in the bosom of an earlier ancestor still, a pre-Polynesian language in Fiji from which it became isolated by a first movement of peoples into western Polynesia, doubtless to Tonga itself, before 1000 BC according to glottochronology.

The message is clear: a Fijian origin; a period of isolation in which slow language changes established the distinctiveness of Proto-Polynesian from other Melanesian or Eastern Oceanic languages; a period of ambitious navigation in which, by accident or design, so distant a place as Easter Island was reached, but in which Polynesian colonization was in all directions: eastward, northward and west into the Outliers.

Archaeology in Polynesia, which it was once thought would never amount to much,[1] is amounting to a great deal. It is still young. Radiocarbon dates are sometimes dubious and misleading, and the earliest now known in any island group do not necessarily go all the way back to the original date of settlement. However, some of the dates already look earlier than those estimated from language; and early levels in several places have pottery, formerly thought to be entirely missing from the arts of Polynesia.[2] It occurs in the deepest layers known in Samoa, and has been found in the Marquesas with a date of AD 350, which may not be the earliest date possible there. Such pottery, together with certain kinds of adzes and of octopus-lure sinkers, gives good evidence linking the colonization of the Marquesas to Samoa. And the date, in turn, would allow for a prompt settlement of Easter Island, which archaeologists think might possibly have been as early as AD 500.

Tahiti may have been settled from the Marquesas, or independently from Samoa, earlier or later; it is not now clear. Evidence of various kinds suggests that Hawaii was twice reached by important

---

[1] For example, this 1939 observation: 'The methods of archaeology, then, are scientifically valid. Whether the systematic exhumation of pre-European Polynesian artefacts is a profitable and urgent task for science today is another question' [256, p. 335].

[2] Pottery was being used in Tonga at the time of European discovery, but the pots were made in Fiji. McKern [166], from his early work in archaeology, concluded that pottery was made in prehistoric Tonga, but the meaning of the fact was not appreciated until lately.

migrations, early from the Marquesas and later from Tahiti, the latter being the migration remembered in tradition. And for the Maoris of New Zealand the story is the opposite: after a first settlement from Tahiti, about AD 750 to 800, there was probably another contact from the Marquesas. In any case, the settlement was not from western Polynesia; specific objects from early levels point strongly to eastern Polynesia. The first Maoris found a giant flightless bird, the moa, which they soon extinguished; they also had to adapt Polynesian culture to a new kind of climate and vegetation, since New Zealand lies far to the south of the tropics.

Roger Green, an archaeologist who has also done much work on Polynesian linguistics, is satisfied that the two kinds of study are telling the same story. In Hawaii, the Marquesas, the Society Islands and New Zealand such things as fish hooks, adzes, ornaments and other items get markedly more alike when they are traced archaeologically back into the first millennium AD, suggesting that they share a common origin from a center in eastern Polynesia later in time than the original spread of Polynesian culture from the west. Such a center at the moment looks like the Marquesas. The older forms in turn converge, in these concrete objects, on Samoa. A few early east Polynesian traits also occur in Tonga, like the quadrangular axe, but Tongan archaeological forms tend to go their own way after the earlier centuries of the Christian era. Samoa, however, looks both ways: after the split reflected in languages there continued to be contact with Tonga, blurring the distinctions which otherwise tend to ally Samoa with central and eastern Polynesia. We may note, as a familiar item, that the ceremonial making and drinking of kava is a trait of Fiji, Tonga and Samoa. It is not found further east, though kava is made in parts of Melanesia and in Kusaie and Ponape in Micronesia.

So there is a coherent outline, which we can place in time between the birth of Christ and the death of Captain Cook. A period of modest voyaging in western Polynesia had seen the split of early Polynesian into parental Tongan and Samoan. Then, from Samoa, came the downwind occupation of the Outliers, small and unoccupied islands to the west, near or far. At the same time something – better canoes or bolder seafaring – led to a single foothold in the east, probably the Marquesas, and colonization of the margins began. These distant groups had some knowledge of one another in recent times, and undertook intergroup voyaging, which however left Samoa and Tonga out. Nevertheless, according to Suggs [235], earliest known levels in the Marquesas have traits which still point all the way back to Melanesia. One example is an early trophy skull with the lower jaw lashed in place in the fashion known particularly in New Guinea.

This is a very bald framework and one should go for details to *The Island Civilizations of Polynesia* by Robert Suggs [234]. The statues of Easter Island, which are more remarkable than mysterious, have been dealt with by better men than I. Nor does it matter whether the voyages which populated eastern Polynesia were more accidental or planned, a recent controversy. Certainly those which first found Easter or Hawaii were fully fitted out and provisioned with the necessary plants for survival, and archaeology [235] shows that they had pigs and dogs from the beginning. The finding itself had to be accidental, and the tradition of undertaking such voyages surely produced a great majority of fatal accidents. (British administrators felt obliged to ban ocean-going double canoes in the Tokelaus entirely because of the propensity of the people to set off on voyages with a virtual certainty of being lost.) The fact is that enough voyages succeeded, and the Polynesians took up all of Polynesia including islands they later abandoned, like Pitcairn. Knowing how they got there, we would still need to know where they came from.

The Polynesian Phenomenon

Older observers were not really misled by what they saw in Polynesia, but only by their own grandiloquent ideas. The foundation of the whole Polynesian establishment – people, language and culture – is becoming gratifyingly clear again as a historical sequence over two millennia, or from about 1500 BC to AD 500. It can be seen as a single well-framed picture, in contrast, let us say, to the interweaving events in the southern Far East, or in the peopling of Melanesia. Archaeology and linguistics are in resounding agreement now, and physical anthropology as well.

The evidence from linguistics, we saw, is that a pre-Polynesian language arrived in Fiji in about 1500 BC or before; and that its speakers were the first people of Fiji because the ancestral line of Proto-Polynesian is 'pure', so to speak, going back to Proto-Eastern Oceanic directly. That is to say, Proto-Polynesian evinces a very broad kinship among Fijian dialects, but almost completely lacks the many contributions which came into Fijian from other sources. This part of the interpretation is very important.

Then with the first isolation of Pre-Polynesian (on Fiji) there began a period estimated by glottochronology as 1,000 to 1,500 years long [189], during which a real, spoken Proto-Polynesian formed. At the end of this time (between 500 BC and the first century AD) Proto-Polynesian split into Proto-Tongic and Proto-Nuclear Polynesian. Proto-Polynesian itself, as reconstructed, had taken form in isolation, over a long period of time. This is evident because, in addition to preserving many original (Eastern Oceanic) words which were replaced in Fijian, it replaced many other words with new ones which are shared by all living Polynesian languages. It could not at this time have been in regular contact with any other language, including Fijian; and it could not possibly have been located in eastern Melanesia. It could only have been developing in Polynesia itself, in the first archipelago to be settled.

Let us be patient and not draw the obvious conclusion, but see what Pawley and Green deduce from the reconstructed vocabulary of Proto-Polynesian. The place was not an atoll group but a high island, judging from words for mountains, cliffs, rivers, lakes and even landslides. It was, from plants named, in the tropics. The people had a specialized set of words relating to marine life, and to sailing and the equipment for it. Other segments of the reconstructed Proto-Polynesian vocabulary are devoted to gardening and to fishing. All the more basic plants of southeast Asiatic horticulture are there, such as yam, taro, banana, sugar cane, coconut palm, etc.; pig, dog and fowl are named. The sweet potato is ambiguous (but see page 216). Interestingly present is palolo, a large greenish marine worm found only as far east as Samoa, Tonga, Fiji and Uvea. It lives in hollows of coral reefs and on the night before or after the moon's last quarter in October (sometimes November) it turns around and shakes off its long tail, which is an egg-casing. This floats to the surface in great quantities at dawn, and everyone is waiting in canoes to eat voraciously while the supply lasts. Cooked it is said to taste like spinach.

At any rate, the palolo worm seems to remove from the running all the island groups of Polynesia not named, since while they have the term they apply it to other creatures. After a little judicious teetering, Pawley and Green admit that the glass slipper fits Tonga best. Thus language insists rather strongly on a colonization of Tonga from Fiji not long after 1500 BC and a further colonization from Tonga after 500 BC – a surprisingly long interval before such a move – of some other Polynesian archipelago. We can only take note that the nearest one is Samoa.

Archaeology insists even more strongly. I mentioned pottery coming into Melanesia; at least three types of non-Lapita wares were present in the eastern islands at early dates. But here we concentrate on Lapita ware, named for a site in New Caledonia where Shutler first used radiocarbon to date it at 846 BC, a sensation to archaeology only a few years ago. Lapita pottery has a distinctive kind of decoration, pricked out on the wet clay with a toothed stamp – as though a comb had been used – producing meanders, arcades, Y-form figures and other common motifs. For surface coloring a red slip was put on, or sometimes a white one; and a white infilling was used some or all of the time for the punctures of the decoration. Golson [87] now recognizes that much, or most, of Lapita pottery actually lacked the punched line decoration but that undecorated pots had the same typical shapes. Finally, because it was fired at low temperatures the pottery is breakable and its surface is easily eroded, removing the coloring slip and perhaps the markings. In this way it differs from other styles of prehistoric pottery in Melanesia, which are of harder texture.

Lapita pottery is proving to be of great importance for prehistory. It is being found, we shall see, on many small offshore islands in Melanesia. But it is earliest in the east, where its meaning for Polynesia has become clear. In southwestern New Caledonia it has been dated probably as far back as 1215 BC and, just to the south on the Isle of Pines, at 905 BC.[1] It is found in the central New Hebrides, though with a later date. On Fiji it has so far been recovered in at least three sites, of which one goes back at least to 1290 BC. Such dates of course are those available from radiocarbon and may not state precisely the time of first appearance.

The same early pottery has now been found all through Tonga,

[1] A single date of over 2000 BC is reported [268] on shells from an early Lapita horizon on this island.

often in large amounts. Lapita decorated pottery, very close in style to the earliest in Fiji, has been traced back to 1140 BC [101]; decoration declined here, stopping entirely in about 500 BC. Only undecorated ware of the same tradition continued until, Groube now thinks, all pot-making ended at about the beginning of the Christian era. By this time prehistory had begun on Samoa, the oldest level known now being dated to 220 BC. Decoration, not recognizably in the Lapita tradition, is present on a few early examples; otherwise pottery is plain, and seems to have come to an end about AD 100. However, on the evidence of twelve small sherds (all that have been found), the art of pottery had reached the Marquesas Islands by about AD 350. Laboratory analysis shows that this pottery was actually made in the Marquesas, not brought along.

In Fiji, about the first century BC or possibly earlier there appeared impressed ware (decorated with a paddle, and later showing finer incised lines). It completely replaced the Lapita style. This might seem like an invasion; however, it is not yet known elsewhere except possibly in New Caledonia. Groube suggests it might have developed out of Lapita in Fiji itself, during several preceding centuries now unknown in the archaeological record. Pot-making continued into present times; in contrast, Tonga neither received nor developed anything but Lapita, and dropped the art two thousand years ago.

The agreement between archaeology and language, as to both pattern and dates, is more than gratifying if not, as we shall now see, complete. Archaeology does what language cannot: it proves Tonga was the first home in Polynesia, with Samoa becoming the second presumably at the time of the primary split in the Proto-Polynesian language that gave rise to Proto-Tongic and Proto-Nuclear. Linguistics does what archaeology cannot: it proves that these occupants of Tonga were Polynesians and nobody else. Both kinds of evidence agree that, whoever else may have in due course come to Fiji, the colonizers of Tonga had lived in Fiji and departed without having been in contact with later comers. However the linguists (Pawley, Green) have tended to emphasize isolation of the Tongans while Proto-Polynesian was incubating. Groube on the other hand suggests that the very close likeness in the earliest Lapita ware of Fiji and Tonga signifies that close communication between them continued while Tonga was being explored gradually. Archaeology would imply that the northern islands of Tonga were colonized only after several centuries, when style within the Lapita tradition had changed somewhat.

Groube, from his digest of the archaeology, has proposed a more important idea: the original people – the ancestral Polynesians – were primarily harvesters of the reefs, not of gardens. In fact he calls the early Lapita-makers Oceanic 'Strandloopers':[1] fishers and shellfish-eaters expanding ahead of horticulturalists (though love of finely-made pots is odd in such people). The evidence is this. In Fiji and Tonga, Lapita ware is found only along the shore, in shell heaps piled up by exploiters of the reef. No pig bones have been definitely detected in these layers; in Fiji pigs appear with the impressed ware, at a later time when the fertile interiors of these large islands were first being settled.[2] In Tonga, pottery of any kind has been found only in these shoreside shell middens. The traditionally dispersed villages of later Tongan culture had not yet made an appearance. On the other hand, in Samoa no shell middens were formed, and the first occupation sites are located inland. In a word, these Proto-Polynesians, after long dependence on sea food, received horticulture, with pigs and the important food plants – yams, taro, bananas – just before the colonization of Samoa.

Another point: ground stone adzes in the shell heaps of Fiji and Tonga, not numerous, are prevailingly oval in section like those of Melanesia; only a very few adzes of quadrangular cross-section (typical of Polynesia) are known from these deposits. In early Samoa, however, as in Tonga of the same period, the new adze forms were evident. It would be premature to say that any connection existed with the greater emphasis on horticulture assumed by Groube.[3]

All this makes us wonder if the conclusions from linguistic evidence need a little readjustment. That evidence suggests long

[1] A graphic if recondite reference to the Afrikaans word for the now extinct shore-foraging relatives of the Bushmen in Southwest Africa.

[2] Golson [82] noted the absence of bones, or other evidence of any food animals from the early (1000 BC) sites then known in Fiji and New Caledonia.

[3] There is no indication, apparently, that the new emphasis on quadrangular-sectioned adzes was due to influence from Indonesia where this trait is also important. In fact, to my inexperienced eye, some Fijian axes from Sigatoka [18] look transitional from oval to quadrangular.

isolation of Proto-Polynesians (on Tonga). It suggests [189] formation of the language on high islands with mountains, streams, waterfalls and so forth; but the habitable parts of Tonga, especially those islands first settled, are flat, raised coralline atolls. It also suggests a broad knowledge of cultivated plants, Pawley and Green believe, though they seem to find a particular stress on words for fishing, boats and sailing, with many specialized terms. But Groube now proposes that a strong horticulture did not appear until centuries after Tonga was originally reached. Perhaps the reconciliation lies in the first conclusion above, and in Groube's other suggestion: that Tonga and Fiji long remained in intimate contact. If so, the required isolation need not have been that of Tonga, but only of the population of ancestral Polynesians in both archipelagos; Fiji supplies the high islands. A degree of relaxation might help with the matter of food plants as well.[1]

Such was the budding of Polynesian culture. We have already looked at the flowering, as adventurers from Samoa made a spectacular thrust to the east, probably into the Marquesas. In these new groups the culture underwent refinement through special developments and adaptations, with food from the sea again becoming important. Tonga saw none of this and, as Roger Green points out, was touched by new Melanesian elements which could not reach eastern Polynesia but which greatly affected Fiji. In this way a new set of cultural distinctions between Melanesia and Polynesia appeared, with the boundary at Fiji, and with Tonga somewhat differentiated from the rest of Polynesia. Incidentally, the legendary structure of epic voyages, great wars and so on probably reflect, not departures from the Persian Gulf, India or China, but happenings in and around Fiji. At all events, it is

---

[1] The apparent absence of pigs in early centuries, and the indications against a developed horticulture seem very important. Pawley and Green can find the words for yams, taro, banana and pig in reconstructed Proto-Polynesian, which means simply that they were in use before Proto-Polynesian broke up, not that they were present continuously from the beginning. Names of the plants do go back to Proto-Oceanic and Proto-Austronesian. But 'pig', as I read it, is a special case. For Proto-Polynesian they give 'puaka', but the derivations from Proto-Oceanic and Proto-Austronesian do not look very good, and the authors view the connection as a possibility only. In Fiji there is 'vuaka' in many or most east Fijian dialects, which Pawley and Green think is one of a number of words which look like later borrowings from Tonga. But we are tempted to ask if it is an original sharing of a word going back to the pig's first entrance, a word whose origin has not been spotted.

now conclusive that Polynesian culture took form in no faraway lost paradise, but on Polynesia's own western border.[1]

Polynesian Bodies and Skulls

So much for the Polynesian psyche – what about Polynesian bodies? As with the culture, the old school favored an Asiatic source and a Micronesian route, while the new school tends to look no further than Melanesia. Green, noting physical variety in Fiji, suggests that 'Among those ancestral to the present-day Fijians, who have been evolving as a distinct population in their own right for several thousand years, there were some groups which could have given rise to the Polynesians' ([98], p. 231). A careful statement, but it removes the problem only to Fiji in the question of the 'ancestral populations'. For the Polynesians – and the Fijians by and large are near them in body form – are simply too different from anything in Melanesia to be derived therefrom by local change in a few thousand years. Let me try to show this.

First there is the pronounced unity of Polynesian physique. The people are tall among human groups generally, with male means centering on 170 cm (5 ft 7 in) or a little more. Body form resembles that of Europeans (and not of typical Melanesians) with a degree of fleshiness; on the whole, skeletal build is sturdy, and some men and women have been very large both in height and girth (reediness is not a Polynesian character). This body form is equally evident in Tongans, Hawaiians and Maoris. Skins are brown, though varying in shade. Hair runs all the way from straight to frizzly but is mostly wavy, rather distinctly so. The face is fairly long and also broad, though not strikingly. The nose is not prominent and the face is a little flattish – all these seem like slight manifestations of a generally Mongoloid character, though sufficiently restrained for the face to seem deceptively European or Caucasoid, and I use 'deceptively' advisedly.

The skull allows other statements of a similar kind. That of Polynesians is relatively large, with a good-sized and vertical facial skeleton. The flattish nasal bridge and the rims of the eye sockets

---

[1] Green makes another point: the evidence is now much against the Polynesians having carried their culture from the west directly through Micronesia, once a favorite theory. The culture boundary between the Ellice Islands (Polynesian) and the Gilberts (Micronesian) appears ever more sharp in recent studies, rather than like a Polynesian–Micronesian transition.

are set well forward on the skull, so contrasting with Melanesians and Australians, in whom the nasal bones are less flat but in whom the lower face is markedly projecting or prognathous. Brow ridges, though often well developed, are less prominent. The cheekbone is high; the base of the skull is broad. A particular feature, often remarked on, is the 'rocker jaw', a mandible with a lower border convex downward, so that if placed on a table top it can be made to rock back and forth like a rocking chair. This form is apparently as common in Easter Island [178] as in other groups [159]. Without going into tabular details, I may say that the same conformity holds for the other aspects I have described.

Acceptance of homogeneity among the Polynesians was not the rule in recent times. For one thing, there were the everlasting traditions of the Manahune, who in some islands were referred to as 'black'. This led a few writers to assume a Melanesian substratum in Polynesia to account for such 'negroid' traits as particularly curly or frizzly hair and broad noses. Other physical anthropologists, however, partook in the reconstruction of Polynesian multiple migrations from the west, in that period when such interpretations were assumed to be necessary. How they were led into this was pointed out some time ago by Shapiro [211], the most experienced student of Polynesian physique. They discerned 'types' in Polynesian communities – this one more Mongoloid, that one more Caucasoid, etc. Or, working with crania, they would divide the skulls arbitrarily into those which were long and those which were round, and again into those more narrow-nosed and those more broad-nosed. Then these divisions, by an unnoticed but prodigiously fallacious leap, became ancestral forms themselves and the hunt for their ancestral homes was on: *where* had the broad-nosed round-heads come from? The answer is simple: from the same place as the narrow-nosed long-heads, because they all came together. Any population varies, and so produces extremes of form within its own limits of variation. Shapiro remarked with courtly restraint: 'The genetic premises upon which these studies have been based do not, unfortunately, bear close examination.'

Though I still have ground to cover I can only say that I know of no indication that more than one basic population ever entered aboriginal Polynesia. By this I mean of course to exclude American Indians as well as assorted samplings of Caucasoids, Indonesians, Mongoloids, Melanesians, or in the cranial studies of R.B. Dixon

[51], such *Urtypen* as Caspians and Palae Alpines, his names for the pigeonholes into which skulls were placed according to roundness or nose breadth. Shapiro [209] permits himself to say that 'Polynesia is astonishingly uniform, considering its variety of habitats and its geographical extent'.

The unity needs to be stressed but not overdone: of course there are local divergences, but these are almost what one might expect on a single island of respectable size. Shapiro thinks that some of the apparent differences are in fact only the result of different workers making errors in measuring noses (a tricky matter), and that the one significant variation is head shape: round in Tahiti and Hawaii and especially long in Easter. He, like others, thinks there may have been more than one wave of Polynesian immigration (though all from a single source), of which the later was more brachycephalic or round-headed. Even here I would enter reservations. In the multivariate studies of skulls in Chapter 3 I was unable to find that shape (round or long) of skulls was an important kind of difference among generally related peoples (for example Europeans), in spite of the fact that it is such an obvious, though not unchangeable, character of particular populations.

Fortunately we can say a good deal more today about patterns of Polynesian difference and likeness, as relating to change over time, to anthropological 'distance' among groups, and to resemblances to Polynesians in the world outside. To take the first point: change over time, we should like to have ancient, well-dated skulls, but these are in very short supply. However, Murrill [178] has studied the Easter Island skulls recovered by the Heyerdahl expedition of 1955–6. These were competently excavated and dated to the Middle (AD 1100–1680) and Late (1680–1868) periods – none from the Early period. Murrill found a close agreement between his skulls and others of unknown date which had been studied earlier; he also detected no difference between the two periods. In addition, he was satisfied that all the crania, earlier or later, were completely Polynesian in character. This is direct evidence of continuity and lack of change in Polynesians over a number of centuries, evidence, furthermore, which is barren of American connections.

'Distances' among Polynesian populations are shown in the general grouping analysis of Oceanic living peoples in Chapter 3. This puts them into three groups: Tonga–Samoa with Marquesas–

Maori; Societies–Hawaii (with the southern Cooks); and Fiji (with one Tongan sample). To this may be added studies by Michael Pietrusewsky [193], who has worked out the same kind of thing on measurements of Polynesian skulls. In other studies [194] he has done the same on two other kinds of material: non-measurable characters of the living, like skin color, hairiness or tooth shoveling; and specific bony variations of the skull having nothing to do with measurements. Though the same island groups are not represented throughout, there is a tendency to agreement. Tonga and Samoa are associated, and both of them with Fiji when the latter is present, all three being set off against all other groups. The Societies make another pivot, to which Hawaii may be loosely allied. The Marquesas and the Maori are more removed, but the Marquesas may be allied to Hawaii in some cases. Easter, when present, appears closest to other marginal groups (Hawaii, Marquesas, New Zealand). But good data are hard to get. I think the analysis on non-measured skull traits is probably the best, being the broadest in number of features used. The tree shown in Figure 6 is appealingly logical; again, Tonga, Samoa and Fiji are distinctly isolated from the east.

As with the Keilor skull in an earlier chapter, we can look at the results when we put extra individual skulls into the framework set up by a multivariate analysis. In the one described in Chapter 3, the Mokapu Hawaiians are the only whole Polynesian population available to construct the basic framework, the 'discriminant

Fig. 6 Relationships of groups based on distances found using thirty-eight cranial features

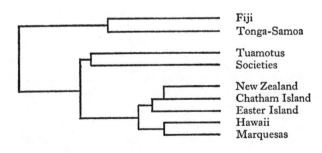

From Pietrusewsky (redrawn) [194]

space'. When seven further single skulls from the Marquesas, Tahiti, or Easter Island, are tested by the formulae from this, all of them are classed as 'Hawaiian': that is, as the only available kind of Polynesian, rather than any of the twenty-odd other possible populations represented from other parts of the Pacific and the world. Three from Tonga, however, are refractory, giving unclear results by stationing themselves in positions not distant from New Britain, Tolais and Chinese. (Caroline and Gilbert Island skulls also act in this way, with 'Ainu' being a possible position for some, which may not really be an atrocious result.) By contrast, a number of skulls from Melanesia – the Solomons, New Hebrides and New Caledonia – all class themselves as either Tolai (New Britain) or Tasmanian. Skulls from Fiji tend to fall into two quite different groups, those which look to the eye to be decidedly Melanesian in character, and those which look Polynesian. Such Fijian skulls as I have tested mathematically class themselves precisely according to this appearance.

This skull study gives a chance to say something about who the Polynesians, or at least the Mokapu Hawaiians, resemble outside Polynesia. (The cluster analysis of the living, we saw, makes them like Fijians, and vice versa.) In both 'distance' analyses using skulls they are far from Melanesians (Tolais). In the first analysis, which includes no other Oceanic groups, the Hawaiians are nearest American Indians; in the other, which includes Asiatics, they are nearest Guamians, Filipinos, Ainus, Arikara, Japanese and Chinese in about that order. These findings, including the separation of eastern from western Polynesians, might be grist for Heyerdahl's mill, like the blood groups, as allowing for an intrusion of American Indians into eastern Polynesia; but I think there are reasons for the American likenesses which are better than direct importation of Indians into the Pacific.

To return to the main point, although we can find a pattern of internal differences, we can see, as Shapiro did, an overall Polynesian homogeneity and a clear difference from Melanesia. Relative roundness of head may be changeable under different conditions, as is known to be the case; and salubrious islands and high gardening and fishing ability may have increased body size everywhere in the islands. Still it would be remarkable if the repeated small expeditions which settled newly discovered groups did not reflect the 'founder principle', that is, did not set up new populations differing slightly in minor ways from the parent. The general sameness of Polynesian outward appearance is thus all the more striking. Nor can we suppose that Polynesian populations, after beginning wide colonization about fifteen hundred years ago, have undergone in every island group the same considerable changes from some quite different – say more Melanesian – constellation of features. It may be laboring the point, but the meaning of the Polynesian unity we can now observe is that we can fairly assume we know the physical appearance of the Polynesians who, nearly 3,500 years ago, came to Fiji and then to Tonga. I also believe that among present-day Polynesians it would be those of the center and of the margins (Tahiti, Hawaii, Marquesas, Easter, New Zealand) who would provide the image better than Samoa and Tonga. Regardless of the 'founder effect', it seems evident that Melanesian, especially Fijian, contact over the centuries has affected the last two groups to a slight degree. To put it another way, as modern Fijians are moderately Melanesianized Poly-nesians, so Tongans, and even less Samoans, are Polynesians much more slightly Melanesianized.

Thus the physical evidence accords with the linguistic and the archaeological. The Polynesians are homogeneous, with slight regional differences corresponding to successive steps in the eastward deployment and in the relative degree of later Mela-nesian effects on Fiji, Tonga and Samoa. The evidence of blood, especially the absence of B, would illustrate the founder effect; it is not necessary to suppose that the first arrivals in Fiji lacked the B gene, though it is possible that in Fiji, Tonga and Samoa it was introduced by later Melanesian contact. Everything seems to conform to the reconstruction of history as we have seen it: arrival in Fiji, isolation in Tonga, and then a major breaking-up as the eastward radiation began. Still rather early, according to the linguists, was the westward voyaging which established the Outliers, the Polynesian-speaking islets in Melanesia. On Poly-nesia's west, a soft boundary formed as new Melanesian culture elements and genes affected Fiji, eventually affecting Tonga much more slightly. In the northwest, as the now fully distinctive Poly-nesian culture occupied the Tokelau and Ellice groups, a hard boundary formed between these and the neighboring Micro-nesian Gilberts, whose population had shared none of this history beginning about 1500 BC.

Like language, physical anthropology accords with archaeology; like language it cannot alone solve problems of prehistory. But it can set some conditions which have not, I think, been given their full due. Some recent students, heavily discounting the old ideas of long migrations, derive the Polynesians from an eastern Melanesian culture hearth, and have tended to favor the New Hebrides on linguistic grounds. But, as physical beings, the Polynesians simply could not have emerged from any eastern Melanesian population; they are just too different genetically. Skulls and the living agree. At least two conditions are thereby imposed: the physical Proto-Polynesians had to enter the area, surely already occupied in part by physical Melanesians, from somewhere else; and the segment of the ancestral immigrant population which later gave rise to the Polynesians proper, and which was evidently sojourning in Fiji, had to be rather well isolated from Melanesian admixture during that sojourn.

The Pre-Polynesian Ancestors Arrive

Here we go back another short step, from what happened after 1500 BC in Polynesia to what happened just at that time, and after, in Melanesia. So far we may argue as follows: the Pre-Polynesians who arrived in Fiji and Tonga were physically Polynesian, distinct from anything which can be called Melanesian. For some centuries they lived on the shore taking food from reef and sea, with limited horticulture, if any, and without pigs. On both counts they did not represent the creeping forward edge of Austronesian-speakers moving east through Melanesia – one of the later movements of settlers described in the last chapter – who were instead Melanesians[1] with full horticulture, pigs, dogs and chickens, getting into the New Hebrides, at least, by 1000 to 2000 BC.

According to Pawley, a Proto-Eastern Oceanic group of languages centered here in eastern Melanesia, beginning to break up about 2000 BC. (Proto-Polynesian of course was one descendant.) It is just in this region that most of the unknowns lie. We might as well go straight to the proposition that the first speakers of an Eastern Oceanic language here were physical 'Polynesians' and Lapita potters by trade, depending heavily on resources of the

[1] Shutler has recovered skeletons of various dates but they have not yet been reported on.

shore and lacking pigs or a strong horticulture. They descended on eastern Melanesia: the New Hebrides, New Caledonia and Fiji, finding Melanesian populations in at least partial possession of the first two but not the last. Groube, as already noted, has called them Oceanic 'Strandloopers'; they might have been also a sort of real 'Sea People'[1] needing no very firm settlements in their existing culture stage. At any rate there was no 'Old Polynesia', but only the successful colonizing of Fiji and Tonga. That is the story we have reviewed; what I am getting at is events in Melanesia, events in fact which would have taken place whether or not there existed a geographic Polynesia as an eventual home for hundreds of thousands of Polynesians.[2] Details differ from what I am saying here; and with the present pace of ideas and publication it is not possible to say who is agreeing with whom, or whom I may be anticipating.

However, if Polynesia did not exist, the events I am proposing and putting together here would now be deeply hidden, and in any case are more hypothetical than the Polynesian side of the story, to which they are an important complement. Still, there are many things we can display which both support the reconstruction and are explained by it. First the hypothesis, then the exhibits.

The Polynesians-to-be planted their way of life undisturbed in Fiji at about 1500 BC or later. Others of their kind reached the New Hebrides and New Caledonia at the same time, where they found occupation somewhat impeded by the presence of gardening Melanesians (Austronesian-speakers). The immigrants may have

---

[1] Another special reference, this time to the little known marauders of the eastern Mediterranean recorded as harassing the Egyptians and Mycenaeans of the Bronze Age. This is highly imaginary, but if the Polynesian epics mean anything, they might mean just this.

[2] Suggestions along this general line have been made in the past. Wurm, for example [41] has put it thus:

1500 years or so after the dispersal of the eastern Austronesian languages through Melanesia, another migration originating in Indonesia, or in what Dyen calls Hesperonesia ... may have reached the center of dispersal of the first migration. ... The new migration wave seems to have spread to parts of Melanesia such as the south coast of New Guinea, the central and south-eastern Solomons, the central New Hebrides, and further to Fiji, Rotuma, and Polynesia. The speakers of these languages are, in many cases, more light-skinned than those speaking languages attributed to the first migration which seems plausible if it is assumed that this new migration wave was of basically Mongoloid stock.

done better on small islands. Nevertheless, they seeded their parental Eastern Oceanic language, or dialects thereof, widely; and they also made Lapita pottery in a number of localities, of which many doubtless remain to be discovered. They did not, of course, overrun the whole region; much of New Caledonia was probably unaffected by them, with its large inland areas already occupied and unappealing to shore-livers.

On the other hand, they themselves at once began to be affected by Melanesian cultural contact and, in due course certainly, by Melanesian admixture, eventually losing their essentially Polynesian genetic nature. And they were given to inter-island movements, by tradition or by economic difficulties. Groups of such Melanesianized people, their languages already becoming distinct, came to Fiji, affecting the Fijian language pattern and beginning to introduce Melanesian genes (probably they were not 'pure' or aboriginal Melanesians themselves). Possibly they caused the replacement seen in Fijian pottery styles;[1] very likely they brought Melanesian food plants and pigs, in time for the ready incorporation of these into the developing Polynesian way of life. (Such a transfer, of important domestic animals and plants into a culture not too foreign, could be almost instantaneous and need have involved no adulteration of the Pre-Polynesian community of about 500 BC to the first century AD either physically or linguistically.) Here we have an answer for the early absence of pigs in Fiji and Tonga, together with a history exactly conforming to Pawley's analysis of Fijian dialects recounted in Chapter 5.

Such movements in eastern Melanesia, however, were not usually toward Fiji. From 1500 BC (or 1492 BC or whatever the right date may be) the original argosy (or whatever the right word may be) was being fragmented and greatly modified. The Polynesian physical appearance was diminished or lost by mixture. Voyaging, however, expanded to the north and west in Melanesia, well into the Solomons. At its extreme, such voyaging carried colonies of the new mixed breed to at least two places in western Melanesia: the northwest coast of New Britain, and the Gulf of Papua in New Guinea. But, in the east, the weight of constant Melanesian influence on the various colonies finally concealed their early nature, until recent studies brought the pattern into view. The

---

[1] Palmer [187] found axes of Melanesian type (oval section) in the Sigatoka site *above* those with Lapita pottery and early quadrangular axes.

exhibits of evidence come from three branches of anthropology.

Physical anthropologists were the first to take note of the signs. In the last chapter I named the places where somewhat Polynesian-like people are to be seen, and they appear in the grouping analysis of Chapter 3: southern New Caledonia; Tanna, Eromanga, Espiritu Santo in part, of the New Hebrides. Far away, the Motu area of Papua has been remarked upon by generations of anthropologists as light-skinned and somewhat non-Melanesian in looks. But such things were simply subjects of speculation – voyages from Indonesia for the Motu people, recent Polynesian admixture for eastern Melanesia. Unfortunately, short of impossible luck in finding many datable skeletons, there is no way of dating such admixtures, assuming them to be that. But I point out the pattern of their distribution and nature.

For language I have simply cited Pawley's report of the distribution of Eastern Oceanic languages, invading the Melanesian domain of the many isolated and diverse Austronesian 'families' listed from Dyen in Chapter 5. Eastern Oceanic is most diversified in the northern New Hebrides and Banks, making this appear an old center for this body of languages: a center which some have taken to be the dispersal point of more expanded groups, like all Malayo-Polynesian, or something equivalent. Broader branches of Eastern Oceanic, Pawley thinks, include all the languages of San Cristoval, Guadalcanal and Malaita (the southeastern Solomons). Further away are two: Nakanai of northwest New Britain (Good-enough, who studied these dialects, suggested in 1961 that this meant a migration from the east), and Motu of Papua. All students place these two with the eastern languages (Dyen puts them in his Heonesian). Altogether, the difference in the present hypothesis is the bringing in of Eastern Oceanic by the Pre-Polynesians from elsewhere, with more local if important effects.

The archaeologists, hunting for places to dig, have a harder time in Melanesia than the physical anthropologists, who generally do not need to look in a tangle of undergrowth for subjects, or the linguists, with their new tapes and old bibles. Their new results are surprising. Lapita pottery, certainly in decorated form, died out in Fiji and Tonga, but it evidently survived longer in Melanesia. What is surprising is the rash of sites with Lapita-like pottery to the west of Fiji or the New Hebrides, up to now found always on small offshore islands (which might be partly a matter of chance and convenience in site-hunting). Here is a list of those reported:

Malo, off Espiritu Santo, New Hebrides, 70 BC and later [108];

Gawa, Reef Islands, Santa Cruz group, 1005 BC and 850 BC [264];[1]

Sohano, off Buka, northern Solomons, 550 BC;

Ambitle Island, Anir group, off New Ireland, date not yet known [264];[2]

Watom Island, just north of Gazelle Peninsula, New Britain, about 500 BC [226]. The Tolai, present occupants of the island, are known from archaeology to be later intruders;

Yule Island, Hall Sound, Gulf of Papua, New Guinea, date provisionally about the first century BC.[3]

The span of dates known is a long one, from 1000 BC to the beginning of the Christian era or later. Obsidian tools have been found at Watom, Ambitle and Gawa and analysis of them shows the source to be identical, indicating trade over long distances. This also suggests that the Watom, and possibly other, dates are too late for the first settlements of such sites, considering the likelihood of this trade together with the earlier Santa Cruz dates.

The obsidian analysis [264] also shows that the one likely source for all of it is at Talasea, on the Willaumez Peninsula in western New Britain. This is just west of Nakanai territory, where the language, we have seen, is considered to be a member of the Eastern Oceanic group. So is that of the Motu of the Gulf of Papua, who have historically occupied Yule Island and the adjacent mainland. Sites found around this last place are of especial interest because, in a good stratigraphic sequence, the earliest pottery is Lapita-like, and is associated with quadrangular-sectioned ground stone adzes resembling those of other Lapita

[1] *Pacific Islands Monthly*, December 1970, p. 39.

[2] Notice in *Annual Report*, 1970, Department of Prehistory, Australian National University, of excavation by W. R. Ambrose.

[3] Information from R. L. Wanderwal, who dug the sites and who has allowed me to cite his views and to refer to a still unpublished paper on the excavations, for all of which I am much obliged to him.

Finds of sites with Lapita or Lapita-like pottery continue to expand. Late additions [274] include Santa Ana, a small island at the eastern end of the Solomons, and Bellona, which today has a Polynesian outlier language. Still others have not been mentioned in print. Dates, as known, fall in the first millennium BC. Authors also appear to be considering possible relations of Lapita to red wares of the west, including those of the Marianas (see below).

sites to the east, and of western Polynesia. These styles are replaced by different ones in later levels.

The concatenation of the three lines of evidence bolsters the hypothetical pattern of a set of movements in Melanesia following arrival of the Pre-Polynesians.[1] The key word is 'following'. The pattern does not mark a migration route, or a series of steps, of the Pre-Polynesians into eastern Melanesia; this would have been the immediate interpretation some years ago, but everything is wrong. The distribution of the western finds looks like a spraying of sites out of a blunderbuss pointing west. Linguistically, everyone agrees on the New Hebrides as the center of events. Archaeologically the dates are of first importance, the western sites being several centuries later than the eastern. (Isolated radiocarbon dates can be deceptive [101] but the solid-looking stratigraphy of Vanderwal's Yule Island sites is persuasive.)

These movements were not from Fiji or Tonga; rather, they were the traffic of the same people who went to Fiji later in the first millennium BC bringing different but related Eastern Oceanic languages, the first Melanesian genes, and pigs. Fiji and Tonga early gave up decoration of Lapita pots, so the westward movements came from an undetermined region of eastern Melanesia where the tradition of decorated Lapita remained vigorous longer, and from which descendants of the Pre-Polynesians could still have physical effects on communities where they settled. One puzzling feature is the quadrangular axes of the early Yule Island deposits, so reminiscent of developed Polynesian forms, of the phase of the late first millennium BC. Still, this is right for the provisional age of the occupation at Yule Island, and perhaps we are too rigid if we exclude the then emerging Polynesians from having any influence at all on the west.

The well-known Polynesian Outliers help to put this in perspective. These are colonies mostly on small and isolated islands or atolls, not near larger islands, and can be easily identified as

[1] The correspondences are far from complete. The Motu area has a language allied to Eastern Oceanic, important Lapita-like early pottery, and non-Melanesian physical traits – all three markers. The Nakanai area has no visible signs of 'Polynesian' physical traits, though the language and pottery markers are there. Tanna and Eromanga, in the southern New Hebrides, on the contrary, have the Polynesian aspects of physique but have isolated languages, and no signs of any pottery at all, past or present. The New Hebrides elsewhere are rife with Eastern Oceanic languages but New Caledonia, with very early Lapita in the south and some Polynesian traits as well, has no Eastern Oceanic languages at all.

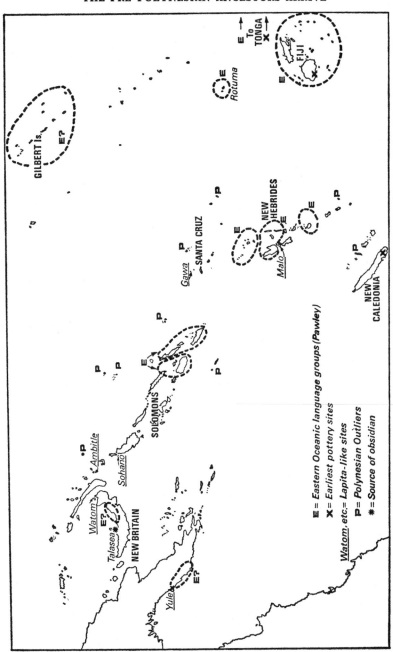

E = Eastern Oceanic language groups (Pawley)

X = Earliest pottery sites

Watom. etc.= Lapita-like sites

P = Polynesian Outliers

✳ = Source of obsidian

12   Melanesian and Polynesian origins: language and pottery.

being distinctly Polynesian in language and culture, if not always in physique. Naturally they were seized on by some early writers as left-overs from the Polynesian 'migration', but linguistic analysis has long since shown them to be closely related and probably to stem from Proto-Samoic. So they are not earlier than the departure of the migrants to eastern Polynesia in the first centuries AD, and probably came originally from Samoa and through the Ellice Islands. Therefore they are clearly distinguished from earlier Lapita bearers from Pre-Polynesian communities in eastern Melanesia and they occupied more isolated islets.

Accordingly, I would view the earlier movements as I have described them: voyages by increasingly mixed descendants of the original Pre-Polynesians, a few hundred to a thousand years after the original invasion of eastern Melanesia. This set of movements was not specifically Polynesian in character (though partly so in physique), like the Outlier colonizers. But it supports the idea of a broader Pre-Polynesian phenomenon. Pawley and Green point to the alacrity with which the actual Polynesians took up any un-inhabited land to the west by occupying the Outliers, and the remark can be extended to the earlier groups. So we assume by this evidence also that Melanesia was solidly occupied, and the implication is that the same was true during the still earlier movement of the Pre-Polynesians into the east.

All the above is one hypothesis, and a hypothesis only, to pull together present knowledge. Archaeology still has much to contribute, and linguistic subtleties are sure to introduce difficulties. But we come to the final question: where did the Pre-Polynesians come from? We cannot think about this until we have considered the last piece of Oceania.

The Micronesians

Micronesia, in the history of popular interest, is Polynesia's poor relation. Very few ordinary citizens can tell you what or where Micronesia is or who owns it; and fewer care. It has been handed about almost casually. Although traders and missionaries of various nationalities poked about in it, all except the Gilberts came under Spanish control for three centuries. When in 1898 the United States ended Spanish power, it took Guam and allowed Spain to sell the rest of her possessions to Germany. In 1914 Japan at no military cost took them from Germany, and in 1944–5 the

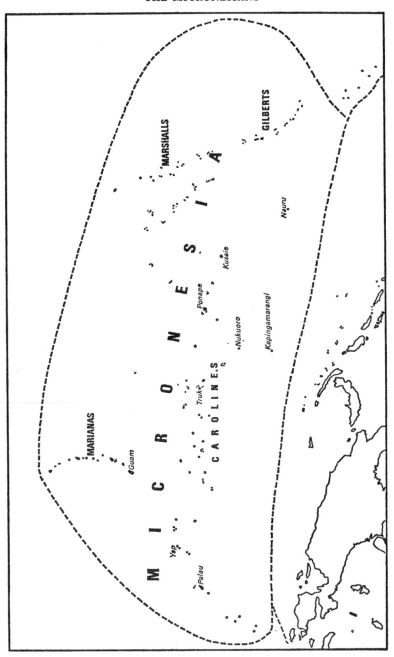

13 Micronesia.

United States at great military cost took them from Japan, and now holds them in trust. Except for such mutual benefits as some military bases, the Micronesians and the American government seem equally undelighted with the situation. But the Micronesians are more used to it.

Micronesia generates little public excitement. There is the stone money of Yap. The toadstool-like limestone remains of the 'latte' structures of the Marianas, and the monumental stone walls of Nan Matol in Ponape, present also on Kusaie, have not set belles-lettres abuzz with talk about settlement by Incas from Peru. There has been good archaeological work but not much of it. The physical anthropology, except for blood typing, is deplorable; there has been nothing to compare with the monographic studies of Polynesian groups, and by and large skulls are extremely scarce in collections. Only the social anthropologists, and increasingly the linguists, have paid Micronesia its due. But social anthropologists normally have a rather cursory interest in prehistory and physique. So the information which might be put together here is of the poorest; one is tempted to say, as does almost every treatise on Oceania, that the Micronesians are 'varied', exhibiting likenesses to Polynesians, Indonesians and Melanesians.[1] That is generally the beginning and the end of consideration of Micronesia's contribution to light on the past. It is quite unjustified.

Let us not despair. What I say about the Micronesians will have to be partly impressionistic, the best I can do. By way of organization I will divide Micronesia into three parts, east to west. The first, with the Marshalls to the north and the Gilberts astride the equator to the south, consists of clusters of atolls which make a line pointing southeast via the Ellice Islands into the heart of the Fiji–Samoa–Tonga triangle. They are Micronesian in language and culture (though Gilbertese may be more closely related to Polynesian linguistically, as a possible member of Eastern Oceanic according to Pawley). The natives are, however, fairly close to Polynesians in appearance. Relatively light-skinned on the average, they can be quite dark from tanning. If either population is darker it is the Gilbertese, I am told by those with long contact with both; but I have not seen particularly dark individuals in

---

[1] In a large Italian survey of peoples of the world [13] the section on 'Polynesians and Micronesians' devotes fifty-six pages to Polynesia and not quite two to Micronesia.

Gilbertese residing in the Solomons, and among Marshallese I
have seen none with very dark skins. Marshall Islands men are
rather heavy set but not tall. They have slanting foreheads but
straight faces, with fairly prominent facial features. Hair is curly
to straight, and in middle-aged men commonly gray. All these
traits are those of Polynesians also, and to my eye Marshall
Islanders do indeed look very Polynesian. In the general crude
cluster analysis in Chapter 3, two sets of Marshallese fall in branch
D2, with Carolinians rather than with Polynesians. This place-
ment probably results from shorter stature, since the other scores
derived from measured features put them nearer to the Tonga–
Samoa group, and specifically to the northern Cook Islands.

The Gilbertese could not be entered into my analysis at all,
because of the wretched state of knowledge. They are, however,
apparently taller than the other Micronesians, being of Polynesian
size. For the rest of their appearance, I can only repeat that, to me,
they look like Polynesians. This is not to say that they, or the
Marshallese, are not different, but that from all I can find out they
fall, physically, in a particularly Polynesian-like category.

The second division contains the whole east–west stretch of the
Carolines with the exception of Yap and Palau. All but Truk,
Ponape, Kusaie and Nauru are atolls.[1] Truk has several moderate-
sized 'high' volcanic islands set in an immense lagoon, a combination which is surely the world's finest natural harbor, as the
Japanese, who based their Pacific navy on Truk, well appreciated.
Ponape and Kusaie consist, in that order, of more high land and
less lagoon. None has an island over ten miles across. Nauru is a
raised atoll.

In the cluster analysis of living peoples, all the groups on
record fall together in one branch. Those in the more typically
Carolinian sub-branch are especially narrow in head, face and
nose (for Pacific peoples); in the other sub-branch, along with
various Melanesians, fall Truk and the neighboring Mortlocks and
Kusaie; these people appear to have smaller faces. Now the
Carolinians, although in many ways recalling Polynesians physically, evidently have varying degrees of Melanesian admixture.
They are somewhat shorter than Polynesians, without being short.
To talk of Truk particularly, people here seem average in size by
our standards and are sturdily built; they can be quite fat, the

[1] Politically, Nauru is not part of the Carolines.

women especially – a Polynesian failing as well – but none are
tall. Appearance ranges from a Polynesian look to a decidedly
Melanesian one; let us say from an 'almond' eye to heavy brows,
deep-set eyes and a short, broad face. Skin color is definitely
darker than in the Marshalls and Gilberts, as dark on the average
as some of the less black Melanesian peoples. Hair, while running
from straight to ringlets, is also frizzy and fine-textured in almost
everyone. (There is none of the juvenile light hair seen in Melanesia.)

I would say, as a present approximation, that the Trukese are a
mixture, not thoroughly stirred, of a moderate-sized Polynesian-
like population and a Melanesian one. I say 'Polynesian-like'
advisedly, as a description, not as an estimation that some direct
connection with Polynesians is involved. The people differ from
Fijians in their smaller size and narrow heads and faces. I cannot
say what uniformity this rough description would have for the
rest of the Carolines. I suspect that the Melanesian aspect is less
pronounced elsewhere, if only from the groupings shown in
Chapter 3; and I think Ponapeans are more Polynesian in their
appearance than the Trukese.

The third division runs north and south along a submerged
mountain chain forming the eastern rim of the Philippine Sea and
consists of three major groups: the Marianas, Yap and Palau. The
Marianas are good-sized basalt islands covered with coral limestone, reefed on the western sides and directly exposed to heavy
Pacific surf on the eastern. Yap and Palau are high islands (Palau
is a bunched group), each surrounded by reefs. Thus these three
bend away from the Philippines in line to the north, with Palau,
the nearest, about five hundred miles to the east of Mindanao. It is
not because of special likeness that I group them together, but
rather because of their being distinct from the rest of Micronesia.
Palau and the Marianas have languages which by Dyen are
ranked as Malayo-Polynesian but, as single languages, strongly
and separately independent; that is to say, each stands equivalent
in distinctiveness to the whole Heonesian subfamily (which
contains Polynesian, Carolinian, Gilbertese, etc.), and to the two
Indonesian subfamilies. Others [31] rate them as 'Indonesian' of
Philippine affiliation. Yapese is still more individual within the
whole Austronesian stock. The three island groups are the only
areas in Micronesia known to have made pottery, the practice

continuing into modern times. The Marianas people were also the only Oceanic growers of rice at the time of contact; however, like the rest of Micronesia, they at no time had either dogs or pigs.[1] Finally, in my analysis of measurements of the living in Chapter 3, the three areas are grouped separate from all other Micronesians. They fall in the 'B' branch with a variety of Melanesian populations, but these are Melanesians whom I believe in most cases to have physical admixture from Micronesians or 'Polynesians'.

I do not entirely know the meaning of the last fact, the separation from other Micronesians physically. I am not persuaded of close community of biological ancestry among the three. My analysis included only Oceanic peoples; if a variety of Indonesian samples had been present, they might have given a different picture; that is, they might have exhibited affiliations unreadable from the one analysis. The three seem to me to diverge from one another in 'racial' nature. Palauans are described by Force [62] as highly variable: light to dark brown skin with reddish tinges, and reddish tinges also in the hair, which is dark brown to black and frizzly to straight. The somewhat Mongoloid look of the eye seen in other Micronesians is less evident here. Build is stocky and short, and pictures are not evocative of Polynesian appearance, recalling rather that of the Philippines, though not strikingly. Melanesian admixture is certainly suggested in all this; according to Force, Palauan folk tales give evidence of contact with Yap, the Philippines, the central Carolines and Melanesia.

As to Yap, the same holds: quite clearly much of a Melanesian character is present in physical traits, on a base which suggests something akin to both Indonesians and Polynesians. There may be an even more positive spread of individual appearance on Yap. A rigid caste system exists – for how long no one can say – and Mrs Inez de Beauclaire suggests ([49] and in conversation) that castaways, who might easily include some Melanesians, were always relegated to the deprived caste. This kind of segregation would tend to preserve a whole configuration of Melanesian or 'Negritic' traits, rather than simply to make their separate emergence from the gene pool more frequent, so that variety would follow caste lines. As far as photographs indicate, men of higher rank are

---

[1] Dogs were present at the time of European discovery in Truk and Ponape, but in the absence of adequate archaeology the antiquity of their presence is unknown.

definitely less 'Melanesian' and more bearded, long-faced and 'Polynesian-like' in appearance. Such a situation makes selection of individuals for a study sample a special problem.

As to the Marianas, there are other obstacles. The Spanish, impatient with local insubordination and insurrection in the sixteenth century, simply cleaned out all the islands north of Rota and brought the Chamorros (the native inhabitants) to Guam, where they could be more efficiently Catholicized, cleansed of native cultural ideas and otherwise brought into the light. Fortunately for anthropology the plan was by no means a complete success. The natives lost the old crafts of pot-making and of constructing sailing outrigger canoes, but they kept their language. The Chamorro population intermarried from this time on with Spanish, Filipinos and Mexicans especially, and is therefore believed to have become much mixed; it also fell drastically in numbers. So, with Saipan finally resettled after over two hundred years, the modern Chamorro population there is not native to the island but simply a sampling of the same kind of population which had developed on Guam, and one which might bear very little relation to the original one.

Nevertheless it may be that the Chamorros have not been as fully denatured as this suggests, if the sample measured on Saipan and used in my analysis still takes the position it does. In addition, blood evidence (Chapter 4) fails to suggest substantial European or Asiatic hybridizing with the Chamorros. The most useful evidence is that of skulls from the pre-Spanish period dug up around latte remains on Guam and preserved in the Bishop Museum, the only respectable group of Micronesian skulls from a single island that I know of. In the family tree in Chapter 3, the male Guam group clusters with the Hawaiians, but this is a result of previous clustering of various far-eastern peoples who are particularly close to one another, leaving the Guamanians to look elsewhere. In the actual distances between groups, those closest to Guam are: Philippines (2·51), Hainan Chinese (2·99), Shang Dynasty Chinese (3·02), Atayals of Formosa (3·30), south Japanese (3·35), north Japanese (3·60) and then Hawaiians (3·78), followed by American Indians and Ainus. Among the female groups (from which Philippines and Shang series are missing) Guam clusters directly with the Hainan Chinese, and the distances from Guam are: Hainan 1·47, south Japan 2·11, Atayals 2·26, north Japan

2·75, Arikara Indians 2·78, Ainus 3·06 and then Hawaiians 3·60. In all cases, of course, Guam is most distant from Melanesians and Australians.[1] Now all this speaks against any special close connection with Polynesians and in favor of broad affiliation with Asiatic or Indonesian peoples, or others of a general Mongoloid extraction, like American Indians. At the same time the skulls, though they have prominent and flaring cheekbones, do not look particularly like such Mongoloids, being rather massive, with strong markings of muscle attachments. (Breadths across the cheekbones are equalled only by Buriats of Siberia; while the root of the nose is not recessed notably under the brows, brow projection on either side of the middle is surpassed only by Melanesians and Australians.) One particular point of importance: shovelling of the incisor teeth (see page 195) is notable for its absence or light development, whereas this is a trait marked in Filipinos, Asiatics generally, American Indians, and to a small degree in Polynesians.

The living people of Rota, the only Mariana natives outside Guam not uprooted by the Spanish, should be nearest the old Chamorro population on the face of it. Such Rotans as I have seen have the broad heavy faces of the Guamanian skulls, evidently with the same kind of flaring cheekbone and well-developed brow ridges. Now all this is going over the Marianas with a fine-toothed comb, in a book which I hope will be read by a few readers less avid than I in such details of shapes and statistics. This is why: many books have been written about where the Polynesians came from but nobody cares a straw where the Guamanians came from. And yet it is probable that they can tell at least as much about the peopling of the Pacific as can the Polynesians. Before bringing it up again, I will give my opinion from the above evidence that the people, at least of Rota, are something like the Ainu in this way: they are left-overs of a time when Japan, the Ryukyus, Formosa and the southeastern mainland of China were occupied by pre-agricultural or simple horticultural peoples, living in much more of a tribal or local organization than recent Asiatics, and varying physically from group to group over a wide range from something as 'Caucasoid' as the Ainu to something as 'Mongoloid', let us say,

---

[1] Two lone skulls from Tinian Island, between Guam and Saipan, classify themselves as 'Guam', from among all the other possibilities named, which is a small sign of legitimacy of the skull evidence.

as the Atayals of Formosa. The original Guamanians probably came close to neither end of this scale, though having some characters of each. They were not, in the classic explanation, a 'mixture of Caucasoid and Mongoloid elements' – they are simply what they are, from past evolution and drift among local groups, as in the picture of New Guinea. The flaring cheekbones are repeated in some skulls from islands in the Ryukyus which, like the Guam skulls, have an almost impartial likeness, in statistical classification, to Japanese, Chinese, Ainus, Filipinos and Guamanians themselves. But I am not thereby tracing the last-named to the Ryukyus.

First Notes on the Micronesian Past

Finally, this third division of Micronesia affords the only prehistory attempted so far. Pottery and building sites suggest good-sized populations and indicate contacts among the three island groups as well as with the Philippines, with Indonesia further to the southwest, and with Melanesia; but they also point to individual local developments. Osborne [186] made surface examinations of extensive prehistoric terraces in Palau but was unable to determine if they had anything to do with agriculture (the rice of the Marianas was absent here), or reflected contact with the Philippines. He allows that they could very well have been for taro cultivation. In a general reconnaissance he found a great many sites with pottery remains in all islands of the group, but he was able to do only limited test digging. Most of the sites would probably fall in the Christian era, which Osborne thinks saw the formation of Palauan culture in parallel but not in close association with the latte period of the Marianas. Standing stones, often with carved faces – no obvious resemblance to the toadstool-like latte structures – are common, as are stone platforms. Not having dates, Osborne assumed an earlier, simpler period of occupation, beginning perhaps 1800 to 1500 BC, with a more generalized kind of Oceanic culture, few or no terraces, and less likelihood of Philippine contacts. This in turn would have been preceded by a period of original exploration of Palau.

On Saipan of the Marianas, Spoehr [231] was able to set up a useful pottery sequence, by more local but more complete excavation. One abundant style, 'Marianas Plain', was associated with the latte-building period, which dates back at least to

AD 845, but was surely being made much earlier also. This same pottery is found on Yap, dated by radiocarbon nearly to the beginning of the Christian era. Among other Marianas styles, Spoehr found two special kinds, apparently pre-latte in date: they have also been found in lower levels of a trench dug on Tinian. One, decorated by grooves filled with lime, may have been imported. The other, Marianas Red, is evidently a common early form. At one site where it occurs, Chalan Piao, Spoehr got a radiocarbon date of 1527 BC near the top of these levels, with four feet of occupation deposit lower down. Connections elsewhere of Marianas Red are not yet known, though Spoehr believes it will turn out to belong to a widespread Malaysian style of red pottery [191]

All this is highly suggestive. In these three places, Palau, Yap, and the Marianas, are found rather isolated and divergent Austronesian languages, as on Formosa. With Formosa, the eastern Philippines and the Ryukyus, they virtually ring the Philippine Sea. Settlement in the Marianas was clearly earlier than 1500 BC, probably substantially earlier, and the same is implied for Palau and Yap, which are on the route toward the Marianas most likely to have been followed by the earliest navigators. And the basic population of the Marianas (as known from skulls) was physically something like various Oceanic and east Asiatic peoples but specifically like none. Although I have too little to go on, possibly the same could be said of the Palauans.

However, the same can certainly be said of the Formosan aboriginals. The work both of Yü and his colleagues and of Chai [32] make clear the considerable inter-tribal differences. Amis of the east coast are the least short, about 164 cm for males, with rather flattish faces and a generally Mongoloid look, Atayals also have such a look, but not the same one, and have the highest frequency of a Mongoloid eye fold. Bununs and Rukais are short and dark, with a much less Mongoloid appearance, but in statistical distance analyses are not at all close to one another. Some tribes slightly suggest American Indians in appearance, others certain Indonesian peoples to the south. If I were to guess, I would think Amis recall Oceanic peoples more than the others. But the important thing is the pronounced physical variation among tribal groups, which accords well with the linguistic diversity of which so much has been made. Without anything more to support the idea just now, we can practically add the Marianas (old) population, the Palauans and the Yapese (the latter after deducting Melanesian suggestions of admixture) to the set of Formosan peoples to make up an assembly of populations, none large or widespread, which show from one to another the kind of local heterogeneity I have just been describing.

In the skull analysis giving measures of 'distance', the male Atayals of Formosa are closest to the Chinese of Hainan Island and of the Shang Dynasty tombs, to south Japanese, and to Filipinos, and slightly less close to north Japanese and Guamanians. Female Atayals are closest to Hainan Chinese, south and north Japanese, and Guamanians (there are no female series of the Shang Dynasty or the Philippines). This affirms the rather general Far Eastern nature of the Atayal skulls, and some likeness to Guamanians, which is also present in certain cranial details although they lack the robustness of the skulls from Guam. Since they constitute the only Formosan skull series available, they are not very informative as to how Formosan peoples other than Atayals might resemble populations elsewhere.

In the last chapter we saw that two, and possibly three, distinct culture groups arrived in Formosa, apparently with rice agriculture, about 2500 BC. The linguistic diversity on Formosa might be even older. So might the physical diversity, since there seem to be more than three physically distinct groups. Of course, four-and-a-half thousand years is a long time, probably ample to allow for progressive physical differentiation on Formosa itself, since the increased linguistic differentiation argues local isolation. But we should also expect that some Corded-Ware descendants, from the period long before 2500 BC, must be among the present peoples on the island, and others in addition.

The Corded-Ware tribes, at least, left evidence of being good with boats, and there must have been other such people penetrating the Philippines and other parts of Indonesia in this pre-rice time of 4000 BC and earlier. Settlers should have reached Palau, Yap, the Marianas and some of the western Carolines in due course. We have nothing to pin a date to (except to say that it was before Spoehr's 1500 BC reading for Saipan); Osborne suggests 3000 to 2500 BC, which seems completely reasonable.

Nor does anything now point to the direction from which the settlers came. Natural conditions favor the south (Celebes, Halmahera) for voyages into Yap and Palau: Osborne points out that the Spanish were in the Philippines (*after* first finding Guam) for over two centuries without discovering Palau, and uses this as an argument against chance voyages from that direction. Archaeology is still sketchy. All the same, pottery of Palau has specific resemblances to that of northern Luzon and of Formosa, though this need not reflect first sources. And some linguists think there are special likenesses between Palauan and Marianas Chamorro, on one hand, and Philippine languages on the other. Physically the people of the three groups are not recognizable as identical with any living Formosan aboriginals, but they do, I believe, give signs of being small populations of the same kind and variety.

That is doubtless the main point; that and the general impression of early settlement along this chain. The rather individual cultures of the historic peoples of the three archipelagos, the diversity and isolation of their languages, and the nature of their physical characteristics, all point to an old establishment of the populations of these western islands and to considerable freedom from overwhelming cultural influences in later periods, if not from such things as random Melanesian admixture coming from castaways and chance voyages.

Migrations and Missing Pieces

The settlements of Micronesia and Polynesia must have been mutually involved; the question is how. We can decide that Micronesians, did not enter Polynesia, nor did Polynesians enter Micronesia.[1] But the Gilberts and the Marshalls have the most Polynesian-like appearance of the people in all the non-Polynesian ocean.

What route did the Pre-Polynesians take into Fiji and eastern Melanesia at about 1500 BC? There are two choices: through Micronesia or, one way or another, through Melanesia. The Outliers are largely between or near the two routes and, I said, have sometimes been taken for vestiges of an original Polynesian migration along that track. They are really an opposite argument: manifesting fully developed Polynesian language and culture, they

[1] This refers to present-day peoples. It is not impossible that the Tokelau and Ellice groups were at one time Micronesian in language and culture, and subsequently Polynesianized.

are a later occupation of places which *should* show signs of Pre-Polynesians but do not.

Let us first hear pleadings for the Melanesian route, recently most favored by anthropologists. It is logical and direct; and along the northern edge of Melanesia the south equatorial counter-current would help eastward voyages along. It also has the lands necessary for keeping domestic animals and plants. Will language and archaeology support the plea?

I think not. Today's archaeology argues a first settlement at the eastern end of the route, and the linguists agree heartily on the dispersal of Eastern Oceanic (or other versions of such a group) from the New Hebrides. Signs of a migration are absent: indications of 'Polynesian' presence in Melanesia, in the westerly Lapita sites, are later than those in the east and result from secondary movements to the west. As with the Outliers, they argue that the very places which original Polynesian voyagers should have occupied along the way were in fact not occupied. There is also another more positive point about supposed way stations through Melanesia. Why was there not more gene exchange with Melanesians, who must have been present in the islands? If we allow for signs of later admixture, as among the Motu, and also for places in the New Hebrides or New Caledonia where, I suggested, the Pre-Polynesians landed in addition to Fiji, there is nothing much left to argue for an original migration. Still more important, in such a series of hops through Melanesia, the ancestral Polynesians would have been the minority party, and modern Polynesians should show a strong Melanesian influence in physique, which they do not.

What about a Micronesian route? It is not in favor with the anthropologists, though after all it was not anthropologists who settled Polynesia. It has obstacles, but perhaps no one of them is fatal, and some of the objections have now been greatly reduced. A considerable one is pottery. No Lapita ware – unless the early Marianas Red turns out somehow to be related, not a great chance as far as I know. It can almost be said that no pottery at all has turned up east of the Palau–Marianas line. Coral atolls seem poor places to look for it, partly for lack of raw material in the first place and partly because, in many of them, hurricanes might have destroyed old deposits. Nevertheless, three or four sherds have been picked up, apparently on different occasions, on Ponape [42] and only time will tell whether they represent a real industry of the past, or trade contact with the west. And the fact is that archaeology has not yet been seriously undertaken in eastern Micronesia, although refuse deposits certainly exist. We might remember that archaeology was slow to start in Polynesia, and thus slow to upset older misconceptions about things like the absence of pottery east of Tonga. As for Lapita ware, it is missing in Melanesia as well as in Micronesia, excepting in those places which seem to have been reached from its center in the east.

Goodenough [89] suggested this principle: that atolls were settled after high islands, and also from them, as a secondary cultural adaptation. From this he surmised that atoll Micronesia was colonized late; that it was ignored by the early people of the western groups (Yap, Palau, Marianas), and was settled out of the southeast from a high island background there: that is to say, from the central Pacific Polynesian homeland. His principle seems valid, but perhaps it can be applied differently.

This brings us to the food problem. Micronesia, with no domestic pigs and with only a few fertile high volcanic islands spaced among the many Carolinian atolls, has seemed an impossible transmission route for the basic Polynesian foods. But the high islands are there. And Groube's hypothesis turns the food argument around. That is to say, if for centuries the Pre-Polynesians of Fiji and Tonga (apparently confirmed for New Caledonia also) were reef-fishers, without domestic animals and horticulture – if in fact they were treating Fiji like a reef atoll, which is virtually what Groube says – then they had already passed through the adaptation to reef and atoll existence. Where else but Micronesia?

It is not possible to suppose that the Pre-Polynesians were entirely bereft of horticulture; and the pottery would be harder to understand if this were so. Here we might too easily write off atoll-dwellers as subsisting on fish and coconuts alone. In Micronesia, however, they do grow taro by laboriously making pits or even 'swamps'; this is possible only in the interior of islands large enough to allow the taro to be protected from salt water. They also grow another species, *Cyrtosperma*, which is more resistant but takes considerably longer to mature. In the east they husband the meat of the breadfruit in large storage pits, just as in Polynesia. Now Groube has found signs of numerous pits like this in his principal recent excavation (Vuki's Mound) of the early period on Tonga, giving good evidence that the Proto-Polynesians were growing either taro or breadfruit, or both. This only makes them more like the Micronesians of the atolls.

Enough of tedious details and cautionary notes. Here, by way of summing up, is a reconstrucion, not free of guesswork. With the peopling of the three major western Micronesian groups, the art of seafaring had become good enough to reach other parts of Micronesia, perhaps by accident of storm or bad navigation, but in some cases carrying food and other supplies. If they landed on atolls, such potential colonies were usually abortive. But some of them reached Truk, Ponape, Kusaie and Nauru,[1] with the panoply of food plants (but no pigs), and these fertile volcanic islands were the next thing to Eden for horticulturalists. They have been so in recent times. On Kusaie, yams and taros took to growing wild, so that the natives have been almost reluctant to cultivate them; and on Ponape the raising of large yams became a game of social prestige, a pastime.

The first voyages happened around 2500 BC, perhaps later. The travelers brought an Austronesian language equal in 'age', or time of original isolation from others, at least to those now found on Yap, Palau and the Marianas. It was the immediate parent of Proto-Eastern Oceanic and of Proto-Nuclear Micronesian, as well as the aberrant present language of Nauru.[2]

So from 2500 BC or after there was a parent colony of Polynesian-like people on one or more of the high islands of the Carolines. Without overpopulation, it is hard to imagine dwellers on a lush place like Kusaie undertaking to adjust themselves to a harsher and more hazardous life on an atoll. With overpopulation, however, on an isolated high island, that is just what they did: applying Goodenough's principle, they learned how to subsist successfully from the reef, and they began to disperse over the atolls in every direction. Some of them about 1500 BC, filtered south through the

[1] Winds and currents, westward along the north shore of New Guinea and turning eastward through the Carolines, would actually foster such movement, voluntary or not. In recent years, part of a wrecked canoe, identifiable as having been made in the Sepik District of New Guinea, floated ashore at Kwajalein in the Marshall Islands, which is further east than Kusaie.

[2] I have no license whatever from the linguists for these assumptions, which are based on their deductions about much later relationships and which they are welcome to reject.

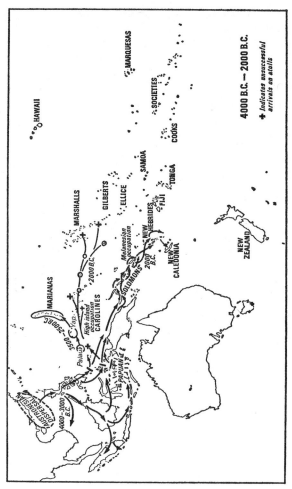

14 Hypothetical periods in the occupation of Oceania, with suggested routes.

(a) 4000 BC to 2000 BC. Dispersal of Austronesian languages begins about 4000 BC from an unknown region in or adjacent to South China, spreading through Indonesia and obliterating most Papuan languages of the area. The impact carries beyond New Guinea into Island Melanesia, with varied small-scale movements reaching Eastern Melanesia (but not Fiji) by 2000 BC or shortly after. Direct movements out of Indonesia reach Palau-Yap-Marianas in the period 3500 to 2500 BC. Voyages in Micronesia succeed in settling on high islands by 2000 BC, but fail to establish settlements on atolls.

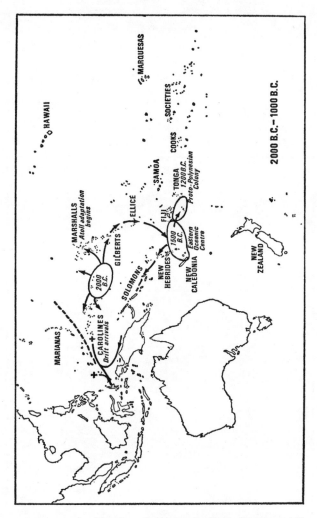

(*b*) 2000 to 1000 BC. Further chance arrivals in western atoll Micronesia continue to fail to establish permanent settlement, but in eastern Micronesia adaptation to atoll exploitation begins after about 2000 BC. By 1500 BC such atoll-dwellers with Eastern Oceanic languages from an eastern Micronesian source reach points in Eastern Melanesia including Fiji. These are primarily reef-fishers and only secondarily growers of atoll-possible foods like taro and breadfruit. By 1200 BC colonists from Fiji reach Tonga. Other settlers move northwest into parts of the southeast Solomons.

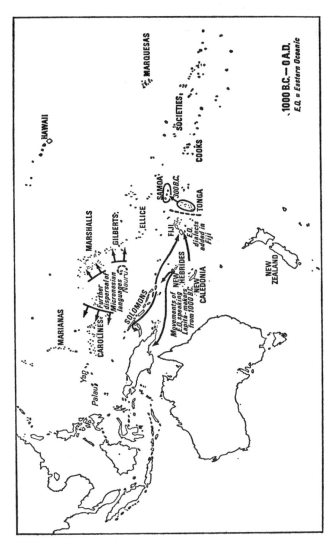

(c) 1000 BC to AD 0. Internal movements of the Eastern Oceanic speakers reach as far as New Guinea and New Britain, making Lapita pottery; others make further settlements in Fiji. All these become Melanesianized by contact. Tonga is now isolated from Fiji and is the source of settlement of Samoa. In Micronesia, atoll occupation has been proceeding westward as well as into the Gilberts and Marshalls.

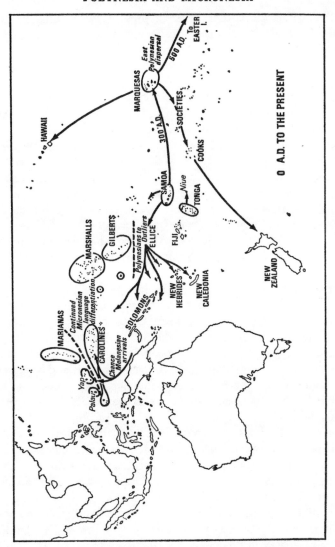

(*d*) AD o to present. Westward movement of atoll-dwellers in
Micronesia continues, allowing survival of Melanesian immigrants
arriving by chance; but Yap and Palau are not affected by this
movement. Following an eastern movement, all of Polynesia is
occupied; westward movement establishes the Polynesian Outliers,
on more remote islands where Melanesian influence is less effective
after settlement.

Gilberts into the corner between present Micronesia, Polynesia and Melanesia, speaking Proto-Eastern Oceanic, making Lapita pottery and living mainly on food from reef and shore; they knew how to grow taro but not how to take advantage of the fertile land in places like Fiji and Tonga.

The rest of this particular story is already familiar. After a thousand years on Fiji and Tonga, these Proto-Polynesians filled out their list of food plants afresh, and they also acquired pigs, chickens and dogs, all at the hands of their Melanesian neighbors. Some of them, certified Polynesians at last, funneled eastward through Samoa and beyond, finally curling back through the Ellice Islands on the northwest, where they faced the Micronesian Gilbert Islands across a clear culture difference resulting from fifteen hundred years of separate history.

Cousins of theirs – Eastern Oceanic speakers in the New Hebrides – still made Lapita pottery, which they carried to other parts of Melanesia. Brothers – real Polynesians – later settled the Outliers. But although, as next-door neighbors, the Gilberts were affected by Polynesian contacts, there was no back movement from the Pre-Polynesian, Eastern Oceanic-speaking center into Micronesia. Rather, the first home at the southeast edge of Micronesia was still, as it had been earlier, a dispersal center in its own right. Having descended from their high island background and once made themselves at home on coral reefs, the atoll-dwellers were increasingly successful, especially in navigation.[1] They had long since gone down into the Gilberts and on into Melanesia. They also occupied the paired chains of the Marshalls, and moved westward back through the long constellation of coral atolls which makes up most of the Carolines, and which begins not much more than a hundred miles west of Kusaie. Thus arose the present languages and cultures of Micronesia, more diverse and individual than those of Polynesia because the dispersal was a generation earlier, so to speak, and because it was less rapid and unified. Variety in physique and language comes partly from this and partly from previous diversity.

The main direction of drift, or at least the longest one, was, as the linguists have been saying, out of the center of greatest heterogeneity in the southeast towards the west. In the last

---

[1] See Gladwin [80] for a fine popular account of Micronesian skill in finding and sighting so bad a landmark as a low atoll.

segment of the spread, the languages from Truk through the remaining Carolines compose little more than a string of dialects together labeled 'Trukic' – a mirror image of what is seen on a grander scale in Polynesia. And this is doubtless a fair picture, letting us suppose that this spread would have been at about the same time as that of the Polynesians. For the separation between the languages of Truk and of Ponape to the east has been estimated by glottochronology (Fischer in [41]) at 1080 BC, not a bad match for the beginning isolation of Proto-Polynesian in Fiji and Tonga. At last, in the far west, where these languages come up against the bastion of old-established languages on Palau, Yap and the Marianas, hoary in their isolation, the contrast is great.

The elusive homeland

This partly imaginary history has something for everyone, both pleasures and problems. For a physical anthropologist it avoids the dilemma of getting Polynesians unmixed through Melanesia; on the other hand I, at least, can see no immediately related population at the western end of the Micronesian line. Not Guam, where skulls of older inhabitants are broadly like those of Hawaiians but narrowly and specifically different.

For linguists there is the spread of Eastern Oceanic out of eastern Melanesia together with the kindred spread of Micronesian languages from nearly the same place, without what is to me the preposterous difficulty of generating eastern Micronesians out of Melanesians. Linguists may also find a clue to the solution of questions about the language of the Gilberts, which seems to puzzle them. But they are likely to voice strong objections, stemming from their reconstructions of ancestral languages, when they find words for pigs and dogs in an ancestral vocabulary that I am trying to place in Micronesia.

Archaeologists suffer most. The central position of Lapita pottery is the puzzle; it has not been found in Micronesia, but then it has not been found anywhere that could serve as a source. (It would be strange if the same could be said in another ten years' time.) Some say it has no known western connections. Others ally it to the Kalanay pottery tradition of the Philippines [222], because of a community of decorative elements. Actual Kalanay pottery is too late, but the motifs were widely scattered in Southeast Asia by 3000 BC, so there might be an indirect connection. In

Chang's formula, such kinds of pottery could all be sparks struck off from late Corded-Ware or Hoabinhian cultures by Lungshanoid influence on simpler horticulturalists.

But this gives us no homeland, suggesting as it does anything from the Philippines southward. More northern origins have proponents: Solheim's maps of pottery analysis have an insistent northern accent. The archaeologists throw us some smaller scraps. Northern (Japanese) connections have been seen in details of fishing gear of the eastern Polynesians (!). More direct links are shell artefacts and ornaments in Tongan archaeology [197] which have a strong kinship with Fiji and New Caledonia but also with Micronesia, especially Yap. And Groube [101] found in Vuki's Mound in Tonga, belonging to the early period, examples of a particular kind of ornament, a 'long unit', a piece of shell with holes drilled at each end. Such ornaments have been found twice elsewhere: in one of the early Fijian sites and (though made of stone) in early levels on Tinian – in the Marianas! [191]

These things sound too specific and direct, and one swallow does not make a summer. I have already suggested how I visualize the physical appearance of the ancestors of the Polynesians and the eastern Micronesians. We have seen the tribally varied living populations of aboriginal Formosa and of Yap and the other western islands. Other such peoples surely existed in the Ryukyus and as far away as Jomon Japan. One more such population, originally of modest size, would be the obvious model for the ancestral group we seek. For its origin point I would look toward the southern end of the spectrum: there may have been people who were more Polynesian-like in the Philippines, just as there were probably earlier Austronesian languages there, since swept away by later expansions.

I doubt that the ultimate origins of the Polynesian forerunners can be made out from what we know now. An important piece of information is added once in a number of years to the picture of earlier and earlier movements and changes; the solution is not found at a stroke. The linguists still have so much to do, and the Lapita sweepstakes are still being run. I am not in the business of guessing what the archaeologists will dig up next; it pays small returns.

And the trail is cold. A conjunction of archaeology, physical anthropology and language has shown us the Polynesian forerunners descending on Fiji. The track of their own ancestors in the centuries before, coming from a home in the west, is lit by no such focussing of evidence today. For the time being, at least, we lose those earlier argonauts; they are in any case merely a piece, and a minor one, in the whole prehistory of the Far East.

Note added in proof: An important treatise has been published by José Garanger (1972, 'Archéologie des Nouvelles-Hébrides', **Publications de la So ciété des Océanistes,** no. 30) which considers many problems of the chapter above but is primarily a detailed report on numerous recent excavations in the central New Hebrides, the supposed core area of the Eastern Oceanic languages. Here the first recognizable 'Melanesian' occupation, with pottery of the 'Mangaasi' tradition (incised and appliquéed decoration), and with pigs but not dogs, has C^{14} dates of the middle of the first millenium BC, the earliest being 645 BC. If a first arrival of Melanesians, this would be later than is assumed herein (1000 to 2000 BC), with different implications for the relations between Melanesians and Lapita-making Pre-Polynesians. However, another non-Lapita style, paddle-impressed ware, is thought to be present in New Caledonia about 800 to 900 BC. Garanger distinguishes a number of prehistoric Melanesian pottery styles; are these multiple settlements, or more Melanesian parochialism?

At the site of Erueti, on the south coast of Efate in the central New Hebrides, Mangaasi pottery marks the lowest levels (645 BC), with Lapita in a later occupation (350 BC). Garanger reports that Golson, inspecting the latter material, suggests that it might represent an arrival from Fiji (where of course Lapita pottery had been in use nearly a thousand years before 350 BC). This supports the idea of continued movements of Lapita-makers in Melanesia. Dare we think that Lapita ware was actually developed in Fiji or New Caledonia? The idea appeals to me just about as much as does Dyen's Melanesian origin for Austronesian languages, which is very little; Lapita seems too sophisticated.

N. M. Blake et al. (1973, *American Journal of Human Genetics*, vol. 25, no. 4), reporting on the red blood cell enzyme phosphoglucomutase (page 69) in Micronesia, give frequencies of .05 to .06 of the gene PHs^a in the western Caroline atolls of Puluwat, Woleai and Ulithi (the last close to Yap). These figures are very low and also suggest no mutual variation because of genetic drift. They contrast with that for Yap (.26), as the same atolls do in language, all being closely related members of the Trukic group (page 101). Phs^a might prove a useful index gene in Micronesia; at any rate this small evidence supports an arrival of the people of the above atolls from the east (see Map 14).

9

The view from Asia

A main goal of the Pacific explorers, from Mendaña on, was discovery of the land and riches of Terra Australis. This was the great continent of the south, which Mercator and others believed must exist, balancing the land mass of the northern hemisphere. The wretched little ships of the sixteenth and seventeenth centuries shackled the voyagers, holding them to a middle track across the ocean. Nobody arrived at Terra Australis. Drawing on this large store of ignorance the highly respected Scottish geographer, Alexander Dalrymple, was able in 1769–70 to publish a study of the voyages, including a demonstration that between Australia and South America the continent must be there, that it was the size of Asia and had fifty million inhabitants. But in the same decade the unimpressionable Captain Cook sailed criss-cross all over its supposed location, going south right into the Antarctic Circle. And that was that.

I have been dealing with lands or countries of the ancient past not visible today, but which we know very well to have existed. Sundaland and Sahulland, with Wallacea between them, are geographical places we must map, however crudely, because we understand that the realities of the present are not those of the late Pleistocene. There was actually a series of such lands, as the seas fell or rose to different levels. We are far from being able to graph them precisely, but geologists and oceanographers – even paleontologists – are constantly working at it and cannot be wrong about the most general features.

Another kind of country such as Old Melanesia or Hoabinhia is even more vague. I have used these as human provinces more than geographic regions, and anthropological Captain Cooks can always make so much seawater out of them in the future. That is quite all right; the usefulness of trying to perceive them now lies in challenging other possibilities. New answers, however gratifying, are less important than new questions. If we bring Hoabinhia and Old Melanesia into confrontation now, it is to hope that further archaeology, covering the range of time from about 15,000 to 50,000 BC will see whether there is any meaning in these provinces; and we also hope that more careful analysis of human skeletal remains will give us clearer notions of who the inhabitants really were. Somewhere in all this lie some basic distinctions for Pacific and Asiatic origins.

In general, I believe there were two fundamental and ancient population complexes in eastern Asia, and we know as little about one, racially speaking, as about the other. As a way of getting into this, take Polynesian origins again. I did not just now nominate an 'Old Polynesia' to match Old Melanesia. Archaeologists and linguists have all but done so for eastern Melanesia after the arrival of the Lapita-making, Eastern Oceanic-speaking Polynesian forebears. They came with skeletons too, but we have not found any.

The usefulness of the achievement is in recognizing further problems. Some are Melanesian. Had *Melanesian* speakers of Austronesian languages already arrived in these islands – New Caledonia, for example? When did they actually bring garden crops and pigs, chickens and dogs, into the region? Did they in fact make possible the conversion of the Polynesian ancestors to the uses of these things? These are untested links in the hypothetical chain of events which sees the entrance and the exit of the Pre-Polynesians on Fiji from 1500 to 500 BC.

The spread westward of Lapita pottery and languages of Eastern Oceanic affiliation may be a hypothesis which has already passed its qualifying exams, rather than a problem. The other real problems take us to Micronesia and to conjectural entrances and exits of Pre-Polynesians there, about 2500 to 1500 BC. A Micronesian migration path seems probable to me, but it depends on the eventual consent of linguists. Perhaps they could use a few rash proposals from outsiders. Not having a true time clock like radiocarbon they are forced to rely on internal evidence and on existing distributions of languages; and physical anthropologists have sometimes been tripped up when they accepted the same kind of limitation to living peoples. Micronesian migrations also depend on the continuing consent of archaeologists, and a future excavation almost anywhere could play ducks and drakes with the whole idea. But I have a word for the archaeologists too: go and dig in eastern Micronesia. Perhaps they have avoided it as unpromising, and one cannot blame them; but for generations they were equally unwilling to dig any substantial holes in Polynesia.[1]

This little sermon is aside from the main point. The real reason I refrained from using a term like 'Old Polynesia' was not from discretion but to avoid implications of analogy with 'Old Melanesia'. For the latter included an entire complex of populations, existing for a long time in a large area. If the Polynesians, by the lights of traditional anthropology, now constitute a whole important race, they got to this point by an exceptional diaspora and population explosion. Thus, going back in time, they and their Micronesian cousins would dwindle down into an originally small genetic strain – perhaps an amalgam of a few related groups, perhaps a quite local group in themselves, but in any case falling into a mere pigeonhole in a much larger complex.

This would have reached from Southeast Asia at least to Japan, and from recent times back to the late Pleistocene when Japan and Formosa, like Sundaland, were periodically connected with the mainland. The whole coastal zone must have been occupied by tribal groups, locally varying in the physical sense, much as in the case of modern Melanesia. Larger subgroupings may also have differed somewhat, but taken all together the population complex could be described by some such term as Proto-Mongoloid. That is to say, traits we now consider as classically Mongoloid – prominent cheekbones, flat faces, very straight hair, prevalence of inner eyefold – were present in muted form and varying degree, about as one sees them in American Indians. And the Indians, by any logic, are in fact emigrants from just such a population matrix, or a part of it, going over the Bering Strait land bridge during the same late Pleistocene period of lower seas. Ultimately, the whole was related to the one from which the Europeans derive, so that in

[1] I quickly except Shutler from this admonition; he has been reconnoitering in the Gilberts and tells me they are not at all unpromising. Janet Davidson has dug on the Outlier atoll Nukuoro with excellent results (though of late date). However, archaeological deposits on atolls are doubtless subject to destruction by typhoons.

features of skull and face there are less profound differences among Europeans, Ainus, Polynesians and American Indians than between all these and Africans on the one hand, or Australo-Melanesians on the other. At least, this is what skull 'distances' say. Within this zone, and not at the same time and place, pottery-making, domesticated plants and rice-growing developed. The domestication, and then seaworthy boats, furnished a series of pulses which sent settlers beyond Indonesia and New Guinea into the Pacific. Within this zone also, the parental form of the Austronesian languages appeared at just the time to be intimately involved in these movements, occupations and reoccupations. A relatively late contribution of this phase and population would have been limited groups going to Palau, Yap, the Marianas, and then to Micronesia and 'Old Polynesia'.

The framework has barely been suggested by the evidence of prehistory. From physical anthropology the evidence is slight indeed. It rests mainly on such things as aboriginal tribes now found in Southeast Asia and Formosa, and on such skeletal remains as those of the pre-Japanese Jomon peoples of Japan. The Ainu are survivors, but other people of the culture were evidently different from the Ainu. The picture is difficult to see because it was changed by important expansions of more specifically 'Mongoloid' peoples from the north, above all the Chinese. With these new empires covering most of the old area, including much of Formosa and Hainan Island, old distributions and tracks were erased, with dislocations and cultural influences spreading south right into Indonesia. So, to get back at last to the Polynesians, their 'homeland', along with those of other Indonesian and Pacific groups, is likely to be unrecognizable.[1]

We assume that the widespread Proto-Mongoloid complex was one of the basic populations. The other such population complex, of course, was that of Old Melanesia, having the same local variety as the other from its earliest to its latest history. Although

---

[1] We may, of course, get further information from genetic markers, not only from skeletons. The distinction of Mongoloids from Proto-Mongoloids is upheld by earwax (Chapter 4). The northern Mongoloids (Tungus, Mongols, Japanese) have very low proportions of sticky wax, while all the supposed Proto-Mongoloids (Ainus, Formosan and Hainan aboriginals, Malays of Malaysia, and all Oceanic groups so far tested in Micronesia or Melanesia) are much higher. Southern Chinese and Ryukyu Islanders, both of whom might represent some absorption of Proto-Mongoloids, are intermediate.

it had extended to New Guinea and Australia well before 30,000 BC, it was essentially Asiatic in that its earliest traceable home was Sundaland; still, at its greatest early extent it took in not only Australia and the islands westward, but the Philippines as well, though not Formosa. Unlike the Proto-Mongoloids it can provide some meager but datable witnesses of its antiquity, in such skulls as Niah Cave and Mungo. For the Proto-Mongoloids, the Liu-Kiang skull of China is probably a good Pleistocene member but we cannot date it in years. The Upper Cave skulls from Choukoutien near Peking are perhaps northern representatives, but they are likely to be late in time, like the Wadjak skulls of Java in Old Melanesia.

Old Melanesia, like the central Pacific, poses its problems. It has, in fact, a large brood of them. Here the reach of prehistory is so long, and the march of discovery has lately been so rapid, that we have more in the way of queries than of well-ordered hypotheses or clear problems. We simply need to know more about tool developments and dates in such places as the Niah and Tabon caves, and about their connections elsewhere. In fact, much excavation and study is called for to shed light on the stone tool cultures which have been found in so many parts of Indonesia but which cannot be pinned down in time. We need to know much more about New Guinea as it took its separate way from Australia, something vastly important for Melanesia. As to language, the students are only beginning to see light where all was darkness in the Papuan morass (they had thrown up their hands and called everything 'non-Austronesian').

Something has got to be done about Solo Man, to place him and his culture more exactly in time and context. It may seem like Conan Doyle's 'Lost World' to think of him surviving among Old Melanesians, but that is what the signs say now. Without this we cannot be satisfied and will go on speculating on a real problem: the existence of two genetic lines of man in Australia keeping their distinctiveness until the end of the Pleistocene, when they probably amalgamated.

A solid problem is the other change in Australia at about the same time. After the impressively long duration of the simple core-and-scraper tools there appeared the finer, more varied work of the small-tool complex. The archaeologists agree that it has no visible Australian parentage and must have come from outside. The dingo agrees with them, because only God can make a dingo, and he (the dingo) likewise appears in Australia at the same time. Golson is willing to consider transmission of both from India, the nearest place where the dingo has a relative and where small tools occurred at that time; today India also has some rather Australian-looking faces. This is a problem of some majesty.

A last problem is more down-to-earth: the western and northern limits of Old Melanesia. We cannot assume that there was a boundary with the Proto-Mongoloid Hoabinhia, complete with guards and customs. More likely there was exchange, genetic and cultural, with the Melanesians partaking in domestication toward the end. Here we must rely on future work of the archaeologists, fervently hoping they will find us skeletons along with stonework. At the moment I see no signs of the Old Melanesian population on the present mainland, with the possible exception of Malaya.

The evidence, of course, is poor and rather late in time. Still, it seems likely that the two population complexes, Proto–Mongoloid and Melanesian, had been present in southeast Asia for a great many millennia. But I shall not go further into origins. We have seen how, in a previous phase of the Pleistocene, men and *Stegodon* were wandering freely through Indonesia on land bridges which have not existed since. That is another story, one not for this book. Even in tracing the Melanesians and others back into the period, four hundred to five hundred centuries ago, when Neanderthal Man still presided over Europe and the Near East, we are waking some really large sleeping dogs. For the time being, there are smaller dogs to worry about, like dingos.

References

1 ABBIE, A.A. 1963. 'Physical Anthropology.' *In* Stanner, W.E.H. and Shiels, H. (eds.), *Australian Aboriginal Studies*. A Symposium of Papers Presented at the 1961 Research Conference, 89–124.

2 ABBIE, A.A. 1966. 'Physical characteristics.' *In* B.C. Cotton (ed.), *Aboriginal Man in South and Central Australia*, part I, 9–46 (Adelaide).

3 ABBIE, A.A. 1968. 'The homogeneity of Australian aborigines.' *Arch. & Phys. Anthrop. in Oceania*, **3**: 223–31.

4 ABBIE, A.A. 1969. *The Original Australians*, 288 pp. (London: Frederick Muller).

5 ADACHI, B. 1937. 'Das Ohrenschmalz als Rassenmerkmal und der Rassengeruch ("Achselgeruch") nebst dem Rassenunterschied der Schweissdrüsen.' *Zeitschrift für Rassenkunde*, **6**: 273–307.

6 ADAM, W. 1943. 'The Keilor fossil skull, palate and upper dental arch.' *National Museum Memoirs*, **13**: 71–7 (Melbourne).

7 ALLEN, J. and HURD, C. 1963. Languages of the Bougainville District. MSS, Summer Institute of Linguistics, Ukarumpa, Territory of New Guinea.

8 BARTHEL, T.S. 1963. Review of *Archaeology of Easter Island*, T. Heyerdahl and E.N. Ferdon, Jr. (eds.), *American Anthropologist*, **65**: 421–5.

9 BELLWOOD, P. 1971. 'Varieties of ecological adaptation in the southern Cook Islands.' *Arch. & Phys. Anthrop. in Oceania*, VI: 145–69.

10 BENDER, B.W. 1971. 'Micronesian languages.' *In* T.A. Sebeok (ed.), *Current Trends in Linguistics*, **8**: 426–465 (The Hague: Mouton).

11 BENOIST, J. 1964. 'Saint–Barthélemy: physical anthropology of an isolate.' *Am. J. Phys. Anthrop.*, **22**: 473–87.

12 BERNDT, R.M. and C.H. (eds.). 1965. *Aboriginal Man in Australia. Essays in Honour of Emeritus Professor A.P. Elkin* (Sydney: Angus and Robertson).

13 BIASUTTI, R. (ed.). 1959. *Le Razze e i Popoli della Terra,* 4 vols. (Turin: Unione Tipografico–editrice Torinese).

14 BIJLMER, H.J.T. (No date.) *Nieuw Guinea,* 109 pp. (Deventer, Netherlands: W. van Hoeve).

15 BIRDSELL, J.B. 1949. 'The racial origin of the extinct Tasmanians.' *Records, Queen Victoria Museum, Launceston,* **2**: 105–22.

16 BIRDSELL, J.B. 1951. 'The problem of the early peopling of the Americas as viewed from Asia.' *Papers on the Physical Anthropology of the American Indian,* W.S. Laughlin (ed.), 1–68 (New York: Viking Fund).

17 BIRDSELL, J.B. 1967. 'Preliminary data on the trihybrid origin of the Australian aborigines.' *Arch. & Phys. Anthrop. in Oceania,* **2**: 100–55.

18 BIRKS, L. and H. 1968. 'Adzes from excavations at Sigatoka, Fiji.' *Arch. & Phys. Anthrop. in Oceania,* **3**: 105–15.

19 BLACKBURN, C.R.B. and HORNABROOK, R.W. 1969. 'Haptoglobin gene frequencies in the people of the New Guinea Highlands.' *Arch. & Phys. Anthrop. in Oceania,* **4**: 56–63.

20 BLUM, H.F. 1961. 'Does the melanin pigment of human skin have adaptive value?' *Quarterly Review of Biology,* **36**: 50–63.

21 BOWLER, J.M., JONES, R., ALLEN, H. and THORNE, A.G. 1970. 'Pleistocene human remains from Australia: a living site and human cremation from Lake Mungo, western New South Wales.' *World Archaeology,* **2**: 41–60.

22 BOWLER, J.M. 1970. 'Lake Nitchie skeleton – stratigraphy of the burial site.' *Arch. & Phys. Anthrop. in Oceania,* **5**: 102–13.

23 BOWLER, J.M. 1971. 'Pleistocene salinities and climatic change: evidence from lakes and lunettes in Southeastern Australia.' *In* Mulvaney and Golson, 47–65.

24 BOYD, W.C. 1963. 'Genetics and the human race.' *Science,* **140**: 1057–64.

25 BROTHWELL, D.R. 1960. 'Upper Pleistocene human skull from Niah Caves, Sarawak.' *Sarawak Museum Journal,* **9**: 323–49.

26 BROUWER, D. (No date.) *Bijdrage tot de anthropologie der Aloreilanden* (Amsterdam: Uitgevermaatschappij Holland).

27 BRUES, A. 1954. 'Selection and polymorphism in the A–B–O blood groups.' *Am. J. Phys. Anthrop.*, **12**: 559–97.

28 BUCK, P. 1939. *Anthropology and Religion*, 96 pp. (New Haven: Yale University Press).

29 BULMER, R.H.N. 1971. 'The role of ethnography in reconstructing the pre-history of Melanesia.' *In* Green and Kelly (eds.), vol. 2: 36–43.

30 CALABY, J.H. 1971. 'Man, fauna and climate in aboriginal Australia.' *In* Mulvaney and Golson, 80–93.

31 CAPELL, A. 1962. 'Oceanic linguistics today.' *Current Anthropology*, **3**/4: 371–428.

32 CHAI, C.K. 1967. *Taiwan Aborigines. A Genetic Study of Tribal Variations*, 238 pp. (Cambridge, Mass.: Harvard Press).

33 CHANG, K–C. 1962. 'Major problems in the culture history of southeast Asia.' *Bulletin of the Institute of Ethnology, Academia Sinica*, no. 13, 26 pp.

34 CHANG, K–C. 1964. 'Prehistoric and early historic culture horizons and traditions in South China.' *In* Chang et al., 1964.

35 CHANG, K–C. 1967. 'The Yale expedition to Taiwan and the southeast Asian horticultural evolution.' *Discovery*, **2**: 3–10.

36 CHANG, K–C. 1968. 'Archaeology of ancient China.' *Science*, 1962: 519–26.

37 CHANG, K–C. 1970. 'The beginnings of agriculture in the Far East.' *Antiquity*, **44**: 175–85.

38 CHANG, K–C. 1971. Review of W.H. Sung, *Changpinian*. *Asian Perspectives*, XII: 133–6.

39 CHANG, K–C. 'Ancient farmers in the Asian tropics: major problems for archaeological and palaeoenvironmental investigations of Southeast Asia at the earliest Neolithic level.' (Sen Festschrift, in press.)

40 CHANG, K–C. and STUIVER, M. 1966. 'Recent advances in the prehistoric archaeology of Formosa.' *Proc. Nat. Academy of Sciences*, **55**: 539–43.

41 CHANG, K–C, SOLHEIM III, W.G. and GRACE, G.W. 1964. Movements of the Malayo–Polynesians: 1500 BC to AD 500.' *Current Anthropology* **5**/5: 359–418.

42 CHAPMAN, P.S. 1968. 'Japanese contributions to Micronesian archaeology and material culture.' *In* Yawata and Sinoto, 67–82.

43 COON, C.S. 1962. *The Origin of Races*, 724+xxi pp. (New York: Knopf).

44 COON, C.S. 1965. *The Living Races of Man*, 324+xx pp. (New York: Knopf).

45 COON, C.S., GARN S.M. and BIRDSELL, J.B. 1950. *Races. A study of the Problems of Race Formation in Man*, 153 pp. (Springfield, Ill: C.C. Thomas).

46 COSTIN, A.B. 1971. 'Vegetation, soils and climate in late Quaternary southeastern Australia.' *In* Mulvaney and Golson, 26–37.

47 CURTAIN, C.C., GAJDUSEK, D.C., KIDSON, C., GORMAN, J.G., CHAMPNESS, L. and RODRIGUE, R. 1965. 'Haptoglobins and transferrins in Melanesia: relation to hemoglobin, serum haptoglobin and serum iron levels in population groups in Papua–New Guinea.' *Am. J. Phys. Anthrop.*, **23**: 363–80.

48 DAVIDSON, J.M. 1968. 'Nukuoro: archaeology on a Polynesian outlier in Micronesia.' *In* Yawata and Sinoto, 51–66.

49 DE BEAUCLAIRE, I. 1968. 'Social stratification in Micronesia: the low-caste people of Yap.' *Bull. Inst. of Ethnology, Academia Sinica*, no. 25, 45–52.

50 DEMPSTER, A.P. 1969. *Elements of Continuous Multivariate Analysis*, 388 pp. (Reading, Mass.: Addison–Wesley).

51 DIXON, R.B. 1923. *The Racial History of Man*, 583 pp. (New York: Scribners).

52 DUCKWORTH, W.L.H. 1934. 'Human remains from rock-shelters and caves in Perak, Rahang, and Perlis from Selinsing.' *Journal Malayan Branch of the Royal Asiatic Society*, vol. 12.

53 DUNN, F.L. 1970. 'Cultural evolution in the Late Pleistocene and Holocene of southeast Asia.' *American Anthropologist*, **72**: 1041–52.

54 DYEN, I. 1962. 'The lexicostatistical classification of the Malayopolynesian languages.' *Language*, **38**: 38–46.

55 DYEN, I. 1963. 'The position of the Malayopolynesian languages of Formosa.' *Asian Perspectives*, **7**: 261–71.

56 DYEN, I. 1965. 'A lexicostatistical classification of the Austronesian languages.' *International Journal of American Linguistics*, Memoir 19.

57 DYEN, I. 1971. Review of Pätzold, K., *Die Palau–Sprache und ihre Stellung zu anderen indonesischen und Südseesprachen* (1968). *J. Polynesian Society*, **80**: 248–58.

58 EMORY, K.P. 1968. 'East Polynesian relationships as revealed through adzes.' *In* Yawata and Sinoto, 151–69.

59 EVANGELISTA, A.E. 1971. 'Type-sites from the Philippine Islands and their significance.' *In* Green and Kelley (eds.), vol. 2: 28–35.

60 FERRELL, R. 1969. *Taiwan aboriginal groups: problems in cultural and linguistic classification.* Monograph no. 17, Institute of Ethnology, Academia Sinica, Nankang, Taipei, 444 pp.

61 FISHER, R.A. 1956. 'Blood-groups and population genetics.' *Acta Genetica et Statistica Medica*, **6**: 507–9.

62 FORCE, R.W. 1960. *Leadership and cultural change in Palau.* Fieldiana: Anthropology, vol. 50, 211 pp. (Chicago: Chicago Natural History Mus.).

63 FOX, R. 1967. 'Excavations in the Tabon Caves and some problems in Philippine chronology.' *In* M.D. Zamora (ed.), *Studies in Philippine Anthropology*, 88–116 (Quezon City: Phoenix Press).

64 FOX, R.B. 1971. 'The flake industries of the Palaeolithic in the Philippines and their persistence in post-Pleistocene times.' Paper presented at 28th Congress of Orientalists, Canberra, January 1971.

65 FRIEDLAENDER, J.S. 1969. 'Biological divergences over population boundaries in South-Central Bougainville.' Unpublished PhD thesis, Harvard University Library.

66 FRIEDLAENDER, J.S. 1971. 'The population structure of South-Central Bougainville.' *Am. J. Phys. Anthrop.*, **35**: 13–25.

67 FRIEDLAENDER, J.S., SGARAMELLA-ZONTA, L.A., KIDD, K.K., LAI, L.Y.C., CLARK, P. and WALSH, R.J. 1971. 'Biological divergences in South-Central Bougainville: an analysis of blood polymorphism gene frequencies and anthropometric measurements utilizing tree models, and a comparison of these variables with linguistic, geographic, and migrational "distances".' *Am. J. Human Genetics*, **23/5**: 253–70.

68 FOX, R.B. 1967. 'Excavations in the Tabon caves and some problems in Philippine chronology.' *In* M.D. Zamora (ed.), *Studies in Philippine Archaeology*, 88–116.

69 GAJDUSEK, D.C. 1970. 'Psychological characteristics of

Stone Age Man.' *Engineering and Science*, **33**: 26–52.

70 GALLOWAY, R.W. 1971. 'Evidence for late Quaternary climates.' *In* Mulvaney and Golson, 14–25.

71 GALLUS, A. 1970. 'The geological age of the earliest stone tools uncovered during the excavations of the Archaeological Society of Keilor, near Melbourne.' (Mimeographed summary of recent articles by Dr Gallus.)

72 GALLUS, A. 1971. 'Results of the exploration of Koonalda Cave, 1956–68.' *In* R.V.S. Wright (ed.), *Archaeology of the Gallus Site, Koonalda Cave*, 85–133. Australian Aboriginal Studies no. 26 (Canberra: Australian Institute of Aboriginal Studies).

73 GARANGER, J. 1971. 'Incised and Applied-relief pottery, its chronology and development in southeastern Melanesia, and extra areal comparisons.' *In* Green and Kelley (eds.), vol. 2: 53–66.

74 GATHERCOLE, P.W. 1969. 'Review of Yawata and Sinoto, 1968.' *American Anthropologist* **71**/4: 771–4.

75 GATES, R.R. 1960. 'Racial elements in the aborigines of Queensland, Australia.' *Zeitschrift für Morphologie und Anthropologie*, **50**: 150–66.

76 *Gilbert and Ellice Islands Colony*. 1968. Report for the years 1964 and 1965 (London: H.M. Stationery Office).

77 GILES, E., WYBER, S. and WALSH, R.J. 1970. 'Microevolution in New Guinea: additional evidence for genetic drift.' *Arch. & Phys. Anthrop. in Oceania*, **5**: 60–72.

78 GILL, E.D. 1970. 'Quaternary shorelines research in Australia and New Zealand.' *Austr. J. Sci.*, **31**: 106–11.

79 GILL, E.D. 1970. 'Current Quaternary shoreline research in Australasia.' *Austr. J. Sci.*, **32**: 426–8.

80 GLADWIN, T. 1970. 'East is a big bird.' *Natural History*, April, May, 1970, 24–34, 59–69.

81 GLOVER, I.G. and GLOVER, E.A. 1970. 'Pleistocene flaked stone tools from Timor and Flores.' *Mankind*, **7**: 188–90.

82 GOLSON, J. 1961. 'Polynesian culture history.' *Journal of the Polynesian Society*, **70**: 498–508.

83 GOLSON, J. 1961. 'Report on New Zealand, western Polynesia, New Caledonia and Fiji.' *Asian Perspectives*, **5**: 166–80.

84 GOLSON, J. 1968. 'Archaeological prospects for Melanesia.' *In* Yawata and Sinoto, 3–14.

85 GOLSON, J. 1971. 'Australian aboriginal food plants: some ecological and culture-historical implications.' *In* Mulvaney and Golson, 196–238.

86 GOLSON, J. 1971. 'The dog in Australian and Asian prehistory.' Paper presented at meeting of Far Eastern Prehistory Association, Canberra, January 1971.

87 GOLSON, J. 1971. 'Lapita ware and its transformation.' *In* Green and Kelley (eds.), vol. 2: 67–76.

88 GOLSON, J. 1971. 'Both sides of the Wallace Line: Australia, New Guinea, and Asian prehistory.' *Arch. & Phys. Anthrop. in Oceania*, **6**: 124–44.

89 GOODENOUGH, W. 1957. 'Oceania and the problem of controls in the study of cultural and human evolution.' *Journal of the Polynesian Society*, **66**: 146–55.

90 GOODENOUGH, W. 1961. 'Migrations implied by relationships of New Britain dialects to Central Pacific languages.' *Journal of the Polynesian Society*, **70**: 112–26.

91 GORMAN, C. 1969. 'Hoabinhian: a pebble-tool complex with early plant associations in southeast Asia.' *Science*, **163**: 671–3.

92 GORMAN, C.F. (Unpublished). 'Cultural adaptations to the topography, plants, and animals of mainland southeast Asia: circa 12,000 to 2,000 BC.'

93 GRACE, G.W. 1964. 'The linguistic evidence.' *In* Chang *et al.*, 1964.

94 GRACE, G.W. 1966. 'Austronesian lexico-statistical classification: a review article.' *Oceanic Linguistics*, **5**: 13–58.

95 GRACE, G.W. 1968. 'Classification of the languages of the Pacific.' *In* Vayda, 63–79.

96 GRACE, G.W. 1970. *Languages of Oceania*. Working Papers in Linguistics, Department of Linguistics. Univ. of Hawaii, vol. 2, no. 3: 1–24.

97 GREEN, R.C. 1963. 'A suggested revision of the Fijian sequence.' *Journal of the Polynesian Society*, **72**: 235–53.

98 GREEN, R.C. 1967. 'The immediate origins of the Polynesians.' *In* Highland *et al.* (eds.), 215–40.

99 GREEN, R.C. 1968. 'West Polynesian prehistory.' *In* Yawata and Sinoto, 99–109.

100 GREEN, R.C. and KELLEY, M. (eds.). 1970, 1971. *Studies in Oceanic Culture History*. Papers presented at Wenner–Gren

Symposium on Oceanic Culture History. Sigatoka, Fiji, August 1969. Pacific Anthropological Records, Department of Anthropology, Bishop Museum. Vol. 1 (number 11), 1970; Vol. 2 (number 12), 1971; Vol. 3 (in press).

101 GROUBE, L.M. 1971. 'Tonga, Lapita pottery, and Polynesian origins.' *Journal of the Polynesian Society*, **80:** 278–316.

102 HAINLINE, J. 1965. 'Culture and biological adaptation.' *American Anthropologist*, **67:** 1174–97.

103 HAINLINE, J. 1966. 'Population and genetic (serological) variability in Micronesia.' *Annals N.Y. Acad. of Sciences*, vol. 134, article 2, 639–54.

104 HANDY, E.S.C. 1928. 'Probable sources of Polynesian culture.' *Proceedings 3rd Pacific Science Congress*, vol. 2: 2459–68.

105 HARLAN, J.R. 1971. 'Agricultural origins: centers and non-centers.' *Science*, **174:** 468–74.

106 HARRISSON, T. 1967. 'Niah caves, Sarawak.' *Asian and Pacific Archaeology Series*, **1:** 77–8.

107 HEATH, B.H. and CARTER, J.E.L. 1971. 'Growth and somato-type pattern of Manus children, Territory of Papua and New Guinea: application of a modified somatotype method to the study of growth patterns.' *Am. J. Phys. Anthrop.*, **35:** 49–67.

108 HEDRICK, S.D. 1971. 'Lapita style pottery from Malo Island.' *Journal of the Polynesian Society*, **80:** 5–19.

109 HEWES, G.W. 1968. 'On Francois Péron: the first official expedition anthropologist.' *Current Anthropology*, **9/4:** 287–8.

110 HIATT, B. 1969. 'Cremation in aboriginal Australia.' *Mankind*, **7:** 104–19.

111 HIERNAUX, J. 1963. 'Heredity and environment: their influence on human morphology. A comparison of two independent lines of study.' *Am. J. Phys. Anthrop.* **21:** 575–89.

112 HIGHAM, C.F.W. and LEACH, B.F. 1971. 'An early center of bovine husbandry in southeast Asia.' *Science*, 1972: 54–6.

113 HIGHLAND, G.A., FORCE, R.W., HOWARD, A., KELLY, M. and SINOTO, Y.H. (eds.). 1967. *Polynesian culture history. Essays in honor of Kenneth P. Emory*. Bishop Museum Special Publication 56 (Honolulu: Bishop Museum Press).

114 HOCKETT, C.F. 1958. *A course in modern linguistics*, 621 pp. (New York: Macmillan).

115 HOOIJER, D.A. 1953. 'Pleistocene vertebrates from Celebes. VI.

Stegodon sp.'; 'VII. Milk molars and premolars of *Archidis-kodon celebensis* Hooijer.' *Zoologische Mededelingen*, **32**: 107–12, 221–31.

116 HOOIJER, D.A. 1969. 'The *Stegodon* from Timor.' *Proceedings Konink. Nederlandse Akad. van Weterschappen*, ser B., **72**: 203–10.

117 HOOTON, E.A. 1946. *Up From the Ape*. Revised edition, 788 pp. (New York: Macmillan).

118 HOSSFELD, P.S. 1966. 'Antiquity of man in Australia.' *In* B.C. Cotton (ed.), *Aboriginal Man in South and Central Australia*, 59–95 (Adelaide).

119 HOWARD, A. 1967. 'Polynesian origins and migrations: a review of two centuries of speculation and theory.' *In* Highland *et al.* (eds.), 45–101.

120 HOWELLS, W.W. 1933. 'Anthropometry and blood types in Fiji and the Solomon Islands.' *Anthrop. Papers, Am. Museum of Nat. History*, vol. 33, part 4.

121 HOWELLS, W.W. 1934. The peopling of Melanesia as indicated by cranial evidence from the Bismarck Archipelago. Unpublished Ph.D. thesis, Harvard University Library.

122 HOWELLS, W.W. 1966. 'Population distances: biological, linguistic, geographical and environmental.' *Current Anthropology*, **7**: 531–40.

123 HOWELLS, W.W. 1970. 'Anthropometric grouping analysis of Pacific peoples.' *Arch. & Phys. Anthrop. in Oceania*, **5**: 192–217.

124 HOWELLS, W.W. 1973. 'Cranial variation in man. A study by multivariate analysis of patterns of difference among recent human populations.' *Papers, Peabody Museum*, vol. 67.

125 HRDLICKA, A. 1928. 'Catalogue of human crania in the United States National Museum Collections. Australians, Tasmanians, South African Bushmen, Hottentots, and Negro.' *Proceedings, US National Museum*, vol. 71, art. 24: 1–140.

126 HRDY, D. 1973. Quantitative hair form variation in seven populations. *Am. J. Phys. Anthrop.*, **39**: 7–18.

127 HULSE, F.S. 1957. 'Some factors influencing the relative proportions of human racial stocks.' *Cold Spring Harbor Symposia in Quantitative Biology*, **22**: 33–45.

128 HUMPHREYS, C.B. 1926. *The Southern New Hebrides*. An ethnological record, 214 pp. (Cambridge: University Press).

129 JACOB, T. 1967. *Some problems pertaining to the racial history of the Indonesian region.* A study of human skeletal and dental remains from several prehistoric sites in Indonesia and Malaysia, 162 pp. (Utrecht: Drukkerij Neerlandia).

130 JACOB, T. 1969. 'The mesolithic skeletal remains from Sai–Yok.' *Archaeological Excavations in Thailand*, vol. III (Copenhagen: Munksgard).

131 JENNINGS, J.N. 1971. 'Sea level changes and land links.' *In* Mulvaney and Golson, 1–13.

132 JONES, R. 1968. 'The geographical background to the arrival of man in Australia and Tasmania.' *Arch. & Phys. Anthrop. in Oceania*, 3: 186–215.

133 JONES, R. 1969. 'Fire-stick farming.' *Australian Natural History.* Sept. 1969, 224–8.

134 JONES, R. 1971. 'The demography of hunters and farmers in Tasmania.' *In* Mulvaney and Golson, 271–87.

135 KEERS, W. 1948. 'An anthropological survey of the eastern Little Sunda Islands.' 'The Negritos of the eastern Little Sunda Islands.' 'The Proto–Malay of the Netherlands East-Indies' (3 papers). *Koninklijke Vereeniging Indisch Instituut*, Mededeling no. 74 (Afdeling Volkenkunds no. 26), 196 pp. (Amsterdam).

136 KEESING, F.M. 1950. 'Some notes on early migrations in the Southwest Pacific area.' *Southwestern Journal of Anthropology*, 6: 101–19.

137 KENNEDY, T.F. 1966. *A descriptive atlas of the Pacific Islands*, 65 pp. (Wellington: A.H. & A.W. Reed).

138 KIRK, R.L. 1965. 'The distribution of genetic markers in Australian aborigines.' *Occasional Papers in Aboriginal Studies*, no. 4, 67 pp. (Canberra: Australian Institute for Aboriginal Studies).

139 KIRK, R.L. 1970. 'Biochemical polymorphism and the evolution of human races.' *Proc. 8th Int. Congress of Anthrop. and Ethnol. Sciences, Tokyo and Kyoto*, 1968, vol. 1: 371–6.

140 KIRK, R.L. 1971. 'Genetic evidence and its implications for aboriginal prehistory.' *In* Mulvaney and Golson, 326–43.

141 KODAMA, S. 1970. *Ainu. Historical and anthropological studies.* Hokkaido University Medical Library Series No. 3, 295 pp. (Sapporo: Hokkaido Univ. School of Medicine).

142 LAMMERS, M.J. 1948. *De physische anthropologie van de bevolking van Oost-Dawan* (*Noord-midden Timor*), 320 pp. (Doctoral Thesis, University of Leiden).

143 LARNACH, S.L. and MACINTOSH, N.W.G. 1966. 'The craniology of the aborigines of coastal New South Wales.' *The Oceania Monographs*, no. 13, 94 pp.

144 LARNACH, S.L. and MACINTOSH, N.W.G. 1970. 'The craniology of the aborigines of Queensland.' *The Oceania Monographs*, no. 15, 71 pp.

145 LESSA, W.A. 1964. 'The social effects of typhoon Ophelia (1960) on Ulithi.' *Micronesia*, **1**: 1–47 (Reprinted in Vayda, 1968.)

146 LESSA, W.A. and JAY, T. 1953. 'The somatology of Ulithi Atoll.' *Am. J. Phys. Anthrop.*, **11**: 405–12.

147 LIN, C.C. 1963. 'Geology and ecology of Taiwan prehistory.' *Asian Perspectives*, vol. 7, nos. 1–2, 203–13.

148 LINTON, R. 1923. 'The material culture of the Marquesas Islands.' *Memoirs, Bishop Museum*, vol. 8, no. 5.

149 LOOMIS, W.F. 1967. 'Skin pigment regulation of vitamin biosynthesis in man.' *Science*, **157**: 501–6.

150 MACINTOSH, N.W.G. 1949. 'A survey of possible sea routes available to the Tasmanian aborigines.' *Records, Queen Victoria Museum, Launceston*, **2**: 123–44.

151 MACINTOSH, N.W.G. 1960. 'A preliminary note on skin colour in the western Highland natives of New Guinea.' *Oceania*, **30**: 279–93.

152 MACINTOSH, N.W.G. 1965. 'The physical aspect of man in Australia.' *In* R.M. and C.H. Berndt (eds.), *Aboriginal Man in Australia*, 29–70 (Sydney: Angus and Robertson).

153 MACINTOSH, N.W.G. 1967. 'Fossil man in Australia.' *Austr. Jour. Science*, **30**: 86–98.

154 MACINTOSH, N.W.G. 1967. 'Recent discoveries of early Australian man.' *Annals, Australian College of Dental Surgeons*, **1**: 104–26.

155 MACINTOSH, N.W.G. 1969. 'The Talgai cranium: the value of archives.' *Austr. Nat. History*, **16**: 189–95.

156 MACINTOSH, N.W.G. 1971. 'Analysis of an aboriginal skeleton and a pierced tooth necklace from Lake Nitchie, Australia.' *Anthropologie*, **9**: 49–62.

157 MACINTOSH, N.W.G. and BARKER, B.C.W. 1965. 'The osteo-

logy of aboriginal man in Tasmania.' *Oceania Monographs*, no. 12, 72 pp.

158 MACINTOSH, N.W.G., SMITH, K.N. and BAILEY, A.B. 1970. 'Lake Nitchie skeleton – unique aboriginal burial'. *Arch. & Phys. Anthrop. in Oceania*, vol. 5: 85–101.

159 MARSHALL, D.S. and SNOW, C.E. 1956. 'An evaluation of Polynesian craniology.' *Am. J. Phys. Anthrop.* **14**: 405–27.

160 MARTIN, P.S. 1967. 'Pleistocene overkill'. *Natural History*, December, 1967, 32–8.

161 MASON, L. 1959. 'Suprafamilial authority and economic process in Micronesia.' *Humanités, Cahiers de l'Institut de Science Appliquée*, ser. V., vol. 1, 87–118. (Reprinted in Vayda, 1968.)

162 MASON, L. 1968. 'The ethnology of Micronesia.' *In* Vayda (ed.), 277–98.

163 MCARTHUR, N. 1967. *Island populations of the Pacific*, 381 pp. (Canberra: Australian National University Press).

164 MCCARTHY, F.D. 1965. 'The aboriginal past: archaeological and material equipment.' *In* R.M. and C.H. Berndt (eds.), *Aboriginal Man in Australia*, 71–100 (Sydney: Angus and Robertson).

165 MCCULLOUGH, J.M. and GILES, E. 1970. 'Human cerumen types in Mexico and New Guinea: a humidity-related polymorphism in "mongoloid" peoples.' *Nature*, **226**: 460–2.

166 MCKERN, W.C. 1929. 'Archaeology of Tonga.' *Bishop Museum Bulletin*, no. 60, 123 pp. (Honolulu).

167 MCNEISH, R. 1971. 'Early Man in the Andes.' *Scientific American*, April 1971, 36–46.

168 MEAD, M. 1967. 'Homogeneity and hypertrophy.' *In* Highland *et al.*, 1967.

169 MOODIE, P.M., BOOTH, P.B. and SANFORD, R.. 1969. 'The Nus – a genetic survey of Tench Islanders.' *Arch. & Phys. Anthrop. in Oceania*, **4**: 129–43.

170 MOVIUS, H.L., Jr. 1944. 'Early man and Pleistocene stratigraphy in southern and eastern Asia.' *Peabody Museum Papers*, vol. 29, no. 3, 125 pp.

171 MULVANEY, D.J. 1963. 'Prehistory.' *In* W.E.H. Stanner and H. Shiels (eds.), *Australian Aboriginal Studies*. A symposium of papers presented at the 1961 Research Conference, 33–85.

172 MULVANEY, D.J. 1969. *The Prehistory of Australia*, 276 pp. (New York: Praeger).

173 MULVANEY, D.J. 1970. 'Prehistory down under.' *Natural History*, April 1970, 44–51.

174 MULVANEY, D.J. 1970. 'The Patjitanian industry: some observations.' *Mankind*, 7: 184–7.

175 MULVANEY, D.J. 1971. 'Aboriginal social evolution: a retrospective view.' *In* Mulvaney and Golson, 368–80.

176 MULVANEY, D.J. and GOLSON, J. (eds.). 1971. *Aboriginal man and environment in Australia*, 389 pp. (Canberra: Australian National University Press).

177 MURDOCK, G.P. 1964. 'Genetic classification of the Austronesian languages: a key to Oceanic culture history.' *Ethnology*, 3: 117–26. (Reprinted in Vayda, 1968.)

178 MURRILL, R.I. 1968. *Cranial and postcranial skeletal remains from Easter Island*, 105 pp. (Minneapolis: Univ. of Minnesota Press).

179 NGUYEN, D. and NGUYEN, Q.Q. 1966. 'Early Neolithic skulls in Quynh Van, Nghe An, North Vietnam.' *Vertebrata Palaeasiatica*, 10: 49–57.

180 OAKLEY, K.P. 1964. *Frameworks for Dating Fossil Man*, 355 pp. (London: Weidenfeld and Nicolson).

181 OLIVER, D.L. 1951. *The Pacific Islands*, 313 pp. (Cambridge: Harvard).

182 OLIVER, D.L. 1954. Somatic variability and human ecology of Bougainville, Solomon Islands. Unpublished MSS.

183 OLIVER, D.L. 1972. *Ancient Tahitian Society* (Honolulu: University of Hawaii Press).

184 OLIVER, D.L. and HOWELLS, W.W. 1957. 'Micro-evolution: cultural elements in physical variation.' *Am. Anthropologist*, 59: 965–78.

185 OLIVIER, G. 1966. 'Révision du crâne mésolithique de Tam-Pong (Laos).' *Bulls. et Mémoires de la Soc. d'Anthrop. de Paris*, vol. 9, series XI: 229–53.

186 OSBORNE, D. 1966. 'The archaeology of the Palau Islands. An intensive survey.' *Bishop Museum Bulletin* no. 230, 497 pp.

187 PALMER, B. 1968. 'Recent results from the Sigatoka archaeological program.' *In* Yawata and Sinoto, 19–27.

188 PAWLEY, A. (In press). 'On the internal relationships of Eastern Oceanic languages.' *In* Green and Kelley (eds.), vol. 3.

189 PAWLEY, A. and GREEN, K. (In press.) 'Lexical evidence for the Proto-Polynesian homeland.' To appear in *Te Reo* (Proceedings of the Linguistic Society of New Zealand).

190 PEACOCK, B.A.V. 1971. 'Early cultural development in southeast Asia with special reference to the Malay Peninsula.' *Arch. & Phys. Anthrop. in Oceania*, 6: 107–23.

191 PELLET, M. and SPOEHR, A. 1961. 'Marianas archaeology; report on an excavation on Tinian.' *J. Polynesian Society*, 70: 321–5.

192 PETRAKIS, N.L. 1971. 'Cerumen genetics and human breast cancer.' *Science*, 1973: 347–9.

193 PIETRUSEWSKY, M. 1970. 'An osteological view of indigenous populations in Oceania.' *In* Green and Kelley (eds.), vol. 1, 1–12.

194 PIETRUSEWSKY, M. 1971. 'Application of distance statistics to anthroposcopic data and a comparison of results with those obtained by using discrete traits of the skull.' *Arch. & Phys. Anthrop. in Oceania*, 6: 21–33.

195 PLATO, C.C. and CRUZ, M. 1967. 'Blood group and haptoblobin frequencies of the Chamorros of Guam.' *Am. J. Human Genetics*, 19: 722–31.

196 PLOMLEY, N.J.B. (ed.). 1966. *Friendly Mission. The Tasmanian Journals and Papers of George Augustus Robinson 1829–1834*, 1074 pp. (Tasmanian Historical Research Association).

197 POULSEN, J. 1970. 'Shell artifacts in Oceania: their distribution and significance.' *In* Green and Kelley (eds.), vol. 1, 33–46.

198 PRETTY, G. 1971. 'The excavations at Roonka Station, Murray River, South Australia, 1968–70.' Abstract of paper given at 28th Int. Congress of Orientalists, Canberra.

199 REINMAN, F.M. 1968. 'Guam prehistory. A preliminary field report.' *In* Yawata and Sinoto, 41–50.

200 REINMAN, F.M. 1970. 'Fishhook variability: implications for the history and distribution of fishing gear in Oceania.' *In* Green and Kelley, vol. 1, 47–60.

201 RILEY, C.L., KELLEY, J.C., PENNINGTON, C.W. and RANDS, R.L. (eds.), 1971. *Man across the sea. Problems of Pre-Columbian contacts*, 552 pp. (Austin: University of Texas Press).

202 ROBERTS, D.F. and BAINBRIDGE, D.R. 1963. 'Nilotic physique.' *Am. J. Phys. Anthrop.*, 21: 341–70.

203 SARTONO, S. 1969. '*Stegodon timorensis*, a pygmy species from Timor (Indonesia).' *Proc. Konink. Nederlandse Akad. van Wetenschappen*, ser. B, **72**: 192–202.

204 SAUER, C.O. 1952. *Agricultural Origins and Dispersals*, 110 pp., Bowman Memorial Lectures, Am. Geographical Soc., New York.

205 SCHANFIELD, M.S. 1971. *Population studies on the Gm and Inv antigens in Asia and Oceania*. Ph.D. Thesis, University of Michigan, 137 pp. (Ann Arbor: University Microfilms).

206 SCHLAGINHAUFEN, O. 1964. 'Anthropologie von Neuirland in der Melanesischen Südsee. I. Die Beobachtungen an lebenden Eingeborenen.' *Archir. der Julius Klaus-Stifting*, **39**: 1/4.

207 SCHMITT, R.C. 1969. 'How many Hawaiians?' *Jour. Polynesian Society*, **76**: 467–75.

208 SHAPIRO, H.L. 1933. 'The physical characteristics of the Ontong Javanese: a contribution to the study of the non-Melanesian elements in Melanesia.' *Anthrop. Papers, Am. Mus. Nat. Hist.*, vol. 33, part 3.

209 SHAPIRO, H.L. 1936. 'The physical characters of the Cook Islanders.' *Memoirs, Bishop Museum*, XII/1, 35 pp.

210 SHAPIRO, H.L. 1939. *Migration and environment*, 594 pp. (New York: Oxford University Press).

211 SHAPIRO, H.L. 1943. 'Physical differentiation in Polynesia.' *Papers, Peabody Museum*, **20**: 3–8.

212 SHUTLER, R. Jr., 1967. 'Radiocarbon dating and man in southeast Asia, Australia, and the Pacific.' *Asian and Pacific Archaeology Series*, **1**: 79–87.

213 SHUTLER, R., Jr., and SHUTLER, M.E. 1968. 'Archaeological excavations in Southern Melanesia.' *In* Yawata and Sinoto, 15–17.

214 SHUTLER, R., Jr. 1971. 'Pacific Island radiocarbon dates, an over-view.' *In* Green and Kelley, eds., vol. 2: 13–27.

215 SIMMONS, R.T. 1956. 'A report on blood group genetic surveys in eastern Asia, Indonesia, Melanesia, Micronesia, Polynesia and Australia in the study of man.' *Anthropos*, **51**: 500–12.

216 SIMMONS, R.T., TINDALE, N.B. and BIRDSELL, J.B. 1962. 'A blood group genetical survey in Australian aborigines of Bentinck, Morninginton and Forsyth Islands, Gulf of Carpentaria.' *Am. J. Phys. Anthrop.*, **20**: 303–20.

217 SINNETT, P., BLAKE, N.M., KIRK, R.L., LAI, L.Y.C. and WALSH, R.J. 1970. 'Blood, serum protein and enzyme groups among Enga-speaking people of the Western Highlands, New Guinea, with an estimate of genetic distance between clans.' *Arch. & Phys. Anthrop. in Oceania*, **5**: 236–52.

218 SINOTO, Y.H. 1970. 'An archaeologically based assessment of the Marquesas Islands as a dispersal center in East Polynesia.' *In* Green and Kelley (eds.), vol. I, 105–32.

219 SKINNER, H.D. 1968. 'The North Pacific origin of some elements of Polynesian material culture.' *Asian and Pacific Archaeology Series*, **2**: 104–12.

220 SOLHEIM, W.G. II, 1958. 'The present state of the "Paleolithic" in Borneo.' *Asian Perspectives*, **2**: 83–90.

221 SOLHEIM, W.G. II. 1963. 'Formosan relationships with Southeast Asia.' *Asian Perspectives*, **7**: 251–60.

222 SOLHEIM, W.G. II. 1964. 'Pottery and the Malayo–Polynesians.' *In* Chang *et al.*, 1964.

223 SOLHEIM, W.G. II. 1968. 'Possible routes of migration into Melanesia as shown by statistical analysis of methods of pottery manufacture.' *Asian and Pacific Archaeology Series*, **2**: 139–66.

224 SOLHEIM, W.G. II. 1969. 'Reworking Southeast Asian prehistory.' *Paideuma: Mitteilungen zur Kulturkunde*, **15**: 125–39. (Reprint as SSRI Reprint no. 34, 1970, Univ. of Hawaii.)

225 SOLHEIM, W.G. II. 1972. 'Northern Thailand, Southeast Asia, and world prehistory.' *Asian Perspectives*, XIII: 145–62.

226 SPECHT, J. 1968. 'Preliminary report of excavations on Watom Island.' *Jour. Poly. Soc.*, **77**: 117–34.

227 SPEISER, F. 1912. 'Reisebericht über Tanna (Neue Hebriden).' *Zeitschrift für Ethnologie*, **44**: 297–8.

228 SPEISER, F. 1928. 'Anthropologische Messungen aus Espiritu Santo (Neue Hebriden). Ein Beitrag zur Pygmäenfrage.' *Verhandlungen der Naturforschenden Gesellschaft in Basel*, **39**: 79–166.

229 SPOEHR, A. 1949. 'Majuro. A village in the Marshall Islands.' *Fieldiana: Anthropology*, vol. 39 (Chicago Natural History Museum).

230 SPOEHR, A. 1954. 'Saipan. The ethnology of a war-devastated island.' *Fieldiana: Anthropology*, vol. 41 (Chicago Natural History Museum).

231 SPOEHR, A. 1957. 'Marianas prehistory. Archaeological survey and excavations on Saipan, Tinian and Rota.' *Fieldiana: Anthropology*, vol. 48 (Chicago Natural History Museum).

232 STANNER, W.E.H. and SHEILS, H. (eds.). 1963. *Australian Aboriginal Studies*. A symposium of papers presented at the 1961 research conference. Published for the Australian Institute of Aboriginal Studies, 505 pp. (Melbourne: Oxford University Press).

233 STEINBERG, A.G. and KAGEYAMA, S. 1970. 'Further data on the Gm and Inv allotypes of the Ainu: confirmation of the presence of a $Gm^{2,17,21}$ phenotype.' *Am. J. Human Genetics*, **22**: 319–25.

234 SUGGS, R.C. 1960. *The Island Civilizations of Polynesia*, 256 pp. (New York: Mentor).

235 SUGGS, R.C. 1960. 'Historical traditions and archaeology in Polynesia.' *Am. Anthropologist*, **62**: 754–73.

236 SUNG, W–S. 1969. 'Changpinian. A newly discovered pre-ceramic culture from the agglomerate caves on the east coast of Taiwan (preliminary report)' *Newsletter of Chinese Ethnology*, no. 9, 27 pp., 4 figs, 16 pls. (In Chinese; English summary.)

237 SWINDLER, D.R. 1962. 'A racial study of the West Nakanai.' 83 pp., 9 plates. In *New Britain Studies*, W. Goodenough (ed.), Museum Monographs (Philadelphia: University Museum).

238 SZABO, G., GERALD, A.B., PATHAK, M.A. and FITZPATRICK, T.B. 1969. 'Racial differences in the fate of melanosomes in human epidermis.' *Nature*, **222**: 1081–2.

239 TANNER, J. M. 1964. *Physique of the Olympic Athlete* (London: Allen and Unwin).

240 TANNER, J.M. 1966. 'Growth and physique in different populations of mankind.' *In* P.T. Baker and J.S. Weiner (eds.), *The Biology of Human Adaptability*, ch. 3 (Oxford: Clarendon Press).

241 THOMAS, R.B. 1970. 'El tamaño pequeño del cuerpo como forma de adaptación de una población Quechua a la altura.' *Proc. 39th Congress of Americanists*, Lima.

242 THOMAS, W.L., Jr. 1967. 'The Pacific Basin: an introduction.' *In* H.R. Friis (ed.), 1967, *The Pacific Basin: a History of its Geographical Exploration*. Am. Geogr. Soc. (Reprinted in Vayda, 1968.)

243 THORNE, A.G. 1971. 'The racial affinities and origins of the Australian aborigines.' *In* Mulvaney and Golson, 316–25.

244 TRAVERS, R. 1968. *The Tasmanians. The Story of a Doomed Race*, 244 pp. (Melbourne: Cassell Australia).

245 TREVOR, J.C. and BROTHWELL, D.R. 1962. 'The human remains of Mesolithic and Neolithic date from Gua Cha, Kelantan.' *Federation Museums Journal*, n.s. **8**: 6–22.

246 TRYON, D.T. 1971. 'Linguistic evidence and aboriginal origins.' *In* Mulvaney and Golson, 344–55.

247 VAYDA, A.P. (ed.). 1968. *Peoples and Cultures of the Pacific*. An Anthropological Reader, 557 pp. (New York: Natural History Press).

248 VANDERWAL, R.L. 1970. 'Prehistoric ceramic styles, Hall Sound, Papua. 'Paper presented at Australia/New Zealand Assoc. for the Advancement of Science, Port Moresby, August 1970.

249 VOITOV, V.I. and TUMARKIN, D.D. 1967. 'Navigational conditions of sea routes to Polynesia.' *Asian and Pacific Archaeology Series*, **1**: 89–100.

250 WEIDENREICH, F. 1945. 'The Keilor skull. A Wadjak skull from southeast Australia.' *Am. J. Phys. Anthrop.*, **3**: 21–32.

251 WEIDENREICH, F. 1946. *Apes, Giants and Man*, 122 pp. (Chicago: Univ. of Chicago Press).

252 WHITE, C. 1971. 'Man and environment in northwest Arnhem Land.' *In* Mulvaney and Golson, 141–57.

253 WHITE, J.P. 1971. 'New Guinea and Australian prehistory: the "Neolithic" problem.' *In* Mulvaney and Golson, 182–95.

254 WHITE, J.P. 1971. 'New Guinea: the first phase in Oceanic settlement.' *In* Green and Kelley (eds.), vol. 2, 45–53.

255 WILLIAMSON, R.W. 1924. *The Social and Political Systems of Central Polynesia*, 3 vols. (Cambridge).

256 WILLIAMSON, R.W. 1939. *Essays in Polynesian Ethnology*. Edited by R. Piddington, 373 pp. (Cambridge: University Press).

257 WOO, JU-KANG, 1959. 'Human fossils found in Liukiang, Kwangsi, China.' *Vertebrata Palasiatica*, vol. 3, no. 2, 109–18.

258 WRIGHT, R.V.S. 1971. 'The archaeology of Koonalda Cave.' *In* Mulvaney and Golson, 105–13.

259 WUNDERLY, J. 1943. 'The Keilor fossil skull: anatomical description.' *Memoirs, National Museum of Victoria*, **13**: 57–69.

260 WURM, S.A. and LAYCOCK, D.C. 1961. 'The question of language and dialect in New Guinea.' *Oceania*, **32**: 128–43.

261 YAMAGUCHI, B. 1967. 'A comparative osteological study of the Ainu and Australian aborigines.' *Australian Institute of Aboriginal Studies, Occasional Papers* no. 10, 75 pp. (Canberra).

262 YAWATA, I. and SINOTO, Y.H. 1968. *Prehistoric culture in Oceania.* A symposium. Eleventh Pacific Science Congress, Tokyo, Japan, 1966 (Honolulu: Bishop Museum Press).

263 YEN, D.E. 1971. 'The development of agriculture in Oceania'. *In* Green and Kelley (eds.), vol. 2, 1–12.

Addenda

264 AMBROSE, W.R. and GREEN, R.C. 1972. 'First millennium BC transport of obsidian from New Britain to the Solomon Islands.' *Nature*, **237**: 31.

265 BARBETTI, M. and ALLEN, H. 1972. 'Prehistoric man at Lake Mungo, Australia, by 32,000 years BC.' *Nature*, **240**: 46–8.

266 BOWLER, J.M., THORNE, A.G. and POLACH, H.A. 1972. 'Pleistocene man in Australia: age and significance of the Mungo skeleton.' *Nature*, **240**: 48–50.

267 CHANG, K–C. 1972. 'Prehistoric archaeology of Taiwan.' *Asian Perspectives*, XIII: 59–77.

268 FRIMIGACCI, D. 1970. 'Une datation par la méthode du C. 14 du site Lapita de Vatcha (près de Vao) île des Pins.' *Bulletin Périodique de la Société d'Etudes Melanesiennes*, Dec. 1970, 43–74.

269 GORMAN, C.F. 1972. 'Excavations at Spirit Cave, North Thailand: some interim interpretations.' *Asian Perspectives*, XIII: 79–107.

270 GREENBERG, J.H. 1971. 'The Indo-Pacific hypothesis.' *In* T.A. Sebeok (ed.), *Linguistics in Oceania. Current Trends in Linguistics*, vol. 8, 808–71.

271 LAMPERT, R.J. 1972. 'A carbon date for the aboriginal occupation of Kangaroo Island, south Australia.' *Mankind*, **8**: 223–224.

272 MULVANEY, D.J. and SOEJONO, R.P. 1970. 'Archaeology in Sulawesi, Indonesia.' *Antiquity*, **45**: 26–33.

273 O'BRIEN, P.J. 1972. 'The sweet potato: its origin and dispersal.' *American Anthropologist*, **74**: 342–365.

274 POULSEN J.L. 1972. 'Outlier archaeology: Bellona. A pre-

liminary report on field work and radiocarbon dates. Part I: Archaeology.' *Archaeology and Physical Anthropology in Oceania*, **7**: 184–205.

275 SCHMITT, R.C. 1971. 'New estimates of pre-censal population of Hawaii.' *Journal of the Polynesian Society*, **80**: 237–243.

276 THORNE, A.G. and MACUMBER, P.G. 1972. 'Discoveries of late Pleistocene man at Kow Swamp, Australia.' *Nature*, **238**: 316–19.

277 THORNE, A.G. 1971. 'Mungo and Kow Swamp: morphological variation in Pleistocene Australians.' *Mankind*, **8**: 85–9.

278 WHITE, J.P. 1972. 'Carbon dates from New Ireland.' *Mankind*, **8**: 309–10.

279 WHITE, J.P., CROOK, K.A.W. and RUXTON, B.P. 1970. 'Kosipe: a late Pleistocene site in the Papuan Highlands.' *Proceedings, Prehistoric Society*, **36**: 152–70.

280 WURM, S.A. 1971. 'The Papuan linguistic situation'. *In* T.A. Sebeok (ed.), *Linguistics in Oceania. Current Trends in Linguistics*, vol. 8, 541–657.

Index